A WOVEN WORLD

A Woven World

*

ON FASHION, FISHERMEN, AND THE SARDINE DRESS

ALISON HAWTHORNE DEMING

COUNTERPOINT
Berkeley, California

A Woven World

Library of Congress Cataloging-in-Publication Data
Names: Deming, Alison Hawthorne, 1946– author.
Title: A woven world : on fashion, fishermen, and the sardine dress / Alison Hawthorne Deming.
Description: Berkeley, California : Counterpoint Press, 2021.
Identifiers: LCCN 2020047970 | ISBN 9781640094826 (hardcover) | ISBN 9781640094833 (ebook)
Subjects: LCSH: Clothing trade—New York (State)—New York—History. | Fisheries—Maritime Provinces—History.
Classification: LCC HD9940.U3 N44 2021 | DDC 338.4/7687097471—dc23
LC record available at https://lccn.loc.gov/2020047970

Jacket design by Nicole Caputo
Book design by Jordan Koluch

COUNTERPOINT
2560 Ninth Street, Suite 318
Berkeley, CA 94710
www.counterpointpress.com

Printed in the United States of America

10 9 8 7 6 5 4 3 2 1

For Lucinda

Things outlast us ... they carry the experience they have
had with us inside them and are ... the book of our history opened before us.

W. G. SEBALD

all was woods seen from a train
no sooner glimpsed than gone again
    but those immortals constantly
    in some measure reassured me

W. S. MERWIN

CONTENTS

✳

A WOVEN WORLD

Prologue

✳

The Unmaking

THE KITCHEN WING OF OUR 1864 CASTALIA COTTAGE HAD BEEN slumping down into the earth for decades. Sill beams laid on bare soil had crumbled, making the walls sink. The shelves that held our dishes and glassware had tilted wallward. The floor listed and rippled like a fun house. A gap had grown between the kitchen wing and the main house, inviting rain, mice, and fearsomely huge black ants to run rampant, each in their season. After my parents were gone, stewardship of the summer place became the price I paid for spending a few months each year in the Canadian Maritimes.

The house, on the other hand, spent the whole year on the stormy seashore of the Long Bank, battered by wind and rain and snow and ice, saturated with fog and salt air, invaded by mold and mildew. The roof shingles were busting up from wear, the old brick chimney sieved creosote into rainwater and snowmelt, making gruesome watercolor abstractions on the ceilings. And while the old fieldstone cellar walls held generally upright, one corner had caved to external forces. The house was unmaking itself. Half of my neighbors told me to finish the job and tear the whole thing down. One hundred and fifty years is long enough, they said. The other half said, How could you tear that house down? It's been here one hundred and fifty years. Who built that house anyway? they asked. Then the stories began. A fisherman grew up here who was lost at sea for a week in his dory. And the crusty quips, relegating me to outsider status though our family had owned the place since 1957. You're livin' in my grandfather's house. The more I learned about the place, the more I imagined the lives that had gone before me and came to feel somehow that I was their keeper. I knew the house would not go down on my watch. At least not the whole of it.

I had the kitchen wing torn down and hired Larry Small to reno what remained. New windows and doors, gut out plaster, insulate, new pine tongue-and-groove boards for the walls. No kitchen. No bathroom. A camp sink. It will become an artist studio for my daughter, who plans to keep our family story moving forward in this place.

Demolition has its pleasures. In two hours a backhoe and dump truck can turn a house into a vacant lot. A few bites through the roof, a few scoops of lath and plaster, smashed windows and linoleum, and the wing was smoothed to bare dirt, an open space on the land as it had been before the cottage was built. The demolition was a catharsis. All those years of dithering about what to do with the ruin, all those years of family argument and avoidance and lack of resources (financial and emotional) gone with the dump truck rumbling down the road. Maybe there were ghosts from the family before us who felt the relief as well. I don't really believe in ghosts as material apparitions of the dead. But our dead do live with us as specters in the mind. What do they ask of us? It seems at the very least they ask for stories that will hold them among the living. This is no less true for our ecological losses than for our familial ones.

Heavy machinery is not discerning in the way it unmakes things. But a carpenter—now that is another matter. Larry worked to strip down the plaster walls of what remained. Having worked on houses old and new on the island for forty years, he kept an eye out for surprises that would emerge from under the plaster. Carpenters around here leave time capsules for those who find their way decades later into the interior of a house. I found "This house built in 1864" written in carpenter pencil on a plank of the old cottage. And the shed had been signed on a ceiling plank by Harry Dunbar, as if it were a painting. Larry keeps up the tradition. He left a time capsule buried in the wall of the boat barn he renovated for me into what I now use for a summer cottage—a secret compartment with a Pepsi can and this, written in Sharpie: "Conversion reno by Larry Small, Aug 9 2013. Gas $1.35/LT. Beer $23.00/Doz. A cool damp summer so far, lots of herring in the weirs, and reports that a great white shark took a big gray seal off swallowtail light . . . cool shit."

The uncanny thing about demolition is the objects turning up that accidentally found their way into walls. A shell button that slipped through a crack, sure. A mouse skeleton, of course. But how did the hand-carved wooden shoe last end up nestled between the wall studs? And the tiny awl with a needle point that fit the prick marks around the last's perimeter? Someone who lived here either made or repaired his own shoes. And the heart-shaped padlock big as my fist, rusted permanently open? The door handle, the tablespoon, the fancy brass hatpin with a big oval cut-glass jewel? Larry had a theory for the hatpin that had fallen down with the plaster and lath of a ceiling he'd demolished. A child picks up his mother's hatpin from her dresser, a precious object, and carries it away to his upstairs bedroom. Mother storms around the house searching for the treasured ornament. There are not many ornaments in a nineteenth-century fisherman's house. The child cowers in fear of being apprehended as a thief. As mother mounts the steep stairs huffing with rage, the child hides the hatpin under a loose floorboard. Voila, it lands on Larry Small's head a hundred years later.

Once we were down to the bones of the old cottage, the beams and planks told stories—planks wider than any tree alive today in these parts, studs cut rough with bark intact on the uncut edge, square-cut blacksmith-forged nails. Larry was surprised to see, at one juncture where mortise and tenon met holding together two beams, that Roman numerals had been punched with a chisel into the wood to match up the six-by-six beams. XII on the rafter. XII on the vertical beam. Match the matching numbers, and the house clicks together. On another—IIII. Cut to fit, then assembled like an IKEA kit, directions right on the structural elements. I don't know why I found this discovery so moving. The maker's hand was evident in so many aspects of the cottage's bones—adze marks on the beams and such—and yet this crisp detail made me feel so much love for the labor that went into the house, for the intelligence and practicality of marking the beams this way as they were cut in preparation for assembling. All you need is one two-inch chisel to mark all the Roman numerals as high as you need to go.

Not all unmaking is so felicitous. Down with the mildew and anger go the order and joy of a family breaking bread together, the binding love of family and place, no matter the hardship. Generation to generation, place brings people together and tells them who they are. Place is a vessel that holds us, Aristotle said. Death unmakes all families in the end; that is our insufferable reality. Yet place opens again, a vessel to contain what comes next.

Unmaking is nature's way of making, picking up the pieces and figuring out how to put them together into a new form. Compost. Leaf mold. Humus. Dead herring for the corn hill. Cow dung for the alfalfa. Mushrooms popping out of a deadfall tree trunk. Stories stitched from scant threads of those who have gone before. Maybe I was just following nature's lead in the demolition, unmaking so I could clear the way for making. I wanted to honor those who had come before me. Since childhood I have felt a kinship with my island neighbors, drawn to their close relationship with the sea, their love of stories and shared memory of those who had made possible their lives in this place. I wanted to hand over my place in better shape than it was when it came to me. This sentiment quickly ramifies into cultural concerns these days when the unmaking of nature races forward in flood, fire, and foolhardy dismantling of that which sustains us and lends beauty to our lives. Just how far can the unmaking go before the making becomes impossible? I have set myself the task of imposing upon that uncertainty some meaning to be found in memory, lost knowledges, the silences of our dead, and the work of human hands that keeps stitching the fabric of life back together whenever it frays.

1

✳

The Sardine Dress

The Costume Institute: Metropolitan Museum of Art. 2016

AMONG DRESSES ADORNED WITH EMBROIDERED FLOWERS, BO-tanical illustrations, glass beads, freshwater pearls, chunks of coral, plastic straws, and ostrich feathers, one stands out for me, a dress made to look like fish skin. This is the dress I have come to see, a simple sheath, scoop neck, long sleeves, made to hug the contours of the body so that a woman might look as sleek and bioluminescent as a fish. Made from black silk crepe, its surface is covered with an imbrication of black and pewter beads, the fish scale motif created with blue, gray, black, brown, silver, and opalescent gelatin sequins. The colors are so subtle that they bleed into one shimmer like the disappearing light a herring casts as it darts through the water. Each scale on the dress is made of five or six rows of overlapping sequins, the tiny sequins in each cluster adding up to a composite scale that has been scaled up from tiny scales shingled over each other with invisible stitches. The dress is all about scale: how micro detail can be patterned into a state of macro elegance and beauty.

When I was a child first visiting Grand Manan Island in the Bay of Fundy, I saw the herring seiners pump torrents of silvery fish through a scaler on their way to the sardine factory. The scales were siphoned off in baskets made of ash wood, the slimy glitter carried to Mearl Pearl in Eastport, Maine. The company turned the scales into cosmetics, nail polish, and automotive paint. The Mearl Corporation ran the last commercial "natural pearl essence" plant in the world. It closed in 2007. Now the sheen in such products comes from mica or plastic. The few boats that continue to harvest herring from weirs or purse seines in the Bay of Fundy, where the herring fishery has tanked in the past decade, dump the scales back into the sea as waste. Fish scales must have been the original inspiration for sequins. That long human hunger to possess the grace in form and movement of animals finds many vocabularies in fashion. Fur coats, alligator shoes, leather pants, feather boas. Silk made from the saliva of worms. The first sequins were made of gold—glam in the Indus Valley five thousand years ago.

The sardine dress is a 1983 design of Yves Saint Laurent. The sequin work hand-stitched at Maison Lesage in Paris took fifteen hundred hours to complete. The dress makes some improvements on nature by adorning the female form in a second skin that projects the graceful and fluid movement of a schooling fish. Perhaps it appeals to a deeply buried atavistic call in us to return to the waters of our ontological past. The dress must have been heavy to wear, but the exhibition manikin does not have to worry. She is headless, handless, legless. She stands on a wheeled base with illuminated details of the sequin work projected onto the walls. The dress catches the light with such intensity that the delicate paillettes perfect the illusion: the dress is made of metal, a gorgeous feminine armor. Metal dress on the wheeled metal shaft of the manikin stand, though of course the dress is not metal at all, merely the illusion of metal, ideal for the woman who shines with the patina of strength. The hem and sleeves are trimmed with a different pattern of sequins. Long ripples rise and fall, rise and fall, like a disturbance on a calm bay, moon-work at play in a field of light. The manikin is standing in an arched alcove that mirrors water's restlessness in shimmering light, though there is no water in the exhibit hall.

My grandmother kept a dress-form manikin in her room. She lived with us throughout my childhood, retired from her business as a dressmaker in New York City. She continued to make her own clothes, an elegant black dress with overlays of lace and insets of moiré silk, a flared floor-length dressing gown in sateen in a print featuring oversized begonias. Her manikin stood on a small table, its torso covered with beige canvas and padding to represent precisely my grandmother's form with its impressive bosom and stout trunk. She never used a pattern, but cut the fabric by eye, laid it on the manikin, stitched by hand the toile that would guide her hand when she sat to work on the treadle-powered Singer to make the finished garment. Marie Bregny had learned the skills from her mother Louisa, my great-grandmother, who emigrated from Paris to New York City in the 1860s and established the dressmaking business that carried the family for two generations under the hands of these women. It ran from the 1870s until sometime in the late 1920s, by which time the ready-to-wear industry had driven such small-scale artistry into obsolescence. At its peak, the business employed sixteen women, many with refined skills—a Hungarian woman who specialized in beadwork and sequins, sleevers, finishers—and it served a wealthy clientele who ordered dresses for each season, custom-made dresses in the current Paris styles fitted precisely to the customer's body.

I have been looking for these two women both long dead. I find myself thinking of them at incongruous moments. A friend describes her mother's unhappiness. Her husband wouldn't let her get a job. "Oh, back then women couldn't ..." I want to argue that there have always been women who defied the odds, but I don't. My argument is not with anyone who acknowledges the limits imposed on women's lives. My argument is with the world's dismissal of makers in favor of manufacturers. My argument is against breakers, who seem everywhere to be rising in influence. A fisherman sits mending his nets before heading out to seine his weir for herring. He passes the shuttle through the grids of twine, knotting each of the four corners of every half-inch square for adding strength. His hands are strong and sure. "How did you learn that?" a younger fisherman asks him, looking on with keen attention. The older man names the one who taught him. It was a family thing, three generations of men, each making the skill he'd mastered look easy to the one coming up. Makers. Whose skill is so perfectly fit to the needs of the job, learned by watching and doing, patience and time.

The sardine dress was made with machine-stitched seams. The sequined embroidery was handmade with stitching techniques mastered in the early nineteenth century using the Lunéville hook, a tool with a wooden handle and small metal hook, making possible work on very delicate fabrics. From a simple chain stitch, a glossary of stitches developed: in rows, in scales, in a river, vermicelli, garter stitch, Riche stitch, Boulogne stitch, bullion stitch, German knot, triple Palestrina, herringbone, lazy daisy, seed stitch, stem stitch, and many more. Maison Lesage has been the steward of opulent embroidery since 1924, when the house took over the Michonet embroidery atelier that had been in business since 1858. The house currently trains more than four hundred students each year, while riding out boom and bust waves in the fashion industry—the excess of the 1980s and minimalism of the 1990s. Its archives hold the world's largest collection of embroidery in the world with seventy thousand samples. Its bead library fills a wall where the *petite mains*, who wear white lab coats and work on commissions for famous ateliers, can select from a color palette to rival Matisse.

François Lesage, who took over the business from his parents when he was twenty ("I was born into a pile of beads and sequins"), described the process of making couture fashion as an ongoing artistic conversation between designer and embroiderer. I do not know the type of direction that Yves Saint Laurent gave for the sardine dress. The dress was made for the Gilda Collection of spring 1983, inspired by Rita Hayworth's role as femme fatale in the film *Gilda*. There is no sardine dress in the film, though there are plenty of sequins. The most celebrated dress in the film is the strapless black satin item Hayworth wore for the "Put the Blame on Mame" number. The dress was a long, side-slit sheath accompanied by shoulder-length black satin gloves, the only thing to come off in a sensual striptease. Hayworth's moves are astonishing, the liquid swing of her hips, the glorious bare arms extended above her head, the flesh aglow from fingertips to the gently contoured terrain of shoulders and clavicles, the effortless taunting sexuality of a woman who adores her capacity to arouse.

To keep the *Gilda* dress from falling when she danced, the designer Jean Louis had to build a harness inside the dress. "Like you put on a horse," he said. "We put grosgrain under the bust with darts and three stays—one in the center, two on the sides. Then we molded plastic softened over a gas flame and shaped around the top of the dress. No matter how she moved, the dress didn't fall down." He designed a large faux side-bow at the waist to disguise the belly she had from the recent birth of her daughter. A glorious artifice of femininity and sexual abandon played by a new mother who is harnessed like a horse beneath the sheen of her gown.

I don't know when the sardines came into play for YSL's *Gilda*-inspired dress. "Sardine dress" was not YSL's name for the dress, though the scales motif is undeniably marine. And Hayworth's moves are nothing if not piscine. She seems to dissolve into movement, conjuring a being graceful as a deep-water creature yet moving in air. While the *Gilda* dress is all about creating sexual appeal, the sardine dress is about something different. The neck is high and modest, the sleeves full-length, very little flesh calls out for attention. But the sleek, tight skin of the dress accentuates an appreciation of form, suggests the capacity for gorgeous movement, while the model remains bound. To my eye, the dress celebrates biomorphism and our human relationship to ancient oceanic kin.

Lesage recounts the direction he received from YSL on another creation: "François, make me something that is like a chandelier reflecting off the mirror with the sky of Paris in the background." Not bad for a man who began as a boy in French Algeria cutting out paper dolls and who ended up one of the world's great designers, working quietly in the very heart of Paris couture at a desk made of plywood wrapped with muslin and set on sawhorses.

Both Lesage and Laurent are gone, though the work of Maison Lesage goes on under the artistic direction of Hubert Barrère. "Hand embroidery is something emotional," he said in a 2016 article by Betsy Blodgett in *Seamwork*. "It isn't a kind of exhibitionism, and its value doesn't come simply from the hours and hours of meticulous work involved. Above all else, it's something that comes from the soul, it makes you feel something, without quite knowing why."

François Lesage rooted that feeling in deep time.

"Self-adornment goes back to the Lascaux Caves! Think of scarification. That's the ancestor of embroidery."

And this: "A country that loses its craftsmanship is a country that is dying."

2

✳

Driving the Cadillac to Valhalla

Kensico Cemetery, Valhalla, New York. 2005

THE WOMAN WHO KEEPS THE RECORDS IS GRACIOUS AND FASHionable. She works at the cemetery amid desks cluttered and close in a big room where office staff tend to schedules and bills and keeping the grounds. I have arrived in my black Cadillac, a car so absurdly heavy I can barely open the driver-side door to get out from my perch behind the steering wheel. I kept thinking there was a body in the trunk or a Magnum under my seat.

"It's the only car we have," said the rental agent in Albany, an airport small enough to make the claim credible.

But I'm an environmentalist, I wanted to protest. I can't drive that thing. I remained silent, facing the inevitable with a nod toward the bizarre irony that I would drive to Valhalla in a funeral director's car to visit my grandmother's grave. I skulked through the wooded hills of the Taconic Parkway. Gray geese by the hundreds groomed the fallow fields. Oak trees gone rusty, and thin white birches making their forecast of snow. The last few red barns of the Hudson Valley's pastoral era lighting up the landscape.

When I arrived at the cemetery, crossing double railroad tracks and turning toward the English Tudor-style house marked OFFICE, six or eight cars like mine were parked in a line along the driveway. A funeral was commencing, a hearse bearing a coffin laden with a thick burden of flowers and on its roof a black-and-white photograph of the deceased, a young, handsome Asian man, framed with yellow chrysanthemums. Men wearing black suits and chauffeur caps waited in the black Cadillacs for their fares to finish the business of their grief. More than one of them gave me a look that confirmed my status as a fraud.

The woman who keeps the records wore a brown sweater set, tawny wool pencil skirt, a small gold cross on a thin chain around her neck, gold hoops in her ears, the contrast stunning between her brown skin and the gold's shine. A screen saver scrolled across her monitor: "IN HIS TIME" and "Gospel Concert." Her manner was calm and professional. She was accustomed to death and did not shrink from its obligations.

"I'm writing a book about my grandmother. I think she's buried here. Marie Bregny Macnab. She died in 1971." I told her about my books and she asked for the titles, my fraudulence beginning to fade.

"Yes, she's buried here." The woman who keeps the records checked and rechecked her screens.

"Have you got a minute?" she asked. She excused herself, went into a back room, and returned carrying a large ledger with marbled cardboard covers. The entries had been handwritten with a fountain pen to fit the ledger's narrow lines. No spreadsheets, no data sets, no digital files. She leafed through the tome, resting her index finger on the name.

"Here's what I found." She made notes on the back of a used index card: the names, dates of burial, dates of death, who bought the plots.

"Section thirty-one. Six-nine-six-zero lot. There are two plots there open for remains, three for ashes. The plot allows for six caskets."

"Yes," I said. "My grandmother was cremated."

She looked at me, paused a beat.

"I'm not supposed to tell you this, but because of who you are, I think you should know. No one witnessed the burial."

"What?"

"It happens more than you'd think."

Suddenly my mother's evasion of painful realities, her benumbing fear of death, didn't seem a particular mark of distinction. Silence in a family can erase a life. Erase a death. How common a story might that be?

"They no longer list Cause of Death in records."

"Because of AIDS?"

"Yes, and because there are so many murders."

What had I come here for? To pay my respects, I had thought, feeling there was debt hanging in the silence that followed Marnie's death. That's the name my brother and I gave our grandmother. My mother once told me that Marnie had wanted us to call her "*ma petite grandmère*" and "Marnie" is what we came up with. My mother called her "Mother." Never Mom or Mommy or Mamá, as my father had called his mother. There was a cold formality to the word. My mother never really cared for her mother, though she gave her a home.

"So, who would have buried her ashes?"

A long pause.

"It says here that she had no heirs."

"That's not right. She was my mother's mother. She lived with us."

I gave her the name of my mother, Travilla Deming. I gave her the name of the funeral home where the body would have been carried from my parents' house in Redding, Connecticut. I knew this must be where Marnie had been taken, because it was the funeral home where my father's body had been delivered in 1990. I had arranged the details, my mother then incapacitated with grief.

"Hull," I said. Like the hold of a ship. Hard to forget a name like that for ferrying the dead.

The woman who keeps the records showed me the form. Heirs: an unchecked box, an empty line. She showed me the affidavit of heirship. Marie Bregny Macnab left no children. She described the plot for six burials purchased on April 22, 1924, by Marie and George Macnab, who lived at 312 West Seventy-Eighth Street, New York City.

"Yes, that was my grandmother, Marie Bregny Macnab, and her husband, George Travilla Macnab."

"On April 23, Julia B. Smith was buried here." She showed me the rectangular plot on the cemetery map. "That one is a body."

"Yes, Julia was Marie's sister. Jou-Jou, they called her. Both sisters were dressmakers. Their mother too. They ran a salon in the city designing and making Parisian dresses."

"Then in 1941 George T. Macnab was buried. That one is also a body." She showed me the plots on the map of the dead. "In 1932 Sarah E. Alliger was buried … a body … here." There were two empty plots remaining.

Who was Sarah E. Alliger and why was she buried with my relatives?

"Here is where your grandmother's ashes are."

She pointed to the spot in the Uncas plot, Section 31, located just off Tecumseh Avenue on a high knoll.

Pause.

"There's no gravestone. You'll have to find it by locating the ones on either side."

She circled the spot on the map and drew little arrows on the lanes for me to follow up the grassy hill through the massive land of the dead.

"There's no marker of any kind?"

Pause. I could feel the woman who keeps the records calibrating her response.

"Your grandmother died on February 9, 1971."

"Yes, she was living at home with my mother and father."

"She arrived here February 19. No one claimed her. There was no funeral. No instructions. And the paperwork said there were no heirs. When that happens, we store them for a year. She was buried in January 1972."

"So, who would have buried her?"

"I don't know. But we can't keep them. They start to smell."

We looked at the dates. The form stating that Marie Bregny had no heirs.

"That's not true. My mother was her daughter."

We entered that into the record.

"Did she have any other children?"

"One stillborn in Mexico by her first marriage, but I guess that doesn't count."

"No, we have to put it down. What year was that?"

"Maybe turn of the century?"

She wrote into the record "one stillborn child around 1900." She handed me the affidavit to take for my mother's signature as heir to the plots.

KENSICO CEMETERY IS A BEAUTIFUL PLACE TO BE DEAD. CRE-ated in Valhalla, New York, a forty-minute train ride from Grand Central Station, the cemetery sprawls over four hundred acres of graceful, rolling hills, land ascending to the highest rise between Long Island Sound and Tarrytown and fronting a mile along the rail line. Built in 1889, when New York City cemeteries were filling up, Kensico was intended to be New York's "Great City of the Dead." A special rail conveyance, "Car Kensico," carpeted and draped in heavy Victorian style, could be hired for sixty dollars to carry the remains and mourners out for the burial. One compartment carried the remains, the immediate family sitting in upholstered chairs lining the walls of the railcar's parlor. A turntable at the cemetery station spun the car around, so that mourners could return to the city "without the slightest contact with the traveling public," as the company advertised. This was meant to be a cemetery for the wealthy and cultural elite. New York in the 1880s flaunted its wealth and turned a good deal of it toward culture. The New York Public Library, Metropolitan Museum of Art, Madison Square Garden, and American Museum of Natural History were all paid for not by taxes but by donations from New Yorkers who intended for their city to rival the great cities of Europe. In spite of massive immigration—one million residents in 1870 swelled to three and a half million in 1900—in spite of desperate poverty and cruel working conditions in the tenements, in spite of cholera and gang wars, New York City was a place exhilarated by its promise. Even the dead could look forward to luxury.

The Kensico founders gave Native American names to lakes and lanes and plots in the cemetery: Dacotah, Powhattan, Katonah, Mohegan, Katahdin, Mannahata, Uncas. They believed the spirit of the land and its ancestral people would lend harmony to the newly dead. Impressive as an advertising slogan, but as a trope the naming carries heavy freight, considering the fate of the tribes. It seems almost a lament. Perhaps it suggests the hope that in the land of the dead all hostilities can be laid to rest.

Downslope from the graves, the old village of Kensico lies flooded under a great reservoir that flows to New York City. The first dam was built in 1885 to impound the Bronx River where the lay of hills and valley were right for holding water. Locals say if they stand on the top of the dam, they can see the chimneys of their great-grandparents' houses ghosting up from the reservoir's depths. Layer after layer of erasure.

During construction of the dam, labor camps were set up for workers. Their train stop needed an address, as Kensico's post office was about to be lost under the reservoir. The postmaster's wife was said to be an opera buff who loved Wagner and Norse mythology. She suggested the name of Valhalla for the new post office, honoring the Hall of the Slain in Viking tradition, where Norse warriors feasted on endless mead and boar stew while awaiting their great and final battle against the World Serpent.

✳

MY GRANDMOTHER WAS AN OPERA LOVER, ATTENDING FRE-
quently when she lived in the city. At our home in Connecticut, on Saturday afternoons she listened to live broadcasts from the Metropolitan Opera
House, singing along with the arias in the soaring thin voice of one not to be
denied her passions. During intermission, she followed along with the Opera
Quiz, though as a subscriber to *Opera News* she would have answered all the
questions before the airing. A sparkling conversationalist well into her nineties, she enjoyed the on-air repartee of the opera aficionados. I think of her
room as a little Europe in our woodland home. She had an ornate cherry sec-
retary desk with mother-of-pearl inlays, a teak chiffonier and dresser, a round
table with decorative floral inlays of blond wood. She kept a covered Limo-
ges porcelain bowl the size of a dinner plate in the center of the table. The
vessel was a translucent white—bone china is made from ground-up cattle
bones, which make the porcelain particularly strong and translucent—with
art deco swirls of embossed gold. Marie loved material culture and collected
it: a "painting" of elegantly dressed women in floor-length gowns, the work
entirely composed of azure wings from morpho butterflies; drawers full of
handmade lace; diamond rings and brooches that she wore as an everyday
matter of style. She also loved sweets and on her annual trips to the city
returned with a white baker's box tied with thin white string and filled with
pastries, each with its special architecture: brioche, éclair, Napoleon, stru-
del, macaroon. She continued these excursions into her nineties—the last
one during the great blackout of November 9, 1965. She was staying with a
friend in the city and, with lights and elevator out, a stranger had carried her
piggyback up the stairs.

The dress-form manikin stood in the corner, clothed in her sheath of
ivory muslin. She stood as sentry, buxom torso weirdly truncated at the
thigh, guarding, it now seems, the history and dignity of a woman whose
life had narrowed down from one of cosmopolitan bustle to the redoubt of

old age. Though her business of dressmaking had folded during the Great Depression, she continued to make her own clothes until the end of her life, dresses fit perfectly to her shape, the cut she knew was most flattering, fitted snugly at the bust and torso, then flaring at the waist into a graceful A-line skirt that flowed over the hips and hovered mid-calf. She had been gifted, my mother told me, at designing clothes for women who had a deformity—a hump on her back or a surgical scar. It was one of the few things my mother told me about her mother's business. Silence, in general, abounded. She'd been ashamed that her mother was a businesswoman and not one of leisure. When I asked about the business, her most frequent reply was "Why would you want to know about that?" I never had the guts to stand up to these imperious dismissals, so now I'm left with silence and an unmarked grave.

"Did she ever want you to help in the dressmaking?"

"She tried, but I was too nervous. I was hopeless."

Marnie was always old to me. She came to live with my parents in 1945, the year before I was born, when she was seventy-three. She had outlived two husbands. The first was Antonio Modesto del Valle, a Cubano living in New York, to whom she was betrothed in an arranged marriage when she was nineteen. They lived in Mexico City. She showed me a framed photograph of her mounted on the horse that had been a gift from the President of Mexico. These were the happiest six years of her life. When her husband died from consumption, she returned to New York to run her mother's business.

And here are the small cloisonné vase and blue Bohemian cut-glass bowl, gifts she handed to me from her private collection. The heavy glass bowl had been a present from the husband of her best friend, Adeline Donché, a corsetiere who made a fortune.

"That terrible man, a strikebreaker," my mother cursed when years later she saw the blue cut-glass bowl on my table. She said it was an ashtray for cigars, and only then did I see the cigar-sized divots along its thick glass edge.

✳

I TOOK TECUMSEH AVENUE UP THE LONG GRASSY SLOPE AS IT meandered through landscaped grounds loud with songbirds, dogwood, azalea. The place looked more like a park or sculpture garden than a graveyard. Kensico has a Tree Walk Guide, each numbered tree with its legend.

White Ash (Olive family) is subject to many diseases which have killed many notable trees recently. The wood is known for its use in baseball bats. Grows to 80 feet.

White Birch, usually called paper birch. Bark layers have been used for canoe and wigwam covers.
Grows 50 to 70 feet.

Gingko. Virtually unchanged on the earth for some 150 million years. One of the few trees that existed during the dinosaur era that is still in existence today. Gingko is one of the most distinct of all deciduous trees.

A forest stream runs through the cemetery. Two lakes grace its hillside lawns. The living find space to contemplate their losses. The dead find room to breathe. Elbow room for the wealthy and accomplished to express themselves one last time. One mausoleum sports giant bronze doors, each with an elegant bronze knocker. On the back wall, a Tiffany window depicts a woodland stream composed of blue glass that meanders under the canopy of a great oak. "The Guide to Notable Burials" reads like a micro-portrait of New York City:

Swing trombonist Tommy Dorsey

Baseball legend Lou Gehrig

New York producer Florenz Ziegfeld

Opera singer Geraldine Farrar

Pioneer aviatrix Harriet Quimby

Broadcaster Fred Friendly

Comedian Danny Kaye

Screenwriter Paddy Chayefsky

Department store magnate Paul Bonwit

Special sections for members of the Actors Fund of America and National Vaudeville Association, some of whom died in poverty

Special section for the Salvation Army where General Evangeline Booth, London's White Angel of the Slums, daughter of the Army's founder, lies buried surrounded by rows of her warriors

Luigi Palma di Cesnola, Piedmontese veteran of the Crimean and U.S. Civil Wars, first director of New York's Metropolitan Museum of Art, lies under a towering monument

Composer Sergei Rachmaninoff beneath an Eastern Orthodox cross

Author Ayn Rand beneath a six-foot dollar sign

I WALKED UPSLOPE TO SECTION 31. I FOUND LOT 6960. THE Suplee family. The Towbins. Simple granite gravestones. A less grandiose

neighborhood of Kensico. An open space the size of six graves was marked with patchy dried grass, a small pile of browned leaves, and tangled among them a half-deflated Mylar balloon tied with red-braided ribbon. The groundsmen had been piling autumn leaves in the one blank spot in the neighborhood. The site was a little trashy, a little threadbare, which was pretty much how I felt knowing my grandmother lay there, a pile of ashes poured into the crematorium's transport container and buried by a gravedigger in order to clean out the storage closet by attending to this stranger who had no heirs. I must have been the first person to ever visit her grave, and this was happening more than forty years after she had died in her bed in our family home.

A flood of images from childhood flickered by my mind's eye: the way she made crepe suzettes for my brother and me when my parents were away for dinner; Swedish meatballs she cooked; blueberries she picked from our forest meadow and made into pie and preserves; canning jars of brandied peaches she put up; being taught how to properly sew on a button so that it would not come loose; sitting on her lap while she bounced her knees and taught me songs, a French lesson in "La Plume de ma tante" and "Frère Jacques," a life lesson in "My Grandfather's Clock." She bounced me on her knees in time with the hymnal beat, tempo and knees halting for the double caesura of poor grandfather's heart, all in good fun.

My grandfather's clock was too large for the shelf
So it stood ninety years on the floor
It was taller by half than the old man himself
Though it weighed not a pennyweight more

It was bought on the morn of the day that he was born
And was always his treasure and pride
But it stopped, short, never to go again
When the old man died

Ninety years without slumbering
    Tick-tock tick-tock
His life seconds numbering
    Tick-tock tick-tock
It stopped, short, never to go again
When the old man died

Marnie always wore a corset, a beige lace-up affair with stays, covering her torso from thigh to bosom. It was neither elegant nor seductive, rather a practical matter of keeping the lines of feminine form clear on her somewhat prodigious form. I think too she found comfort in the corset's embrace. She tucked a small pink silk sachet into her cleavage, in which she kept a few dollars folded very small. She pinned this to the inside of the corset. She advised me always to do this to keep myself safe in the city if my purse were stolen. Because of the corset, her body felt hard when I sat on her lap or embraced her. I didn't feel the soft warmth of flesh while in her arms, but they offered a stiffened version of intimacy and I welcomed it.

On the grassy hill below, a funeral procession wended along one cemetery lane. A Black family walking together, the old and the young making their way to a place of farewell. Another procession traced a farther lane, the family, perhaps Japanese, dressed in black with white silk sashes. After the burial, they walked in the opposite direction, all the sashes gone.

I stood beside the silence of the unmarked grave. A grave not sanctified by ritual or love. I could see why Marnie would have chosen Valhalla to bury her sister and later her estranged husband. I could see why she would have wanted this to be her resting place. A cosmopolitan woman, a purveyor of high fashion, an entrepreneur, world traveler, lover of opera and finely made things. I gathered up the Mylar balloon and some cedar chips used for mulch. I wanted evidence, though of what I could no longer be sure. The birds were going crazy, singing away as dusk came down like a lid.

3

⁎

The House Built of Herring

Castalia, Grand Manan, New Brunswick.

IN THE NORTH ATLANTIC, WHERE I HAVE SPENT SUMMERS ON Grand Manan Island at the mouth of the Bay of Fundy since I was child, herring (*Clupea harengus*) migrate in shoals a mile or more long, millions of fish that know how to keep the just-so distance from each other while racing and turning and feeding as one shining mass. Herring are lean and muscular, silver with blue-green flashes on their dorsal sides. They have big eyes, small heads, and bulldog jaws. Their journeys span the water from North Carolina to Greenland, moving from spawning to feeding grounds and then into deep water for wintering. They are wily group hunters, feeding on *Calanus finmarchicus*, tiny crustaceans rich in oil that are the predominant zooplankton in the northern sea. Herring practice synchro-predation (less lyrically known as "ram-feeding") in fearsome bands of synchronized swimmers that keep the distance between them equal to the jump distance of their prey. When the copepod leaps to escape the predator, it lands right in the open mouth of another herring. Thus, the prey shape the social structure of the herring.

Fish have shaped the social structure of the island too. Traditionally, men spent weeks at sea. Women stayed at home to tend house, kin, finances— all the family business. Traditionally, men considered it bad luck to have a woman on shipboard. This wasn't the only superstition arising to counter the peril of working at sea. Don't wear corduroy. Don't bring a bologna sandwich. Canadian geographer Joan Marshall wrote about the island's gender dynamics in her cultural study *Tides of Change on Grand Manan Island: Culture and Belonging in a Fishing Community*. Women, she found, became skilled and adaptable, managing the household in the men's absence, then ceding the authority when the men returned. The roles are changing now as more women take to the sea in the booming lobster fishery. Thus too are the prey determining changes in the social structure of the predator.

There are plenty of predators adept at gobbling herring: hake and whales and, most adept of all, humans. Yet still, herring mean abundance, their conservation status of least concern to marine biologists. Try telling that to the weir fishermen of Grand Manan, where herring have been the foundation of a thriving culture that made this island of twenty-five hundred souls the sardine capital of the world in the 1880s, when islanders packed one million boxes (twenty thousand tons) of locally caught and processed fish for export. In the 1930s nearly a hundred weirs—the graceful structures of sixty-foot-tall stakes, birch top-poles, and twine that capture fish as they school shoreward to feed—skirted the island's shore. When our family began visiting the island in the 1950s, there were still dozens of weirs, smokehouses operating in each of the island's five villages, and a sardine factory in Seal Cove.

By 2015 weirs had dwindled to nine, and as I began writing about the fishery in early summer 2016, there was no sign of work on the Cora Belle, Iron Lady, Mystery, Jubilee, or many other sites. A boat went down the previous fall in the Turnip Patch, likely due to the hull being staved in by a broken weir stake. It's unlikely the weir will be rebuilt. Perhaps a few more will go in, built by dreamers who hate losing the old ways and know that herring can change their minds about where they will migrate. The smokehouses are all shut down and dilapidated, the sardine cannery too, as corporate interests have taken over the processing and marketing of fish. What herring are caught by seiners in deeper waters of the Bay of Fundy are churned up to become fertilizer, feed for farmed salmon, or bait for the lucrative lobster industry that is booming. There may be herring in the sea, but for reasons of their own and our making, in recent years they have rarely visited the island's shores. The herring could come back, but, with only nine or ten weirs looking to rebuild and climate change promising nothing good for the cold-loving species of the bay, it's clear that a certain handmade, place-made way of life is nearly over.

As a child, I fell in love with herring and the brush weirs islanders build to harvest them. In photographs of our family's first visit to the island in 1956, I clutch my trusty Brownie Hawkeye camera, carrying it everywhere as if a survival kit. Was this the start of my poetic imagination, an insistence to see, to fix the flow of time into stills, to mark what seemed to matter both to inner and outer worlds? The photo that has survived from my career as a nine-year-old documentarian was taken when the family rode out to Whale Cove to watch men seine the Mystery weir. The four-by-four creased and worn image shows nothing but fish and men, the seine net raised to become nothing but bounty, a teeming silvery mass of fish struggling for their lives, as the men who raise the nets struggle for theirs. It was beautiful and terrible and thrilling.

That first summer, my mother and father purchased a house on the island. My father said we could not afford to buy it, though the cost as I recall was fourteen hundred dollars for the cottage and ten acres. My mother said, We'll use Frances Shedd's money. My mother had befriended the librarian in Wethersfield, Connecticut, inviting her to our home for Thanksgiving and such. Shedd was elderly, single, and without family. When she died, she left her modest estate to my mother. A few stocks and an antique Governor Winthrop slant-lid desk. The desk sits today in my guest room in Arizona. The librarian's modest stocks bought us an island home.

The Castalia cottage was a hard-luck house, built in 1864 by James Smith, a local fisherman and farmer. The foundation was constructed with stones pulled out of the wooded hillside, the beams adze-hewn from black spruce downed on the same hill. Perhaps Smith had an ox or team of draft horses to help. Certainly, he had neighbors working by his side. Weathered cedar shingles covered the exterior walls like fish scales, each fog-loving shingle hand-split from the timber of a water-loving tree. Though the cottage faced the sea, the two rooms on the front side of the house had only one casement window each, the rooms small and dark, but easy to heat with a wood stove in the basement and a big grate in the living room floor to let the heat rise. No concern for the spectacular view of the sea in front of the house played into the construction. This place was built by a fisherman who knew his environment, steep-roofed so snow and ice would slide off. "Build a stay against storms and cold," he might have told himself. "You'll see plenty of water working on it."

A hand pump pulled fresh water from the stone-lined well into the cast-iron kitchen sink, the wastewater piped out into the rhubarb patch. The house had no "flush." An outhouse stood about thirty yards from the shed door. A long walk in a snowstorm. I'm sure there were chamber pots in the bedrooms. By the time we acquired the place, it had been abandoned for years. The walls peeled with stained wallpaper and crumbled with failing plaster. One wall, having lost its cosmetic finish, revealed a layer of house-wrap made from strips of birch bark. The front door—planks. No porch or deck, just a block of cement that ran like a dead-end sidewalk from one corner of the house to the other. No one uses front doors on the island. The shed on the back side of the house, cluttered with boots and tools and coffee tins full of nails, was the welcoming entrance for all. The sheds traditionally were a place to hang the oil-clothes when men came in from the sea. Commercial oilcloth or oilskins came into fashion in the nineteenth century, when fabric was treated with linseed oil or tar to keep the fishermen warm and dry. I imagine that indigenous people of the North for centuries must have used seal oil or whale oil to temper their clothing on hunts. I don't suppose the old sheds ever lost their stink of fish oil and tar. Those clothes must have stood up on their own without a man inside them, so stiffened by oil and salt and fish scale.

A gnarled lilac tree stood in our yard, its trunk surrounded by a mat of English thyme. A half dozen knobby ancient apple trees ringed the yard. The place had been in the Smith family for ninety-three years, though we bought it from Harry and Nina Dunbar. I think she had been a Smith before marriage. There were three small bedrooms, one downstairs and two up the steep narrow stairs—like those heading up from a boat's galley—with a white-painted birch sapling for handrail. Glossy white, heavy marine paint. I heard that seven people had lived in the house: mother and father, uncle, and four children who must have slept in beds together packed like sardines. I heard that a woman who lived in the house had put stones in her pockets, walked across the road and into the bay, and drowned herself. I heard that a man who lived here was lost at sea off Newfoundland's Grand Banks and that he survived a week adrift in his dory. The island lives by stories. Some of them are true, the one about the fisherman among them.

Mantford Smith was the man's name. In 1887 six islanders were drowned when a rogue squall swamped their dories. Only he among the Grand Mananers, the nineteen-year-old son of James Smith, survived, saying little about the event until he was eighty-two years old, when he agreed to be interviewed by a reporter from *The Saint Croix Courier*. One takes life seriously on a fishing island. One learns when to remain silent and when to tell a story.

The Grand Banks are legendary fishing grounds on the great Atlantic shelf that twelve thousand years ago was part of mainland North America. This plateau, submerged in shallow ocean when the last Ice Age melted and the sea rose to drown the eastern shore, runs from Cape Cod to Newfoundland. The Gulf Stream and Labrador Current meet here, creating ideal conditions for zooplankton on which the fish feed. The region has long been prized for the abundance of its fish. The American Museum of Natural History reports that by the year 1000, Basque fishermen from northern Spain had established an international trade in salt fish harvested from the Grand Banks. They kept the region a secret from other Europeans for five hundred years—though it was no secret to the First Nations people of the North Atlantic or, as some called it, "the herring pond." In 1497, when Giovanni Caboto, who we know as John Cabot, set off on an English vessel in search of a spice route, he found a thousand Basque vessels plying these waters. Legend has it that fish were so abundant, they could be scooped from the water with a bucket. The gold rush in the Grand Banks fishery lasted a millennium. Overfishing and climate change have diminished many species in the region. Ocean warming here is happening faster than in 99 percent of the global oceans. Four times faster. And the pace of change is accelerating. "The problem with the people ... out here on the headlands of North America," writes Mark Kurlansky in *Cod: A Biography of the Fish That Changed the World*, "is that they are at the wrong end of a 1,000-year fishing spree."

Well into Mantford Smith's time, the bounty prevailed. The *Nellie Woodbury* was after cod. The schooner left North Head on Grand Manan on May 22, 1887, and was out 116 days under sail. They fished for cod all along the way to Grand Banks, and the fish were plentiful. They had twenty-eight hundred bushels of salt aboard to cure the fish. Off the coast of Newfoundland, the mothership anchored in shallow water, the dories that had been stacked on deck were lowered down, each rowed by one man who long-lined until his boat was full, then returned with the haul to the mothership. Twenty-one dories, twenty-two crew.

It's difficult to picture how many vessels worked the waters of the Grand Banks in the nineteenth century. How many ships traversed from one continent to another, pushed on the winds of commerce, emigration, exile, enslavement, appetite, adventure, and risk. How much human life depended on the sea and people's ability to make vessels and nets and ropes and sails and salt, and to read water and sky and stars. Their ability to survive unimaginable hardship. The shipwrecks alone give a feel of the scale of maritime enterprise and risk. The Maritime Museum of the Atlantic reports that for Nova Scotia alone there were twenty-five thousand shipwrecks between 1583 and 1999. In the year Mantford Smith was lost in his dory, seventy-six boats were recorded as wrecks on Georges Bank alone (an area the size of a bloated Massachusetts that is the most westward region of the continental shelf). Reasons included "missing," "stranded," "foundered," "abandoned," "wrecked," "ashore," "stove in," "burnt," "collision," or "misstayed." Mostly schooners. Also brigantines, brigs, barques. One dredge. A handful of steam vessels, but nearly all were propelled by sail. Vessels out of or headed to Boston, Philadelphia, New York, Brazil, Argentina, England, France, Ireland, Scotland, Newfoundland, Guyana, Bermuda, and the Bay of Fundy. A veritable United Nations of wrecks. "Cause of event" cited:

Fog

Fog and smoke

Ice (one in January, one in May)

Snowstorm

Struck object

Navigation error: mistook lights, total loss

Leak

Broke mooring

Mechanical failure

Stress of weather

Collision

Judgement error

Misstayed (referring to the ropes that stabilize a ship's masts)

Fire. Cargo: coal. Crew many hours in boats. On fire. Gale.

Current

Unknown: Drifted ashore. Total loss.

Missing: At sea

The data take no account of dorymen lost to fog, swells, squalls, current, or judgment error.

The *Nellie Woodbury* encountered one of the severest gales seen for many years. At eight thirty in the morning, Captain Fred Hodgkins saw the barometer fall. He fired a signal for the men to return to the ship. The fishing was good and the men continued. The barometer fell further. Captain Hodgkins fired another signal. Some returned, others did not. George Bass held up a cod, gave it a pat, laid it down, set lines, and went to work as though no warning had been given. It wasn't the first time the crew had hung on after a warning signal. The captain had upbraided them for it. "Some of you will get drowned yet by your recklessness."

The storm broke at nine, fierce swells rising and fog falling over the dories. The sea grew rougher, the breeze harder, and soon "all was commotion." Men jumped to their oars. Seven got on board the mother ship. The captain cut and ran for the others, managing to rescue six from their boats. "The others," reads the account in the *Eastport Sentinel*, "six in number, owing to the density of the fog, the blinding seas, the fierceness of the gale and the unmanageableness of the vessel, could not be reached or found." Six Grand Mananers were drowned when the rogue squall swamped their dories.

Mantford Smith was the last man rescued. He had been blown twenty to thirty miles from the *Nellie*. As the story came to me through island legend, he was adrift for a week in his dory. However long the rescue actually took, surely every minute was a trial. After keeping silent for over sixty years about the event, Smith recounted his experience to *The Saint Croix Courier*. When the gale blew in, he rowed for the *Nellie* until one of his metal rowlocks split. He made a drag out of the anchor, thwarts, and warp. He dumped overboard a half ton of fish he had caught. He got in the bow of his dory, keeping "his tiny craft head to it and sailing before the wind." Laprille Hopkins, the mate, however, a man with twenty years' experience at sea, "sat in the middle of his dory and tried to keep it stern to the wind. No one was able to figure out why he did this."

For the men who made it back to the *Nellie,* the going was rough. The sails were in ribbons.

Breaking seas boarded the vessel until her waist was full of surging water. One man was washed into the scuppers and nearly drowned before he was rescued. Another was jammed beneath the windlass with such force that a number of ribs were broken. The helmsman, lashed to the wheel, was comparatively safe. Some of the last dories were sighted, but only momentarily. Spray and spume from the ragged-topped wave crests almost obliterated them from view.

Smith continued to bail until exhaustion compelled him to quit.

The ship removed plugs from her cod liver barrels and spilled a large quantity of oil out of the scuppers and into the sea. "This smoothed the waters for a considerable distance," Smith reported. By the time he was found and a rescue rope passed over his dory, he clutched the line for an instant but lost his grip. By the third throw, he had it.

"I didn't have the strength of a mouse, but I tied the rope around my waist and soon was pulled alongside the Woodbury and yanked on deck. I was so frightened I could not stand up."

He'd watched Laprille's dory founder.

High sea broke close unto him raising his dory by the stern almost perpendicularly and throwing him into the sea, where he sank. He came to the surface barely, just once, threw up his hands, went down again and disappeared entirely.

"I shall never forget seeing Laprille's arm sticking out of the water," Smith reported, "after his dory capsized and his attempt to wave goodbye to me as his head went under."

It took the *Nellie Woodbury* eleven days to sail back to port in Maine. Of the Grand Mananers on the crew, Mantford Smith was the sole survivor. The following October he returned to sea with the same captain.

In 1864 James Smith built a house on the Long Bank of the Castalia shore on Grand Manan Island. He raised four children, one of whom was lost at sea for a week and returned to shepherd this property on to his descendants. He hauled the stones from the woods. Cut the timbers from the hills. The shingles that lap one over the other like herring scales were cut from the grove of cedars, the remnant of which still stands rooted in my woodlot. By circumstance and luck, this house has come to me. I have become the steward of what stories I can find that have dwelled in this place.

4

✳

Camel Hair Coat

Cashmere wool truck. *Photo by profeta, courtesy of iStock.*

I'M SORRY THAT SOMEWHERE IN EVOLUTIONARY HISTORY OUR distant ancestors dropped their pelts, leaving us with only the cranial crown and genital thatch. Human nakedness is a marker of our separation from the other terrestrial mammals, for most of us a mark of embarrassment, for some a mark of shame. How must those early generations of hairless ones have envied their hirsute elders with their full-body fur. Or perhaps they ridiculed them as atavistic boneheads. To pillage, etymologically speaking, is to strip of hair. We were pillaged. Left vulnerable in thin skin. To survive meant to invent and cooperate. Our ancestors traded fur for big heads, community, and imagination.

Roland Barthes says we wear clothes for four reasons: protection, modesty, ornamentation, and signification. We dress to create ourselves, transform ourselves; to seduce or impress or intimidate or entertain or warn others. We dress for work. We undress for bed. Or we dress to be undressed. We dress down for home. We dress up for company. We dress to be seen. We dress to be invisible. We dress for armor. We dress to belong. We dress to stand out. We dress to join a team. We dress to signify our class or gender or ethnicity. We dress to mask our class or gender or ethnicity. Everyone wears jeans. We dress to please our parents. We dress to defy our parents. We dress to lure a mate. Every day we decide how we will dress. It is not always an easy decision. We stare into the closet. We stare into the mirror. Is that me?

Why did I spend two hundred dollars recently to buy a long A-line cotton knit skirt (ivory with abstract indigo scrolling), an asymmetrically zippered indigo sweatshirt, and a dressy forest-green rumpled crepe skirt that I imagined would flow with the breeze? Versions of myself to hang in the closet in the event they coincide with what I wish to become on a given day. In my twenties, I dismissed fashion along with everything else of the industrialized world I could jettison. I lived in poverty in northern Vermont raising a daughter. I grew our food. I made corduroy trousers for myself and refused to buy a zipper. Buttons and button holes would surely do. I made dresses for my daughter. I made her a quilt in a starburst pattern. The choice was about frugality and resistance to the demands of capital. Easy, since I had none. It was about learning to make do and to make what I could not afford to buy. It was about valuing the modest work of my hands. It was an expression of a particular time and place. It was a fashion statement, if fashion is what we make of what we are given.

But *couture* is a word I have only recently come to feel part of my lexicon. I have begun using it to describe the dressmaking business run by my great-grandmother Louisa Bregny and later her daughter Marie Bregny in

Manhattan from the Gilded Age to the Great Depression. They created custom-made dresses for a wealthy clientele, ran a small business employing up to sixteen women, cut cloth without patterns following the Paris designs of the season, invited the customers to fittings in the parlor. Perhaps a touch of peach brandy? Sometimes they outfitted entire wedding parties. Those were the nights my mother remembers, her mother cutting cloth on the dining room table until midnight while she retreated to the bedroom cutting photos of movie stars out of magazines. Among their customers were the Steinway sisters. Sadly, that is the only name I know from a clientele that spanned fifty years. There is a lot I do not know, but I am resigned to find in fragments a picture of the whole. Perhaps this is a rationalization for the fact that I am not a good enough sleuth to turn up more factual material about the business. Perhaps these women's lives have left little trace. And yet they lived remarkable lives, accomplished and courageous women who rode the Gilded Age right on into its waning.

Nearly everywhere I looked in Manhattan, I did not find Louisa. She would have landed at Castle Garden, the immigrant port of entry prior to Ellis Island. Immigration records from the years she would have arrived were destroyed in a fire. I was always told that she came to New York alone, intending to move to Mexico. By the time she arrived in New York, it proved no longer safe for the French to go to Mexico, so she stayed and later married another French émigré. Recently I came across an oral history by one of Louisa's grandnieces, who said that Louisa had come to New York on her honeymoon. This became a pattern: wherever I looked I did not find much evidence. Wherever I found story, I found a counter-narrative. Record of her marriage? Yes, but the official New York City document dates the marriage in 1886—more than a decade after their three daughters were born.

After years of erasure and contradiction in my search, I found my great-grandmother's name listed in the Trow Business Directory for New York City in each year from 1878 until 1908: "Louisa Bregny, dressmaker." I laughed out loud in joy at the microfiche reader, where I had bent my head in supplication. I noted the business address for each year, beginning in 1878 at 272 West Eleventh Street and tracking north with the city as it grew. The facts bore out at least part of the story: Louisa Bregny ran a dressmaking business for at least thirty years in Manhattan. What does that tell me? There were thirty-five thousand dressmakers in New York City at the time. Most of them worked in tenement sweatshops. Few ran their own businesses. Fewer yet with a résumé including having been a dressmaker for Empress Eugénie, formidable second-in-command (and wife) to Napoleon III.

"She ran an haute couture business," I tell people, though I shouldn't be-cause in France the term is protected by law. Since 1868, when the Chambre Syndicale de la Haute Couture was established, the phrase refers to ateliers making exclusive custom-fitted clothing tailored to the wearer through a se-ries of fittings. This control of designer branding came to Paris with Charles Frederick Worth, the Englishman who brought innovation to French fash-ion culture. In addition to individual custom-made items, he launched the House of Worth, where models showcased the season's designs. Customers could order the dresses on display in the fabric and color of their choice. He was the first brand-name designer and had the organizational sophistication to know that such branding should be protected from imitation. So, the Chambre Syndicale saw to the task and continues to do so. Fashion houses found eligible each year as *haute couture* must meet these criteria:

1.   Design made-to-order for private clients, with one or more fittings
2.   Have a workshop (*atelier*) in Paris that employs at least fifteen staff members full-time
3.   Have at least twenty full-time technical people, in at least one work-shop (*atelier*)
4.   Present a collection of at least fifty original designs to the public every fashion season (twice, in January and July of each year), of both day and evening garments

As to my great-grandmother Louisa Bregny, she may have left Paris around the time this system of brand control was enacted. It is easy to imagine that she resented the new constraints on her livelihood, particularly in seeing a man—an Englishman—taking over precincts of artistic making that had long been the purview of women. Perhaps she foresaw commercial opportunity in America. Perhaps after the French claimed Mexico, she saw Mexican flags waving in glee along the Seine and was swept in enthusiasm that France had a brazen foothold in the New World. I do not know why she crossed the Atlantic, only that she must have been motivated by a powerful drive to escape circumstances that constrained her and that she had an intuition she would succeed. I know too that she must had have help, financing, connections.

I WAS FOUR OR FIVE YEARS OLD WHEN I HAD MY FIRST QUASI-couture experience. I stood for fittings on a small upholstered stool in Marnie's room. She adjusted the darts, shaping the curve at the waistline of the coat, though at that age I had no waistline. She had me turn and turn to mark the hem. I can feel her hands holding me steady as the little stool wobbled. The wool was snug against my chest then flared out around my knees. Was the coat too tight or do I just remember how it felt as I began to grow out of it? The winter coat was the golden beige of a camel with a brown velvet collar that fit close to the neck. The buttons were covered too with brown velvet, one single row down the middle. She made a bandeau hat, which tied under the chin, of the same brown velvet. I hated the hat and its irritating bind. I would not remember this, my first dress coat, if I had not found a photograph of me wearing it. But the photograph remembers me. I am standing beneath the big double-trunked hickory in our front yard in Avon, Connecticut. I look uncomfortable, as children often do when dressed up in finer clothes than those for playing, the clothes suggesting a seriousness they do not yet quite understand.

I loved that big hickory. It stood on a small knoll in the lawn, the trunk wide at the base, then splitting into two trunks about three feet up. The bark, a soft rippled gray, same color as the squirrels that mastered its height and taunted with their chittering. In the fall the nuts scattered on the ground, hard and blond. I tried a few times to crack them open with a rock but failed. They were little tokens of mystery. I knew they had value, but what kind of value was this that could not be obtained? So many objects in the outdoors of my childhood trigger reflection—acorn, flagstone, pine cone, partridge berry, British soldiers my mother and I would gather to place in a terrarium—my inner life wed to those woodland surroundings.

I understood the camel coat to be a gesture of love and care. Recalling it, I can feel someone dressing me, the awkward process of shoving my arms into the snug sleeves, standing still to be buttoned up, the strange feeling of a body being jostled into comfort and safety, not wanting to stand still for that. Someone dressed me—what a strange and cold way to speak of it. That someone would have been my grandmother during the fittings. My grandmother had a knack for making a game of ordinary things. Stupid little games that entertained. Like when she taught me how to make a bed, she folded the bedspread back to lay the pillows down, then folded the bedspread over the pillows, tucking a seam under the pillows to make it tidy. "Tucka-tucka-tucka," she sang as her hand worked along the pillow line. I don't remember any games in the fittings for the coat. What I remember was that it was special and that made me special. As awkward as the fittings felt, I understood them to be a form of love.

In writing this, I begin to wonder why we called it a camel coat. The style was popular in New England in the 1950s. When I was a teenager I admired the look. It seemed simple, classic and elegant, a Katharine Hepburn coat, and that brand of femininity appealed to me. No one else in my family had a camel coat. My father's dress coat was a gray wool herringbone, my mother's a muskrat fur (middle-class mink—she went for flair), my brother's, I don't remember, but a bomber jacket would have suited him, and my grandmother's a black Persian lamb.

In the New Testament, Matthew says, "And the same John had his raiment of camel's hair, and a leathern girdle about his loins; and his meat was locusts and wild honey," describing the arrival of John the Baptist, who came preaching in the wilderness of Judea. I have to admire the sweet homoeroticism in that meat description. But it is the camel hair reference that I am after, wondering how deep in history a camel-hair garment can be found. Traditional herdsmen of the Mongolian steppe, the few that remain, follow the animals and harvest the wool dropped during their molting. The fur comes off in huge clumps and very fast during the springtime. The herdsmen stack the wool on trucks and use it for coats and for the outer walls of their yurts. Camel hair shows up in an undershirt worn by Richard the Lion Heart to protect him from being chafed by his armor during the Crusades. Antarctic explorer Admiral Richard E. Byrd wore camel hair for warmth. Camel coats were popular in England and the United States in the 1920s, when polo players would throw a loose-fitting camel coat over their shoulders between chukkers. The coat had no buttons but was a wrap style with a wool belt that tied at the waist. Soon the fans were wearing camel coats and Ivy League students were wearing them. By the late 1920s and 1930s, the camel coat, according to *Gentleman's Gazette*, was "the overcoat that had the biggest impact on men's fashion." It fell out of favor in the 1950s when trench coats with detachable linings took over in popularity. But Ralph Lauren, a sports fan who launched his Polo brand in 1967, continues to offer camel hair coats each winter in a range of styles.

Camel hair used in fabric comes from double-humped Bactrian camels, which are native to the steppes of Central Asia. The wild Bactrian camels are critically endangered, but there are two million domesticated Bactrians now producing wool for commerce in China, Mongolia, Iran, Afghanistan, Russia, New Zealand, and Australia. These animals grow a long shaggy coat with coarse guard hairs on the outside and soft fleece underneath. The fleece has a hollow space inside the fiber that insulates. The combination of fibers protects the camel in the harsh climates where they originated, where temperatures can range dramatically from −40°C to 40°C. The fleece is prized for fabric and often blended with other fibers, lamb's wool, or cashmere (which comes from Kashmir goats). The fleece can be shorn or combed or gathered by hand from shed wool during the molting period in spring.

Fashion is change, fashion is modernity, fashion is replacing the wild with style, fashion is the made thing, fashion is the mode, the craze, the fad, the trend, the now.

I think the lining of my camel hair coat was brown satin. A thick, silky satin. I can feel it, cold when the coat came out of the closet, embracing after it warmed to my body heat. The hem and buttons and finish work on the collar were stitched by hand, the seams joined on the treadle Singer, the machine on which I too learned to sew, a machine I think of now with deep familiarity and love. The smell of steel lubricated with oil, the leather belt that connected the treadle with the drive mechanism when you rocked the wrought-iron treadle with your feet, the gold filigree details in the black metal, the little bobbin case that looked like a bullet, so beautifully designed to hold the thread with just the right pressure and loosen it up through the feed dogs to meet the thread coming down from the spool pin, through the thread guards, tension regulator, and presser foot to lace upper and lower threads into an unbreakable chain.

5

✳

A Portrait in Five Portraits

Marie, Julia, and Celestine Bregny, 1885. *Photo courtesy of the author.*

New York City. 1885

SMUDGED AND GHOSTLY, THE SISTERS ARE BARELY LEGIBLE across time. No one is smiling. All are dressed in lace. The photo is fitting for a story that resists being told. But I am patient, having given up on un-

reliable sources and turned to fragments. Does that really say where I am in
this quest to know a woman—Marie Bregny, buried in an unmarked grave in
Valhalla, New York—who happens to be my maternal grandmother? How
do I come close to her in space and time? How do I mark her life as an act
of resistance to death? As an expression of continuity and belonging. This is
why I write and stumble through my not knowing, resigned to find in fragments a picture of the whole.

William Merritt Chase in his studio at 51 West 10th Street.
Photo by George C. (George Collins) Cox (1851–1902),
courtesy of Museum of the City of New York. 58.74.1

Greenwich Village's character as a refuge for artists was fixed in 1857
when the Tenth Street Studio Building was constructed between Fifth and
Sixth Avenues, solely to meet the needs of artists. The idea of American art
was not yet taken seriously among art connoisseurs, Europe still the nexus
in the minds and wallets of collectors. In 1878, the Paris Exposition would
include a section of American Art, and times had changed. The studio build-

ing was designed by architect Richard Morris Hunt, the first American to study at the esteemed École des Beaux-Arts. He supervised the renovation of the Louvre for Napoleon III before returning to New York. Hunt's design featured a glass domed central gallery with studios radiating outward.

Not really a bohemian redoubt, the Tenth Street Studio drew leading artists. Winslow Homer rented a studio, as did the Hudson River School artists Frederic Church and Albert Bierstadt. William Merritt Chase opened a studio there in 1879, where he worked with his greyhound lounging by his side. The studios were cleaned up and opened to the public on Saturday afternoons, when the well-heeled and well-dressed came to consider the new works.

This was the New York of my grandmother's childhood. Her mother, Louisa de St. Isle Bregny, immigrated to New York from Paris in or around 1870 and settled in Greenwich Village. The French community was small, not organized, relatively prosperous. France meant art. America meant business. Little Italy, Little Hungary, Little Syria were a mile away. Bleecker Street was known as French Town, with Café de Paris, Au Chat Noir, and Taverne Alsacienne as gathering places. France meant culture and class. Some of New York's best restaurants of the era printed a French version of their menu. Some were printed only in French. Art and fashion looked to Paris for direction. Old New York was fading: a few farm animals still lounged in the grass—gaggle of geese, full-teated goat, Jersey milk cow—but Greenwich Village was increasingly the hub of creative enterprise.

Marie's father, Arsenne, who had also immigrated from France, had many jobs over the years, none sounding like a career. He is listed in census records over the decades as "crimper," "leatherer," "merchant," "agent for book house." In 1888, he used stationery that bore the header, "Prof. A. Bregny & Co., Sole Manufacturer and Sole Proprietor, Prof. A. Bregny's Anti-Asthmatic Powders." So it seems he was also a scam artist. By then the family had moved to 218 West Forty-Eighth Street. Prof. Bregny's product must not have done the job, because family lore says he suffered terribly from asthma and had to sleep upright in a chair in his last years.

The financial anchor for the family was Louisa, whose dressmaking salon employed up to sixteen women in a home-based business, eventually including my grandmother and her sisters. I have seen no letterhead for Louisa's enterprise—though I do have an envelope with an engraved return address: *Mmes Bregny et Cie., 314 West 58th Street, New York*. That would place the letter around 1905, when their business address is listed at that location. Still the French branding, of course, as mother and daughters Bregny continued to run the *compagnie*.

So many lost trades and goods caught my eye as I spun reel after reel of microfilm, year after year after year coming into the small frame of light, then passing: water wheels, cordage and oakum, French calf skins, hominy, artificial eyes, buffalo robes, bonnet frame makers, importers of cuppers and leechers, gutta-percha goods, corset makers, silver chasers, wagon makers, tinsmiths, barrel dealers, willowware, boot crimping, cod liver oil, importers of walking canes and Nobby natural sticks, hay and manure fork manufacture, horse collar makers, lace menders, cork cutters, cotton gin bristles, diaphanis Haarlem oil (genuine), oculists and aurists, boiled silk, ship biscuit bakers, coopers, last makers, thimble makers, tripe dealers, drove yards, Paris white.

The grainy photo of the three sisters may be a first communion portrait, all three girls dressed with virginal veils of floral lace, their bangs freshly clipped. Marie is the smaller girl on the left, looking directly into the lens, her gaze deep and intense, a refusal to be sentimentalized. Raised Catholic in a French-speaking family, her confirmation into the faith did not carry her to eternity. Marie left the church as a young woman after a priest grabbed her breast. Where did I learn this? Perhaps from my mother, a very defended woman who would rarely speak about her mother. She resented being raised by a working woman, when classmates at the private school her mother struggled to afford came from families in which women had leisure to spend with their children. Often when I asked my mother about her childhood, she rebuffed me. Any bits of story that trickled through this dam were quenching.

"What did she cook for you?"

"My mother didn't cook. She was a working woman."

"What did you eat for breakfast?"

"I don't know."

"Really?"

"Oh, stewed prunes and hot cocoa, I guess."

Marie became a Christian Scientist, as did her sisters Celestine and Julia. Science, as she would call it, saved them, strengthened them, a faith established by the entrepreneurial Mary Baker Eddy that promised the self-sovereignty of Divine Mind as instrument of healing: "Life in and of Spirit . . . the sole reality of existence." Illness is illusion. So too is death. Science was a system of belief attractive to a woman of strong will.

Marie lived to ninety-seven, refusing medical treatment except once, when at ninety-three she suffered from a debilitating bout of pneumonia. My mother arranged for the local doctor to make a house call. He prescribed an antibiotic. She took one pill, said, "They're setting me back," and refused to take more. Her fever spiked. She became delirious. "There are three crows sitting on the dresser," she complained to my father. "Please open the window and let them out." He did and she lived.

Marie Bregny, New York City, date unknown. *Photo courtesy of the author.*

Is this an engagement picture? Marie looks the right age and suitably embellished in lace to advertise her feminine beauty. It's likely her mother designed and oversaw the making of that confection of a dress. There is a restrained formality in the pose. Her mouth seems to be either holding back a smile or gritting in determination. The eyes are fearless. Maybe she's laughing at the hat, the lace, the whole fem get-up. She did love hats. I can imagine she chose large ones because she was so short—"four foot ten," she used to boast, as if no one could believe how much vivacity could be contained in so small a package. She did not feel small to herself and projected that confidence through bold style.

In 1894, at eighteen, Marie entered an arranged marriage to Antonio del Valle, twenty years her senior. That was three years after her sister Julia sued her own suitor. Michael E. Kelly ran the marble yard outside of Calvary Cemetery in Queens where Arsenne was buried. As the story goes, they met when Julia accompanied Louisa to look for a monument for Arsenne's grave. A news article—the only news article I've turned up about any of the Bregnys—cites "a suit for $5,000 damages for breach of promise." Julia and her mother "said they had witnesses to prove that on numerous occasions Mr. Kelly introduced Miss Bregny as his intended wife." Kelly made frequent visits to the family, at Louisa's invitation—"earnest entreaties" per Mr. Kelly—and he frequently took his friends. Shortly after he stopped visiting, he was surprised to receive from Louisa a bill for one hundred dollars for dinners furnished to him and his friends. He said the whole thing was "a clear case of blackmail."

I suppose Louisa was not about to be scammed. Her oldest daughter, Celestina, had run off to marry a gandy-dancer on the railroad, a man who turned out to be a lowlife drunk. I don't know the disposition of Julia's lawsuit, but she ended up marrying for love. To a chauffeur, much to her mother's disapproval. Louisa expected her daughters to rise in class through marriage, not fall. Louisa had had enough of those shenanigans, so she took the marriage of her youngest daughter into her own hands.

Antonio del Valle was Cuban, "a nobleman," though it turned out he was "a black sheep." That's how my mother described him, though she has proved to be an unreliable narrator of her family's story. Antonio had shamed his family, she claimed, and so they sent him away to live in Mexico. But Antonio and Marie hardly lived the lives of shamed exiles in Mexico City. They had a cosmopolitan life—Marie's happiest six years. She and Antonio were friends with Porfirio Díaz, the president of Mexico. Those were the years of Díaz's dictatorial rule, when he championed economic growth at the expense of rural and disadvantaged indigenous people. Díaz himself was a mestizo of Mixtec descent. During his long term in power he flipped from being a champion of the indigenous to becoming their oppressor. Marie's social world was in his aristocratic orbit. Marie said Díaz found her so charming that he gave her a horse as a gift. Once when I was a teenager—she lived in our Connecticut home throughout my childhood—she showed me a framed photograph with her standing proudly by the little bay *caballo*'s side.

Genealogical records suggest that Antonio was a doctor of medicine and as a young man made a generous donation to the Department of Natural History at the University of Havana to support poor students. Marie was his second wife, his first dying in Spain in 1900. Perhaps in that fact lies the scandal that tarnished his name. I can't imagine the Bregny family sanctioning their daughter's marriage if they had known the groom was a married man. I don't know much about Antonio and Marie's life in Mexico. She said that when they went to the opera, he took his Chihuahuas in the pockets of his dress coat.

What else? Marie had a stillborn baby. I recall having seen a photograph of a dead baby wearing christening clothes. Or did I imagine that? Antonio died of tuberculosis. And that's about all I know. Except that, when cleaning out my mother's house for her final move, I found a red clothbound set of six novels, the complete works of William Thackeray, each volume stamped with the name Antonio M. del Valle. Why did he have those books? Why did Marie keep them? Perhaps Marie and Antonio shared the novelist's satirical take on high society, understanding their own position to be contingent and precarious. I can't help but make something of it, this shred of evidence suggesting something they valued.

Thackeray seems right for them. He portrayed outsiders who are trying to get inside, people living and loving on the margin of high society but absolutely central to its existence.

Marie del Valle, Mexico City, 1896. *Photo courtesy of the author.*

Immigrants were flooding into New York City during Marie's childhood. Mostly poor people, migrant workers, displaced by industrialization, famine, exhaustion of their land. They hoped to escape the confines of class that bound them at birth in Europe by coming to a nation where through work anyone could rise from poverty to wealth. Thus did commerce beckon. Many were rural people lacking the skills for urban life. In his book about the experiences of migrant workers in Europe and the erosion of the peasant class, *A Seventh Man,* John Berger writes:

> The inhabitant of the modern metropolis tends to believe that it is always somehow possible to scrape a bare living off the land—unless it is a desert: or a dust bowl. The belief is part of the Romantic idealization of Nature, encouraged by the fact that the city lives off a surplus transported from the countryside and amassed in the city where it suggests the wealth of a cornucopia. The belief is far—in every sense—from the truth. Nature has to

be bribed to yield enough. Peasants everywhere know this. Rural poverty means that there is nothing to bribe with. It is not a question of working harder. The further working of the land is withdrawn as a possibility.

They came from Italy, Ireland, Germany, Russia, Poland, Hungary. New York City in 1870 = 1 million; New York City in 1900 = 3.5 million. They came, twenty thousand per week. Shopkeepers, fasteners, coffin makers, glaziers, miners, blacksmiths, clerks, millers, bricklayers, cotton fasters, seamen, coachmen, curriers, loom sitters, servants, boot makers, coopers, glovers, sign makers, bakers, brewers, porters, locksmiths, saddlers, bashers, butchers, servants. In my grandmother's youth, it was a city of shopkeepers, fasteners, bricklayers, and coffin makers. And an occasional lady or gentleman. A boatload of one hundred servants arrived from Ireland, most of them housed on deck for the journey. A boatload crammed with one thousand. How many died on the two-month voyage? Many immigrants arrived sick on "coffin ships."

Walt Whitman, walking by the docks as the torrents arrived, sang the joy of "the body electric" in this flood of newcomers. Embrace, embrace was his anthem.

> The man's body is sacred, and the woman's body is sacred;
> No matter who it is, it is sacred;
> Is it a slave? Is it one of the dull-faced immigrants just landed on the wharf?
> Each belongs here or anywhere just as much as the well-off—just as much
>   as you;
> Each has his or her place in the procession.

His joy at seeing the dignity in every person is a central part of the American creed. The reality for many was joyless. Jacob Riis reported on New York's slums in 1890 in *How the Other Half Lives*. The tenements of the Lower East Side housed three-quarters of the city's population. A million immigrants lived in the tenements. Buildings that had housed five or six families were torn down and replaced with buildings housing twenty families. In the late nineteenth century, Riis wrote that the Lower East Side had the highest population density on earth, "China not excluded." Tiny rooms with no windows or water. Shared outhouse in the yard. Streets known as Ragpickers Row, Bone Alley, Bandits' Roost, Blind Man's Alley. "Few glad noises make this old alley ring," Riis wrote.

Climb a dark hallway, burlap for wallpaper, pressed tin ceiling—seven thousand people in the building—oilcloth floor, home and sweatshop in three small rooms with no window and no water. OK, maybe one window. Huge pot on kitchen woodstove for boiling diapers. Water hauled—from where? The front room, smaller than a master bathroom today, became a cramped mini-factory by day, the family working up to fourteen hours a day, runners bringing stacks of machine-cut fabric, parts for garments to be assembled and returned to the manufacturer. Children worked alongside parents. Families took in boarders. Stitcher, finisher, presser. There were quotas to meet. If you have four dresses to go and it's the Sabbath, do you stop to light candles and pray or do you finish the dresses?

The worried wealthy—"Will I die from consumption if I buy the ready-made dress?"—didn't have to worry. They had custom dresses made by their personal dressmaker. Choose the style, choose the fabric, choose the embellishment, choose the hat to match, choose the fit, choose the length. A thimble of brandy, perhaps, while leafing through the season's fashion book from Paris. Life in the tenements was not about choice. Lint in the poorly ventilated sweatshops led to brown lung disease. Taverns and bars and whores. Twenty-five thousand pushcarts on the streets selling apples, chicken wings, beets, potatoes, lumps of coal.

At the same time, the other New York thrived.

Vogue, 1895:

From what I see of late, luxury is, if possible, growing apace, in the face of the financial calamities of which everyone complains. This state of affairs has attained such a point that small fortunes are spent on an opera cloak, a dinner dress or a ball toilette.

... furs, laces, seed-pearls, brilliants, gold and silver passementerie, are all pressed into service to help trim fin de siècle opera cloaks.

Some of these wonderful and fairy-like sorties are made of flowered and embroidered Louis XVI satins, lined throughout with grebe, marabout, or lophophore feathers.

The coloring is so near perfection it seems ... that milliners and couturieres have turned into artists, while artists are doing their best to be hailed as first class couturieres.

A woman in full toilette reminds me of the great confectioner Pihan's bon-bons, sweet inside and delightfully enveloped.

The Gilded Age, Mark Twain called it, for the shiny veneer that covered darker truths. The Civil War had been good for business in New York. Guns, medicine, ships, tents, steel blades, uniforms all put demand on markets. Business soared. Invention accelerated. The Civil War spurred steel and mining and railroads and shipbuilding and the first standardized sizes for clothing— an efficient way to provide uniforms for the troops. The Vanderbilt mansion went up on Fifth Avenue and Fifty-Seventh Street, 130 rooms, a French-styled chateau. The "Ladies' Mile" shopping district grew up on Broadway between Fourteenth and Twenty-Third Streets. Real estate values doubled between 1860 and 1870. Wealth moved north; business followed. And so, the two intertwined forces of growth leapfrogged their way uptown. As soon as the wealthy moved on, buildings once thought of as mansions were torn down to make "French flats" or apartment buildings. So many places, so many people, were treated as disposable to the thrilling advance of the metropolis.

New York City had been a zone of transformation since the Dutch took it over from the Lenape. A trout stream had become Canal Street. An Indian path had become Broadway. A tobacco field had become the Greenwich Village of brick rowhouses. A burial ground for plague victims had become Washington Square Park. The average American family lived on four hundred dollars a year, while palaces went up on Fifth Avenue. Hat shops and dress shops followed. Immense amounts of money were spent on dresses and parties.

A woman's body was an emblem of a man's stature. It was a canvas on which wealth could paint its fantasies. No expense was spared to make that stature clear in the most grandiose terms. The Patriarchs were a group of twenty-five men from old New York money. Each hosted a ball with a guest list of four hundred. Guests arrived at eleven, had supper at midnight, and danced quadrilles until four in the morning. By Lent, the wealthy set went to Europe for a few months, the women visiting the atelier of Charles Frederick Worth for consultations about the next season's ball gowns, dresses of baroque detail and craftsmanship, gigantic multi-layered confections. A weekly fashion report that I turned up at the New York Historical Society offers this ornate description:

Fashions from Paris, September 1866

Robes of white lawn with leaden-gray stripes vandyked above a jupe of the same material which is frequently vandyked itself; or of a lilac and white taffeta on a lilac jupe with a trimming of white lace, and a loose jacket of the same material as the jupe and similarly trimmed. For dinner and evening we have robes of thin watered silk, with brilliant color strips on a white ground, the train long, the corsage quite plain, with a band of the same color as the stripes of the robe, the sleeves very tight and especially so at the wrist. Other robes of gauze de Chambéry, of a pale green or mauve tint, and worn over a jupe of white taffeta, the corsage being of white embroidered muslin.

All is change in fashion. As the twentieth century neared, a more sim-plified elegance began to take over from the frilly and tiered and beribboned elaborations of the late nineteenth. The skirt's circumference narrowed—more of the torso outlined by the cut of fabric. Before this the dresses had been tight above the waist, then falling to a fat bell, emphasizing a mystery below the female waist. Now the dress was fitted to the hip, then flared in a graceful flounce of tiers, ruffles, tucks, and ruching. Here a train sweeps from the left side of the skirt and folds under a sort of floral apron, then reemerges and comes around to tie and drape—a kind of feminine bandage or bondage so gentled and subtly wrapped, the apple green flowered "apron." These clothes make a mockery of male dress and servant's dress and even furniture—here a curtain tassel, here a row of three oversized bows, here something belted and buttoned in ornate and useless ways. The body an in-strument of cultural commentary—simultaneous adoration and suppression of female form and beauty and stature.

When Marie returned to New York from Mexico City in 1900, a young widow, the wealth party was still rolling and the city growing skyward. Sweatshops still thrived. By 1910, New York had 450 garment factories em-ploying forty thousand workers. But the Bregnys retained their couturiere salon—stitcher, beader, sleever, finisher, presser, a girl who worked as runner all day securing fabric samples from the garment district. Marie joined her mother and sisters in the business. Marie had a gift, my mother said, for cut-ting fabric with no pattern, for designing with respect for a woman's flaws—a surgical wound, a burn scar, a humped back. She knew how to work folds and tucks and drapes and corsages so that the eye would be drawn away from the unsightly, so that a pleasing form would embellish one less so. She followed the fashion books each season from Paris, a full-color page for each dress de-sign. Were these licensed versions or knockoffs she was making? Customers arrived by chauffeur-driven limos. They ordered six or eight dresses, chose fabrics from the samples, and returned for fittings. My mother remembers "destitute French counts" (were those her words?) coming to the door to pick up gowns and deliver them to the mansions.

Perhaps the Bregnys made dresses for some of the guests at the infamous 1903 dinner party hosted by C. K. G. Billings at Sherry's Restaurant. Thirty-six guests dined on horseback, trays attached to the saddles. They sipped champagne in tubes that ran from their saddlebags. Even the horses had a dinner party, their feed served to them in a trough. Perhaps the Bregnys made dresses for the party hosted in honor of a woman's dog, the canine guest of honor wearing a $15,000 diamond necklace.

It's often said that there were two New Yorks during the Gilded Age, that of the wealthy and that of the poor. There was a third: the maker class of artisans, tradespeople, and professionals—dressmakers, civil engineers, milliners, corsetieres, jewelers, teachers, blacksmiths, silversmiths, accountants—a striving class that could imagine for itself, if not wealth, then at least respectability and dignity in their work. The maker class essential to the performance of commerce and wealth that drove the city.

Marie as Carmen, New York City, 1912. *Photo courtesy of the author.*

The caption is written in Marie's hand in black ink with a fountain pen. It's strange that she titles the photo in the third person, as if bearing witness to a life other than her own and simultaneously claiming it as having been taken at "my home." This is a message for those who come after her. And this is the address for which she received a mortgage in 1905, my guess with collateral of both the business and an inheritance from Antonio she brought back with her from Mexico.

Her second husband, George Macnab, had courted Marie for five years. They met at the Alliance Française, both of them eager to keep up their French. From his letters to her it's apparent that his interests in her were passionate. He was a civil engineer for the City of New York, later supervising the construction of bridges and roads in North Carolina. Marie grew impatient with the courting. "Is this going anywhere?" she asked. He fell to his knees and wept. "Marie, forgive me. I am already married." He gave a story compelling enough to convince her—his wife was ill or mad or some such. He attended to the situation and they married in 1908. But George was not a good man, by my mother's account. As a child, he'd burned down a barn in Pennsylvania. As a father, he was largely absent.

But Marie had charm and wit and worldliness. She was a competent businesswoman and a skilled artisan. Since returning from Mexico, she had taken over the dressmaking business from her aging mother. Business directories begin in these years to list the Bregny Sisters or Bregny Mmes et Cie rather than Louisa Bregny as dressmakers. Strangely, even after the marriage, George and Marie continued to live in the Bregny household at 314 West Fifty-Eighth Street with her mother, sister Julia and her husband, various boarders, and their Italian cook Charlie Melino. Perhaps that was in the interest of the business, but it must have been cloying for George. The photo of Marie posing as Carmen was taken about the time when George walked out on Marie and their two-year daughter Travilla, who would become my mother.

"The whole story is manifest in every event." That's what I have written on a Post-it note, and I do not know the source. If that's true, then the portrait of Carmen is the story of Marie's life. *Carmen*, the opera premiering in Paris the year Marie was born, is the story of a free and defiant woman who follows her passions where she will. It was radical for its time in portraying the lives of an underclass of Roma smugglers and workers in a cigarette factory. Carmen has a wild spirit. She tosses a flower at José to seduce him, then tells him that love is like a rebellious bird and cannot be easily captured. In the last act, as Carmen pursues her love for another man, José murders her. He'd rather see her dead than free.

Whose idea was it that Marie pose as Carmen, a torrent of eyeletted petticoat frothing out beneath the fringe of her Spanish shawl, one shoulder bare? Marie certainly has the look in this photo of a woman not easily captured. She seems hard, strong, sure of her seductive power and of her self-possession. This is a dark Carmen. A don't-fuck-with-me Carmen.

George was an amateur photographer. My mother once found crotch shots he had taken of Black women sitting naked with their legs spread wide. Later in life my mother asked George why he had left them. He said he was afraid he would love her too much. Near the end of her life my mother said, "I'm a very strange person. Something terrible must have happened to me when I was very young. Do you think my father abused me?" It's possible. Such matters were not discussed in her childhood home. But I sometimes wonder if Marie had made it clear to George that she would not tolerate debasement and so won her freedom.

Marie with daughter Travilla, 1909. *Photo courtesy of the author.*

What a strange setting in which to place a four-month-old for a portrait of mother and child, posing her on a boulder on the steep decline beside a city street. The hat wins the day, a feather plume five times the size of Marie's head, a fountain of ostentatious glamour. When I asked a cousin what she remembered of Marie, she said, "A formidable woman." Brilliant pale blue eyes, jaunty attitude, always making an entrance with something witty to say. My mother hated this about her mother. She said it embarrassed her. "She never had time for me." Marie rarely held my mother, having read that it was unhealthy to do so and acquiring a special swing to hold her so that touching was kept to a minimum. Even in the photo, her touch is not tender and maternal, but rather that of a stagehand placing an object to grace the scene.

She wears a pleated overcoat so fitted it looks like a dress—the grosgrain ribbon along the front pleat opening in a gentle V toward the divine triangle. Or is the ribbon stitched onto the dress underneath? The coat has decorative silver buttons at the waist, non-utilitarian buttons, fitting for an artist whose body could become the work of art. Her face is radiant with the glow of oxytocin. But it is the hat, that grandiose pilferage of avian display that says, "See *me*, see what *my* body is capable of, but do not define me by motherhood alone."

6

✳

Herring Our King

AS A CHILD, MOTORING OUT WITH FISHERMEN TO SEINE A WEIR, sturdy fishing boat rolling with the swells as if the vessel were riding on the back of a great breathing animal, I felt the pull of working on the water, the beauty and bounty and risk of hauling subsistence out of the sea's abundance. Grand Mananers have used their knowledge of the prodigious Fundy tides and habits of herring to build fixed weirs along the coast where herring feed. Large stakes—timbers sixty feet tall or more, some spliced together with metal collars to obtain the length—are driven into the seabed, topped with birch poles and encircled with twine. The weirs are a commercial-scale adaptation of aboriginal brush weirs built at stream and river mouths along the Atlantic coast. Passamaquoddy had fished the shorelines of the region for thousands of years before European settlers arrived. Into the early twentieth century, they paddled from the mainland to Grand Manan, making seasonal encampments to harvest porpoise and shellfish. It appears they made no permanent home on the island, though some locals say that Grand Manan was used as an old folks' home for the Passamaquoddy. There are no large predators, no poisonous snakes, no threat of war. The aged could be brought to a peaceful place to live out their last days.

The earliest documented weir in the region—and possibly in all of North America—is the geoarchaeological site of Sebasticook Lake in Newport, Maine, reported in a 1994 article in *Archaeology of Eastern North America*. There, through ground-penetrating radar and other technologies, a survey has been made revealing more than six hundred wooden stakes driven into stiff glacial mud at the lake inlet. The stakes have been radiocarbon dated to about seventy-eight hundred years ago. The weir was most likely used to catch alewives, an anadromous relative of herring that migrates up freshwater streams to spawn.

Weir fishing by settlers to Grand Manan goes back about two hundred years. The structures reflect a melding of cultural practices from both sides of the Atlantic. The island was populated during the American Revolution when Loyalists left or were exiled from their homes in the colonies and came north. These settlers brought with them from the British Isles a history of weir fishing going back eight thousand years. The craftsmanship of contemporary weirs speaks of layer upon layer of skill and learning, discernment and cross-cultural conversation, a process lost to history and evident only in the graceful heart-shaped twined structures that give definition to the island's coastal waters. Weirs in the Bay of Fundy look like Earth art, graceful forms that defy the formless water. Rippling shadows fall onto the water from the top-poles, nets glow as sun meets them or turn into gauzy haze with fog. The weir's fence—a kind of stem leading off the main structure—heads toward shore to divert shoals of racing fish into the enclosure. At night the herring come to shore to feed on plankton that have risen up from the depths in their daily feeding migration. Once deflected by the fence, the fish are channeled into the weir's bunt, where they circle, entrapped.

A fixed-gear method of fishing has natural limits built in, unlike deep water seiners that can chase the fish into ever more distant and deeper waters. The inshore fishery must wait until the herring come to shore. When and if the fish do so, the shoals can be massive and the harvest bountiful and joyous. A seine net is brought into the weir and with a diver's guidance dropped to the bottom, gathered together, and pursed up to raise the fish. When the purse seine rises from the bottom, the water begins to boil, a slow churn below the surface. The net comes slowly to the surface, winched up over the roller, a team of men leaning and hauling over the gunwale. The fish, all glitter and contained velocity, thrash against their confinement in the rising net. At first just a scrim of fish can be seen below the surface, then the net rises and begins to dry up so that it holds nothing but fish, a black swirl flashing with white and silver and blue glints, fish scales falling and drifting like spilled stars over the water. It is hard to understand the beauty of the weir, the joy on the faces of men with fish fever, father and sons and grandsons fishing together for twenty, forty, sixty years, the catch pumped into a carrier ship to become sardines for soldiers or refugees or urban pescatarians or to become bait for a thriving lobster fishery. Everyone pulls for a big harvest, and when it comes, what follows after the exhilaration of labor is satisfaction and rest.

HERRING—"THE SILVER DARLINGS" IN SCOTLAND, "THE SILVER of the sea" in Sweden—have been the most important fish in the world. Nearly every culture along the North Atlantic coast fished for them with stone and brush weirs long before the first Europeans arrived. The Irish built fish traps to catch herring eight thousand years ago. Amsterdam in the fourteenth century was said to be "built on herring bones." The French and British tangled in the 1429 Battle of the Herrings. British wharves in the fifteenth century, and New England wharves in the nineteenth, stood lined with barrels of salted herring stacked high like cordwood. Henry David Thoreau wrote of these barrels as "fuel to maintain our vital fires." By 1884 tiny Grand Manan Island in the Bay of Fundy with its twenty-five hundred residents had become the world's largest supplier of smoked herring. They developed an international trade shipping the fish to the Caribbean and South America.

Herring are one of the most abundant fish in the seas, their two hundred species of least concern to conservationists. Linnaeus called them "copiosissimus piscis"—the most prolific fish. Herring travel in seasonal migratory journeys that may cover two thousand miles. They migrate in huge shoals that hold billions of fish, flickering fields of motion that can extend nine miles long and two miles wide. A researcher in the Gulf of Maine reports echograms of a school one mile long and fifty meters deep. Vast clouds of fish race near the water's surface, filtering plankton through their gill rakers, following a schedule and map for which no instrumentation is needed, following what nature writer John Hay called "the earth's timeless schedule." Their journey exists among many ceaseless flows of migration that characterize the planet: herring, wildebeests, arctic terns, monarch butterflies, and human beings. The continents themselves know the experience of drift.

There is still a romance about the weirs for islanders who value the cultural capital they represent. But the only residents who build them now are those who do it out of love, not economic feasibility. It's not that the herring have been overfished. That happened in the 1960s when new technologies for finding fish in deeper open water boomed and the fishery crashed. But with conservation legislation coming in 1976, the herring rebounded. Herring can come back quickly, because they are vastly abundant. That means random gene variants can be of minor importance. And herring are adaptive. They can breed in spring or fall; they can adapt to high salinity, as have herring in the Baltic Sea. As long as herring have zooplankton to feed on, they thrive and rebound from setbacks. The market too rises and falls. Demand for smoked and canned herring has declined, but market for herring as bait is booming as lobsters move north for cold water. Wars and disasters help the fishery by creating increased demand for sardines, a low-cost, high-nutrient meal-in-a-can. Soldiers on active duty can pop a pull tab on a tin of sardines with no additional hardware required and get a protein-rich meal.

The reason remains unclear why herring seem to have nearly stopped coming into the bay or why, when they do arrive, they have stopped coming to feed along the island's shoreline. I asked Andy Pershing of the Gulf of Maine Research Institute about this. He said, "It has to do with the feed." Herring prey has diminished in the Bay of Fundy due to warming seas and changing currents in the ocean. No zooplankton, no herring. No one knows what the future of this fishery will be, an uncertainty troubling many waters under the influence of global climate change.

CLIMATE CHANGE. GLOBAL WARMING. GLOBAL WEIRDING. NO one is in love with the language we use to describe the complicated and troubling state of the planet. People tend to shrug their shoulders in dismay when the words pop up, as they do now ubiquitously. In a 2016 lecture in the University of Arizona's Earth Transformed series, climatologist Jonathan Overpeck, a member of the Intergovernmental Panel on Climate Change that won the 2007 Nobel Prize for its work on global warming, described the dramatic changes in our understanding of the planet over the past decade and offered evidence-based, if modest, ground for hope. The Earth has changed—oceans, land, and atmosphere. It is changing faster and faster. The scientific community is entirely confident about the reality of global warming, a steady pattern of increase since the beginning of the Industrial Revolution accelerating in the past century. Global sea level rise is up eight inches over the past century and expected to rise four feet by the end of this century—*if* we curb emissions.

If we continue with business as usual—pulling all the fossil fuel out of the ground and releasing the carbon into the atmosphere—seas will rise from thirty to two hundred feet. Currently, 90 percent of the trapped heat goes into the ocean, where it is stored and keeps us from baking. For how long can the ocean keep up with capturing excess carbon that people are putting into the atmosphere? The North Atlantic and the Southern Oceans are changing fastest. Waters in the Gulf of Maine are warming four times faster than the global oceans, thanks to the melting of Greenland ice. As the seas warm, they expand and the waters rise. Coastal flooding days have more than doubled in the United States since the 1980s, the increase caused by human-induced climate change. By the end of the century there will be major transformation of coastlines. We may lose 30 percent of Florida—Tampa, St. Petersburg, and Miami. With sustained drought, the Southwest will have no sustainable water supply.

What else lies ahead? "Uncertainty," says Overpeck. It depends how much more greenhouse gas we throw up into the atmosphere. How confident is he of these conclusions? "I'd bet my house on it." He says. "Not just my old pickup truck. My new pickup truck. My wife's Prius."

But, he says, the beauty of climate change is that we know about the problem in time to act. The question is not if we are leaving the fossil fuel age, but when we will do so, how quickly, and how justly we can do so. Our choices are adaptation—meaning we deal with the changes; mitigation—meaning we slow or stop the changes; or both. If we do nothing, we guarantee more suffering and loss, more climate refugees and political instability (as we've seen in Syria, whose extended conflict is owed in part to the prolonged drought that drove agrarian citizens by the millions off their land and into the cities where they found no means of support), and more grief than makes any sense as a matter of choice.

Overpeck sees the next decade as one of profound transition, like that from horses to cars or from whale oil to fossil fuel. Electric vehicles, solar, and other green solutions are advancing fast. Fuel made from farmed microalgae is being developed, a fuel that would take carbon out of the atmosphere, not release fossil carbon from the earth.

At the Paris climate conference in December 2015, nearly two hundred nations pledged to work as a planet to cut emissions and reconvene to review how they are doing. Five years later, the answer was "not so good." Not one nation had lived up to its pledges for carbon reductions. Australia in the winter of 2020 became the hellscape of climate denialism with wildfires driving people and animals into desperation and death. Economic drivers are moving faster than climate legislation—wind and solar technologies and green building trades mark the growth curve in jobs. In spite of the moral failure in global leadership—and the unconscionably weak U.S. response to climate crisis—wind and solar technologies are soaring. China has more solar energy capacity than any other nation; the United States comes in second. Within a decade, electric vehicles will be cheaper than gas ones.

We can watch fantasy after fantasy of apocalypse in the movie theaters, and these days on the U.S. news, but the anti-apocalypse is happening right here and right now, and it too is speeding up.

HERRING HAVE HAD A HISTORIC ROLE IN FEEDING PEOPLE. VIking and Roman middens host heaps of herring bones. Herring were the staple food of medieval Britain, known, writes herring historian Mike Smylie, as "the potato of the Middle Ages." In France, according to Smylie, the first mention of a herring fishery appears in a charter of about 1030 of the Abbey of St. Catherine near Rouen, allowing a saltworks near Dieppe to pay the abbey "five milliards" (five billion) of herring—either a tax or tithe. Welsh fishermen in the fourteenth century paid tithes in herring for Mass to be said on their behalf. Salt herring, along with cornmeal and a little salt pork, kept enslaved Africans alive on Southern plantations; Frances Fredric wrote that he was given one salt herring for breakfast during the winter months. Herring fueled the Industrial Revolution as the staple food of coal miners and mill workers. Herring have been caught, salted, barreled, dried, and smoked for centuries. Napoleon, seeking to keep his army alive long enough to satisfy his military ambitions, awarded a cash prize to the inventor who first sealed herring in glass jars, the first instance of "canning." This was followed shortly by preserving fish in actual tin cans. Though "herring" and "sardines" are generally synonymous, they are not really the same thing. In New England and Atlantic Canada, a juvenile herring becomes a canned sardine, but in Sardinia, a pilchard becomes a sardine.

Herring shape cultures and cuisines. In Amsterdam, herring partisans eat raw filets raised between thumb and forefinger, head tipped back, slipping the shiny flesh into their gullets like herons. They accompany the herring with raw onion and beer. In Norway, herring aficionados eat pickled herring on crackers accompanied with aquavit. In Palermo, sardine lovers enjoy pasta with sardines, pine nuts, raisins, and parsley accompanied by a robust primitivo from Puglia. And I remember my father on Saturday mornings, after playing tennis with some Grand Manan fishermen, sitting on the sun-splashed deck we added to the cottage, enjoying a beer and leathery brown kippered herring from the smoke stand in Seal Cove, the kind of cured fish that used to be packed ten pounds per wooden box and shipped to the tropics.

Since I have begun paying attention to herring, I have found them in unexpected places: as *sardinillas* in a Basque restaurant in Paris, served in a rectangular tin can, lid peeled back to display the splendid geometry of fish packed stem to stern and stern to stem, their bones softened into slightly crunchy calcium candy, and their flavor a delicate smoke.

I'd gone to Paris in November 2015 with my daughter Lucinda to look for traces of our ancestor, my maternal great-grandmother Louisa de St. Isle, who had been a dressmaker for Empress Eugénie and later emigrated to New York City, where she ran an haute couture business during the Gilded Age. We did not know that we were walking in Paris among people who hoped to kill us—or anyone else they could kill just for the theater of killing. Their weapons did not find us, though we walked days later among the memorabilia left by mourners outside the Bataclan—photographs, candles, bicycles, children's drawings, flowers, and (most strangely perhaps) cotton bolls on the stalk—and we wept for them. Lucinda would have been at the concert, if she had known about it. She'd scanned the paper for music but failed to spot the Eagles of Death Metal billing.

"If I'd seen it, I would have been there. It would have been cool to go to a concert in Paris."

"I would have gone with you, just for the experience."

Instead we had a quiet dinner a few blocks from where the explosions and gunfire went off.

We did not find our ancestor. But we found herring presented in an up-scale parody of what had long been a subsistence food.

I LIKE FOOD THAT TELLS A STORY. HONEST FOOD. I DON'T LIKE liars. Apples that shine with airbrushed perfection but lack the tart and tactile snap of a small winter Baldwin. Tomatoes that please *Vanity Fair* but taste like the paper on which their advertisement is printed. I like food that connects me to a place. In Alaska I might eat halibut and huckleberries. In Arizona I might eat tomatillos and chiltepins. In Maine, steamer clams fresh out of the tidal mud. In Wyoming I might accompany my ranch-to-restaurant elk burger with a salad of greens grown in Jackson Hole's futuristic Vertical Harvest indoor garden. But the least appreciated food I enjoy is herring.

Food has cultural meaning and class associations. The humble herring is a carrier ship of cultural meaning and class association. Herring is fashion. Looked down upon as poor people's food, a herring swims onto my plate in New York City at an Upper West Side Mediterranean restaurant, a slender silver filet served as an *escabèche* appetizer, shiny skin up, lying in a marinade of vinegar and fresh herbs. Sardines lie beached on my Sicilian salad in a fancy foothills restaurant in Tucson. But by and large I am sorry to say that herring are not prized as haute cuisine.

In the *Grand Manan Cook Book*, compiled in 1979 by the Grand Manan Hospital Auxiliary, I find numerous recipes for the fish that made this island thrive for two hundred years.

Potted herring: Fill bean pot with herring, 1 tablespoon mustard, 1 teaspoon salt, ⅛ teaspoon pepper. Cover with vinegar and bake 1 hour.

Baked boneless herring: Place smoked herring in casserole. Barely cover with milk. Dot with butter. Bake 20–25 minutes at 350 degrees. A bay leaf may be added if desired.

Kippered snack rarebit: 1 tin kippers, 2 tablespoons butter. Heat and stir in 3 tablespoons flour. Add slowly 1½ cups milk. Cook until thick. Then add ¼ teaspoon salt, ¼ teaspoon Worcestershire sauce, 1 tablespoon prepared mustard, 1½ cups diced cheddar cheese. Add kippers last and serve hot on 4 slices buttered toast.

There is a recipe for Finnan haddie—not herring but nonetheless a marker of the old ways—a lightly smoked haddock first popularized by a fish curing house near Findon, Scotland, and prized since the 1600s.

Finnan haddie in milk: 2 or 2½ pounds Finnan haddie, 2 tablespoons butter, ½ cup milk, heated. Wipe fish with damp cloth. Place in a shallow baking dish and almost cover with cold water. Simmer on top of stove or in oven for 10 minutes. Drain. Add milk and butter. Place in oven to keep warm but do not leave long enough for milk to curdle. Garnish with parsley.

The cuisine of necessity, an optional bay leaf or sprig of parsley the only flourish. I suspect the cookbook dates back to earlier iterations. The opening chapter, titled simply "Fish," is introduced by an epigraph from the Irish poet and folklorist Alfred Perceval Graves, the nineteenth-century Alan Lomax of Ireland, Wales, and the Highlands, who gathered traditional songs and renewed public interest in the music indigenous to those places. I found several versions of the tune with a quick search. This one sounds best to my ear.

Herring Our King

Let all the best fishes that swim in the sea,
The salmon and turbot, the cod and ling,

Bow down the head and bend the knee
Before fine fresh herring our king.

Then lads and lasses come begin
Your "hungamar féin am sowra lin";
For 'tis we have tempted summer in
At the tail of fine fresh herring.

Thro' all the winter we ran to rack,
For sure the herring was out of sight!
But oh! Upon his silver track
The moon she winked last night.

It was in with the sails and away to shore,
Away, away with the rise and swing
Of two stout lads at each smoking oar,
After fine, fresh herring, our king.

Oh, there we hunted him full to land,
In hissing shoals hot haste along;
And then behind him from strand to strand
We spread our nets so strong.

Such kissing of hands and waving of caps
Was never seen from girl and boy,
As he leapt by scores in the lasses' laps,
Fresh herring our hope and joy.

That line of Irish says, "'Tis we have brought summer in." So potent is
the relationship between men and herring that it has the power to change
the climate. Oh, such is the abundant power of man over nature—the root

of all desires for power—that the harvesting of herring can inspire a reluctant summer to arrive. The lasses in the tune undoubtedly were "the herring lasses" who traditionally moved from village to village, port to port, working outdoors on the docks to bone and clean herring as the catch came in on boats.

The old *Grand Manan Cook Book* offers also a cuisine of anatomical intimacy—people knew the bodies of the meat they ate, and the meat they ate was fish. It's well known that halibut cheeks are prized in maritime communities as the very sweetest part of that species' anatomy. But cod tongues? The book offers recipes for both fried and baked tongues—both oddly calling for 24 cod tongues. Perhaps that is the count of fishes batched for commercial market.

Fried cod tongues: 24 cod tongues, ½ cup milk or 1 egg, ½ cup flour, ½ teaspoon of salt. Wash tongues with a damp cloth. If salt tongues are used, soak them in cold water for ten minutes. Dip tongues in milk or slightly beaten egg, and roll in sifted flour. Fry in hot fat three to five minutes. Air bladders (sounds) may be cooked with tongues by the same method.

Who knew that a fish had a sound and that a person could eat it? More aptly, the question might be, who *learned* that a fish had a sound and a person could eat it.

The new *Grand Manan Cook Book* has no publication date. The cover reads "Grand Manan Island" and "Hands helping hands across Grand Manan." It was published sometime, my guess would be, around 2010. It has no chapter for fish. In the Main Dish section there are recipes for Mom's Salmon Loaf and Salmon Fritters (made with canned salmon), Chinese style country ribs, boogie woogie beef, Cajun chicken fettucine, curry beef stir fry, chuck wagon chili, Hawaiian meatballs, Swiss steak, Nova Scotia sauerkraut pork. It is the hodgepodge cuisine of the industrialized marketplace. Other than Deer Chop Hurry (1 cup ketchup, ½ cup water, ½ cup packed brown sugar, 1 package dry onion soup mix, 1 medium onion, chopped, deer meat) there is nothing that speaks of this land and this sea out of which citizens of this place pulled their livelihood for centuries. Certainly, having more choices than herring, onions, salt, potato, and milk to concoct meals with marks culinary progress. But other than a recipe for brown sugar–glazed salmon filets (farmed salmon being the only kind available on the island and not prized by locals who know too much about the toxic brew that goes into the cages), the new cookbook says either nothing or everything about the current state of the local culture and its changing relation to the sea.

The question remains why herring are missing not from the cookbook but from the weirs. As the bay warms, fish may be sticking to cooler water offshore and eschewing the shallows where they used to feed at night and in their passage become trapped in the weirs. In 2012, marine biologists who monitor zooplankton in the Bay of Fundy brought up sample containers nearly empty of these organisms that are the foundation of the marine food chain. Ocean currents and acidity are changing with the planet's warming. Even before the oceanic changes became apparent, herring were known to establish big triangular patterns of migration from feeding to spawning to wintering grounds that last decades, and then to abandon them for another plan.

On June 30, 2016, I watched the *Strathlorne*, the first of a fleet of six herring carriers built in 1965 to service the growing seining fleet working deeper waters in the bay, torn apart by a bucket loader at the island haul-up on Ingalls Head. Built in Blacks Harbour, New Brunswick, the ship was 54 feet long, 16 feet wide, and carried 55 hogsheads of herring. She had a square stern and high sides so she "could easily 'brace up against' the seiner in all kinds of weather," writes John D. Gilman in *Masts and Masters: A Brief History of Sardine Carriers and Boatmen*.

The loader took a bite out of the wooden hull—surprising to me how bright the wood was beneath the surface, just like fresh cut timber. It was said that the carrier's stern was too rotten to repair, even to be converted into a pleasure boat. And with demand down for carriers, down with the catch, the company isn't about to invest in restoration. So down she goes into the bucket loader's mouth and up she goes into the dump truck's backside, into the oblivion of lost trades. How many millions and billions of herring were pumped up from the sea into her hold, delivered to smoke stands and sardine factories now gone? Well, that's history. The herring swim where they will out there in the deep in search of prey.

7

*

Brook Trout Dress

Alison and trout, 1956. *Photo courtesy of the author.*

ODD THAT I REMEMBER THIS DRESS AS HAVING TINY RED POLKA
dots and red plastic heart-shaped buttons running all the way down the middle. Those details are lost in the photo. This may be the last dress that my
grandmother made for me. I can feel the smooth tight weave of the cotton,
how it hugged my waist and the cap sleeves puffed out a bit at the shoulder
seams. I remember the squared neckline. I had a waist but not yet breasts.
I remember that body and how easy it was to move around in. Things got

more complicated in adolescence. I remember that hair, fine and silky. I remember that joy in my father's trout catch, the bounty and beauty laid out before me.

The car in the photo is our old lime-green Studebaker station wagon. My father was a beloved performer on radio, TV, and stage in Connecticut. He got the car on discount from a dealer who ran advertisements on his radio program, a morning show that offered music, news, comic skits that he wrote and performed. Most common among these was his banter with sidekick Bessie Bossie, the pet cow who accompanied him to the studio. Ben—my brother and I always called him by his name, never Dad or Father or Papá, as he had called his father—published a children's book about the character, a country cow who longs to be a city sophisticate, goes to New York and dons high-style fashion, gets a manicure and pedicure and facial, only to learn that this urban animal is not who she is. She ends up coming home in the rain, mascara running down her cheeks and fancy frock wilting in the downpour as she finds sorrowful comfort among the herd where she belongs. After all, she is a country cow. The cow in the studio was a cardboard can that tipped to make a mooing sound, but Ben worked it into a living breathing buddy. Sometimes he'd emcee a county fair and bring along a real cow on a halter, introduce her as Bessie. One publicity photo shows him in hunter's top hat riding a Jersey cow in mockery of the pretentious hunt club set. He was born into rural Connecticut, an artistic family that homeschooled the kids, an unconventionally literary family that wrote and performed plays on the lawn and published a newspaper called *The Woodchuck Weekly or The Ornithorhynchus*, each kid and adult with a byline: Chippy Hacky and Old Possum, etc. Theirs was a childhood full of self-mythologizing fun, and my father carried that spirit into his adulthood.

In his youth, Ben spent a few years in New York City studying to become an actor. He toured with the road company of Clifford Odets (not so glamorous—they slept in barns and ate pie at diners for dinner) and he played Herod in a Broadway production of Oscar Wilde's *Salome*. Mostly he had bit parts in big shows, riding the subway from one gig to another, hoping for a break. But it was radio where he found his voice.

The early days of broadcasting in the 1930s were a pioneering time. No one yet knew how to fill all that electrified silence. My father had an actor friend who got air time on a New York City station. "Ben, I've got dead air. Come down to the station and read some poems. I've got a guy who can play cello." So, Ben read the love poems of Hafiz with a weeping cello at his side. A young woman, lonely child of a dressmaker, heard his voice and swooned. She sent a love letter to him, disguising her name and address. He read the letter. "I must find her," he said, but he could not decode the identity. Two doomed but destined romantics, lost to one another in the city of dreams. One day he was visiting a friend, a woman who had gone to the Veltin School for Girls with my mother. They were bored and looking for something to do. "I know this fascinating girl. I'll take you to visit her, but you must promise this will not be the last time I see you." When they arrived at Travilla's door, she recognized his voice. "Oh, no, I never wanted to meet you!" My mother always knew how to use words to keep her distance from what made her feel vulnerable. They both had felt abandoned, my father caught as a teenager in his parents' wounding separation, as my mother had been when her father took off when she was a toddler. They recognized something in each other that was beyond words. And so it was for their lifelong marriage, an enabling escape into the safety of each other.

My father, ever the country boy, loved trout fishing. I remember him getting up before dawn. The comforting rustle in the island cottage as I lay in half sleep and he went about the business of making coffee, gathering gear and tackle box, the ratty khaki vest stained with fish guts and lined with pockets for flies and swivels, the wicker creel. For years after he died, I kept the little beat-up plexiglass box of his trout flies that I found in the woodshed. Kept the laminated fishing license with its rusty safety pin for attaching to the vest. Talismans of his presence that lasted long into his absence. Things can offer a silent communion with those who are lost. An apparently worthless object—a stained fishing license twenty years expired—becomes a wordless treasure. You know you will have to let it go, but not yet.

These days I could buy online all the trout flies I ever wanted and even the feathers and beads, chenille and threads I needed to tie my own. Yes, it's true: one click to deer belly fur, squirrel tails, rabbit strips, dead dumbbell eyes, fish skull sculpin helmets, Hungarian partridge skin, goose biots, peacock swords, ringtail pheasant tail clump, turkey quills, calf body hair, and jungle cock feathers. All the deceptive mechanisms meant to trick the trout to bite a steel hook. I love the words on that shopping list, but no meaning, no feeling, inheres in those objects. My father's flies were handmade, figured out from watching what trout fed on in the dawn hours. Objects put to use, then put to rest, yet still carrying emotional freight.

My father fished for pleasure and solitude. I imagine his time beside a woodland stream as regrouping his spirit from the demands of work and family. A time to savor sun-dapple and hermit thrush fluting. A time to contemplate water's passage, the metaphor for life. He brought home the stringer of trout and also a woodland quietude. He loved a window of solitude out of which to gaze. Yes, he loved our home too, a place in which he was so often the source of comfort and charm. Yes, my father was a charming man, who could warm a room with his presence. Fans of his radio and television shows felt the warmth and wit of his public persona. But he was ours at home.

My mother coated the spangled trout with cornmeal and fried them with butter in the cast-iron skillet. She was a good cook. I think often of the particular way she would cut carrots to cook them, then toss them with parsley, or cut up a whole chicken to broil and fry the livers in butter, or peel the chestnuts for Thanksgiving turkey dressing—a recipe that came from her mother, who likely got it from *her* mother. A family recipe from France. Chestnuts, sweet potatoes (pale, not garnet), and sweet Italian sausage. The fennel seeds in the sausage infuse the meat with fragrance. I think often of the particular wild flowers my mother would cut for bouquets to fill a small vase—daisy, clover, vetch, orange hawkweed flowers, buttercups. Flowers that others might consider weeds. She loved to claim them as treasure, inspect them with a magnifying glass, see the godliness in their beauty.

The domestic sphere was not my mother's primary ambition. She was a playwright and theater director, taught speech and dramatics at the Ethel Walker School in Simsbury, Connecticut. It was talent and luck that brought her to this work. She did not attend college, though she had the chance to go to Vassar, for which her elite secondary education had prepared her. But she was reckless and passionate in youth. She wanted to leave the confines of her mother's home and business, but she didn't want college. Instead, she traveled by train to Rancho Santa Fe, California, to live for two years with her aunt, Marie's sister Celestine. She rode horses through the orange groves, drove with dates to San Diego for Saturday night hotel dances, and sunbathed on pearly beaches.

"Mother sent me to California," she said, "to get me away from that terrible Venezuelan." Was this the man who lived in their apartment building who had wanted to teach her "how to handle a penis"? By the time she returned to New York at age twenty, she was living in a fantasy world of séances and lonely walks to the Fulton Fish Market. She took her dates to a speakeasy restaurant and concocted half-baked tales of romance like the one I found in her letter from that time about the arctic explorer who had promised to take her to the wild North. "And I just might go!" she teased, in her cat-and-mouse courtship with my father. But it was my father who won her—actor, poet, playwright, writing in those days a play about Pan in which he played the be-fluted muse of the woodlands.

The lawn on which those trout were laid in the photograph is the yard in front of our Grand Manan cottage, indestructibly old turf, as now the memories seem to be. I can feel myself, a lifetime away from those childhood years, running outside in my white cotton polka dot summer dress at the whisper of the Studebaker rolling into dirt driveway, my father beaming and smelling of trout—fresh forest scent—laying the dozen spangled fish out on the grass to photograph and catching my ten-year-old joy at the bounty. I can see the blue-haloed red spangles of trout skin swimming in the sunlight. I am thankful for a family in which no one said, "Don't get grass stains on your dress, don't touch those smelly things." No. I was welcomed into this earthy joy, and it has never left me.

My mother says I was inconsolable for the first three years of life. I think she was always a little bit afraid of me, stiff and unsure how to comfort me. "Some kind of attachment disorder," my analyst said, when I asked what diagnosis he'd put on my insurance claim, after I'd showed up saying, "I have a terrible mother." But after those first three years of wailing, my mother says, I became a bubbly enthusiast, running up to strangers to tell them in my "little cracked voice" how wonderful the world is. What changed me from inconsolable to exuberant? Look at this girl, so well cared for in her homemade dress that spreads out to meet the lawn where she kneels before the stringer of fish, her hair curled, silky, brushed, held back from falling into her eyes with a bow-shaped barrette.

My earliest clear memory of emotional contradiction comes from about age five. I wake in the night. The house is dark and silent, loneliness overtaking me. I climb out of bed, my doughy legs so short I have to turn my body around, face the bed, and hold on to the covers to get my feet to reach the floor. I pick up my little yellow wooden baby chair and carry it down the hall and around the corner to my parents' bedroom. I plant the chair on my mother's side of their bed and wait. I watch my parents sleeping, listening to the soft animal sounds of their breath, the scent of them rising in the night—a sweet, warm sourness in the breath—knowing comfort in silence.

What happened next? What did I want to happen? I had learned early to keep my distance—my mother's voice could be a harsh instrument—though I must have longed to climb up and nestle between their two warm bodies. I must have wanted to be congratulated—"Such a big girl to carry her chair all this way in the dark!" To be scooped up by love in celebration of that accomplishment. Or is that the adult I have become speaking? Seeking love in my accomplishments? The girl, eternally present in memory, is equally afraid to be alone in the dark and to ask for comfort. She sits in her dilemma like a dazed monk and refuses to close her eyes, the quiet house sheltering her solitude.

Love came in material things—never a day without three good and healthy meals. I think with longing about the way my mother sliced zucchini in thick rounds, then sautéed them in garlic, the way she sliced potatoes to panfry them crispy brown, and London broil cooked medium rare, my father slicing it at the table and spooning up the juice to feed us our "tonic." Never a night without a kiss goodnight. Is that a material thing? It seemed so, the perfunctory peck. This was our family in a nutshell: the charming father, the difficult mother, the angry brother ("Rodney, stop squinting," my mother carps when we pose for a family photo, though it isn't a squint so much as a scowl of unhappiness that goes unrecognized, my brother learning as I did that pain is to be borne in private), and to complete the family portrait, me as wonderstruck girl. "Who raised you?" the analyst asked, when I described feelings of emotional abandonment. "Nature raised me," I said.

Summer camp. The Connecticut hills. Cumulous oaks and maples surround the glassy surface of the lake. At a distance the water looks black. Beneath my small hands, paddling forward, cupping down and pulling back, it sparkles, mica flecks drifting in the sunlit water. Transparent minnows scatter below me. I can see clear to the bottom, gold and tawny sand, a few thin ribbons of weed teasing the current. I know better than to swim into the water lilies wobbling on their ropey stalks. Who wants to touch down in the slime that anchors them or get an ankle tangled in vines? No, I am going for the distance, pulling arm over arm, legs scissoring, head turning in perfect rhythm with my breath, in love with the beauty of a body in motion, no resistance, the landscape of my childhood a refuge then as now it remains in mind. Earth is a place of joy for me.

The whistle, shrill and precise, breaks my aquatic stride.

"Hey, fish!"

Head up, I startle to see how far I've come from shore where the other kids are gathering up their towels and sandals and heading back to camp.

"Hey, fish!" the camp counselor yells. "Get back here!"

I'm a good kid, a compliant kid, a kid who follows rules. I don't really know how to be a social animal, but I know rules. I make the turn, feeling the sting of disapproval, and head back into the melee of the kid world, teasing and tickling and joking about "short-sheeting" the counselor's bed, whatever that means. I'm more at home in the water pretending to be a fish, though I don't really know anything about fish either. It's just that I want to be immersed in the beauty of the world, pull myself through it by my own strength, and revel in the sensation of weightlessness.

This girl in the white summer brook trout dress did not know such questions were to be asked—Who raised you?—this girl who is living in me and joins me at the desk as I write, making it possible for the noise of the world to subside. The force of nature—its insistence on growth, healing, invention, the sheer bounty of what's there for the taking (so many trout brought home for breakfast!) raised me. The dress seems now to be a statement of this pure and robust energy, a declaration of childhood joy without the taint of loss and irony and knowledge of the wounded and wounding adult world. A field of white cotton broadcloth, crisp and clean, red hearts stitched in a line from neck to knee, bodice fitted snug to define the waist, square, low-cut, open neckline that telegraphs the décolleté of the woman to come.

8

Le Travail des Femmes

❋

MY CHILDHOOD NEST WAS A TUMBLED DOWN CHATEAU. AT ITS corners, the same height as the main building, were four square towers with roofs like church steeples. The south side had no windows, only loopholes in the towers, which made the building look like a tomb or a castle, depending on the point of view. A long time ago, people called the place the Fortress, but when I lived there it was usually called the Tomb . . . To the west were the hills and wood of Suzerin. When the snow was deep, wolves would creep from the woods into the Tomb through gaps in the wall, and they would howl in the courtyard. Our dogs would answer them, and this concert would last until the frozen morning. All was well at the Tomb, and I loved those nights.

LOUISE MICHEL, *The Red Virgin: Memoirs of Louise Michel*, translated by Bullitt Lowry and Elizabeth Ellington Gunter

THE REGION OVER WHICH HER [EMPRESS EUGÉNIE'S] PARTICU-lar authority was exercised comprised several rooms, entirely surrounded by wardrobes in plain oak, with sliding panels, in which all the various articles of clothing were arranged in perfect order. Four lay-figures, exactly measured to fit the dresses worn by the Empress, were used to diminish the necessity of too much trying on, and also to prepare her toilet for the day. Orders were given through a speaking-pipe in the dressing-room, and the figure came down on a sort of lift through an opening in the ceiling, dressed in all that the Empress was about to wear. The object of this arrangement was to save time, and also to avoid the necessity of crushing the voluminous dresses of the period in the narrow back-staircases.

ANNA L. BICKNELL, *Life in the Tuileries Under the Second Empire*

SINCE WOMAN IS AN OBJECT, IT IS QUITE UNDERSTANDABLE that her intrinsic value is affected by her style of dress and adornment. It is not entirely futile for her to attach so much importance as she does to silk or nylon stockings, to gloves, to a hat, because it is an imperative obligation for her to keep up her position.

SIMONE DE BEAUVOIR, *The Second Sex*, translated by H. M. Parshley

THE SEVENTEENTH-CENTURY FEMALE "UNIFORM," WHICH HAD consisted of more or less elaborate bodices, petticoats, and skirts layered to suit the weather and status of the wearer, gave way to dresses. The dress-wearing fashion was expensive and impractical (because the pieces could not be worn, washed, or replaced separately), but was adopted surprisingly quickly, and it helped create an increasingly distinctive branch of the clothing industry, a subspecialty that women workers were able to carve out as their own. Seamstresses could tap a growing market, and many female clients, including wealthy and powerful women of the aristocracy, had a vested interest in the seamstresses' independence and success.

JUDITH G. COFFIN, *The Politics of Women's Work*

ONCE MY GRANDFATHER OFFERED ME TWENTY SOUS A WEEK IF I would promise not to steal anything again, but I found I lost too much money on that deal and I refused. I had filed some skeleton keys to open the cupboards where pears and other fruits were kept, and I used to leave little notes there in place of what I had taken. I remember one read: "You have the lock, but I have the key."

MICHEL

EUGÉNIE'S FIRST TRIUMPH WAS TO POPULARIZE THE CRINOLINE. Invented in 1856, the "cage-crinoline" was a bell-shaped petticoat stiffened with hoops of steel wire that replaced the petticoats previously used to create width. "Crinolinomania" conquered France, Britain and the United States within months.

SEWARD

THE EIGHTEENTH CENTURY BROUGHT RAPID CHANGES IN THE production and consumption of clothing, changes that helped establish Paris as the "grand foyer du travail féminin" ... At its low end, the "poor and pitiable" linen workers whose sheds hung from the wall along what is now the rue de la Lingerie at the center of les Halles caused the guild considerable headaches. The widespread perception that these linen workers were trafficking in sex as well as table linens and shirts had long made the guild particularly emphatic about its moral function.

COFFIN

PROSTITUTION WAS A COMMON WAY FOR POOR GIRLS TO MAKE ends meet. In 1836, ... the Conseil de Salubrité declared there were over 3,500 prostitutes in Paris, and a further 35–40,000 working on a clandestine basis ... At the bottom of the hierarchy was the *grisette* ... [who] often worked in the clothing industry or sometimes as a florist, and used prostitution to supplement her meager income. The synonymy between the garment trade and prostitution became a cliché that aroused knowing smirks, but the stereotype was based on statistical fact. So frequently was it proved accurate that it gave this class of prostitute her name: *grisette* derived from the inexpensive grey material from which working-class women's dresses were made.

CATHERINE HEWITT, The Mistress of Paris

THE EMPRESS CHANGED HER CLOTHES SEVERAL TIMES A DAY, and never wore a formal gown more than once. Every six months she gave the discarded dresses to her ladies, who sold them for a high price—often to Americans since there was a good market in New York where they were hired out—and at least one imperial gown appeared in the stage of a Paris theater.

SEWARD

SMART APPEARANCE IS A WEAPON, A FLAG, A DEFENSE, A LETTER of recommendation.

DE BEAUVOIR

ONE DAY, WHEN I WAS PERHAPS SIX OR SEVEN YEARS OLD, WE drenched Lamennais's *Paroles d'un croyant* with our tears. From that day on, I belonged to the masses. From that moment, I climbed step by step from Lamennais to anarchy. Is there further to go? Of course, because there is always more to come, there is always further to go, always progress to make in light and liberty.

MICHEL

THE HABIT WHICH THE EMPRESS HAD ADOPTED, OF WEARING NO covering on her head during the Sunday high mass, was a sore grievance to the clergy, who in vain quoted the instructions of St. Paul addressed to women. But she listened to no remonstrance—as, indeed, was usually the case when anything suited her fancy or her convenience.

BICKNELL

NAPOLEON ALLOWED HER 1,200,000 FRANCS A YEAR, OF WHICH 100,000 went on her wardrobe, the rest on presents, pensions for retired servants and, above all, charity . . . Eugénie was not just attempting to please her husband but putting into practice her own extremely practical form of Christianity.

SEWARD

AND SO HERE IS LOUISE MICHEL. SHE IS A MENACE TO SOCIETY, for she has declared a hundred times that everyone should take part in the banquet of life.

MICHEL

THE EMPRESS LOOKED PARTICULARLY BEAUTIFUL THAT EVE-ning; she wore a Marie Antoinette head-dress of powdered hair, with a small round cap of scarlet satin adorned with emeralds and diamonds, surmounted by a heron's plume. Her costume was of magnificent Lyons silk stuff of black and gold, opening at the sides over a scarlet satin underskirt; the bodice, cut square, was bordered with large emeralds and diamonds.

BICKNELL

THROUGH ADORNMENT . . . WOMAN ALLIES HERSELF WITH NA-ture while bringing to nature the need of artifice; for man she becomes flower and gem—and for herself also. Before bestowing upon him the undulations of water, the warm softness of furs, she takes them herself. Her relation to her knickknacks, her rugs, her cushions, and her bouquets is much less in-

timate than to the feathers, pearls, brocades, and silks she blends with her
flesh, their iridescent hues and their soft textures make up for the harshness
of the erotic universe that is her lot; she values them the more, the less her
sensuality finds satisfaction.

DE BEAUVOIR

AT THIS TIME THE EMPRESS BEGAN TO TAKE AN INTEREST IN
political matters, and it was thought advisable to humor her in this new
fancy, as a means of diverting her mind from other problems to be solved of
a more inconvenient kind. She had held the nominal office of Regent during
the Italian war of 1859: as she might be called upon to do so again, she was
now allowed to be present at the councils.

BICKNELL

EUGÉNIE ALWAYS INSISTED THAT IT WAS HER IDEA TO CREATE A
Mexican Empire and that she first suggested it to Napoleon in September 1861
when a young Spanish diplomat, José Manuel Hidalgo (a friend since childhood) was staying at the Villa Eugénie. For some time Hidalgo had been begging her to persuade her husband to send an army and save the Mexican upper
classes from the godless revolution that was confiscating their estates.

SEWARD

PARIS WAS A SORT OF FAIRYLAND, WHERE EVERY ONE LIVED
only for amusement, and where every one seemed rich and happy. What lay
underneath all this, would not bear close examination—the dishonorable

acts of all kinds, which too often were needed to produce the glamour deceiving superficial observers.

BICKNELL

SOMETIMES EUGÉNIE WORE A HUGE DOG-COLLAR OF PEARLS, FOR which she had a passion, in particular for rare black pearls from Mexico. Until then, black pearls had not been much prized, but when her interest became widely known their price soon overtook that paid for the finest white ones.

SEWARD

THE MONTMARTRE VIGILANCE COMMITTEE LEFT NO ONE WITHout shelter and no one without food. Anyone could eat at the meeting halls, although as the Siege continued and food supplies became shorter, it might only be one herring divided between five or six people.

MICHEL

THE EMPRESS'S FIRST LARGE-SCALE CHARITY WAS PAID FOR with the 600,000 francs that the municipality of Paris had offered her as a wedding present. Instead of spending the money on a diamond necklace as they suggested, she used it to found and endow an orphanage for girls in the Faubourg Saint-Antoine, a notoriously poverty-stricken district.

SEWARD

OFTEN I CRIED, TOUCHED IN MY HEART BY SOME QUICK IMAGE OF progress, art, or science, and my grandfather, with great tears in his eyes, too, would put his hand on my head, which was more tousled than one of our dogs.

MICHEL

DURING THIS PERIOD OF PERSONAL POWER SHE WENT TO VISIT the penitentiary for young offenders. In this establishment five hundred boys from ten to eighteen years of age were kept in solitary confinement. The object put forward was the prevention of criminal contagion; but for young children often arrested only for begging and retained because they had no decent home to go to, the life was one of moral torture.

The Empress was painfully impressed, and took up the matter with her usual warmth. After conquering considerable opposition, she succeeded in having these children transferred to agricultural penitentiaries, where they work in the open air, and together, under supervision. The results have proved very satisfactory.

BICKNELL

EACH OF THESE MINISTERIAL MEETINGS, WHICH ARE HELD IN the Salle de Conseils, is presided over by the Empress Regent, who displays the same grace and intelligence in her new position as she has hitherto shown in all those to which her high station called her. All documents hitherto signed by the emperor now bear the sign-manual of the empress Eugénie.

SEWARD, as quoted in *The Illustrated London News*, June 11, 1859

MY PITY FOR EVERYTHING THAT SUFFERS—MORE PERHAPS FOR the silent beast than for man—went far, and my revolt against social inequalities went still further. It grew, and it has continued to grow, through the battles and across the carnage. It dominates my grief, and it dominates my life. I have been accused of having more solicitude for animals than for people.

MICHEL

"THE PUBLIC JUDGE BY EXTERNALS AND THOUGHT I WAS ONLY interested in smart parties and fashion, dresses and jewellry," Eugénie recalled. "I was blamed for being frivolous. If only they could have seen my notebooks."

SEWARD

WORK IS THE PEOPLE'S ONLY PATRIMONY. THEY MUST WORK OR BEG.

COFFIN. Echoing Adam Smith, cited in Bloch, L'assistance et l'état

9

*

The Stone Weirs

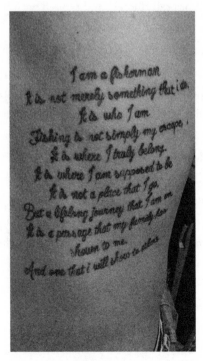

Fisherman's tattoo. *Photo courtesy of the author.*

I FIRST HEARD ABOUT THE STONE WEIRS FROM A YOUNG PILOT, scion of the founder of Atlantic Charters, the small local company that runs Grand Manan's island flight service. He had set up a table at the farmers market one Saturday morning in June. He was selling sightseeing tours of the island. A hundred bucks for a flyover of the whole twenty-five-kilometer-long forested rock pile. At low tide, you can fly low enough to see the remains of the stone weirs in Cow Passage, he said. I met the claim with skepticism. A stone weir seemed an unimaginable effort of handmade labor. I'd seen no mention of stone weirs in the Grand Manan Museum's history of island fishing, no remnants marking the shallows the way the poles of abandoned weirs can be seen ghosting up out of the water, sentinels of the island's past.

Herring weirs, though in decline, have illuminated the island's shores for centuries. Built from tall timbers and topped with birch saplings, strung round with black twine, Fundy weirs catch the light and the fog and swell as if their purpose were to be the fixed thing that makes you pay attention to all that changes. Brush weirs were built by aboriginal people in the region and have a history in the United Kingdom, Japan, and Australia deep back in time. Native Hawaiians built fish ponds in shallow waters offshore. Most of the fishermen I asked about stone weirs on Grand Manan gave me the same skeptical look I'd given the pilot. It's easy to feel herring weirs slipping from memory, knowing there were eighty-six weirs in 1939 and now there are only nine or ten in operation. Many islanders feel the loss as personal. Everything local feels personal on an island with twenty-five hundred residents. When the ambulance blares down the island's one main road, heads turn. It's carrying someone they know. Death and injury are not anonymous in such a place. Ghosts abound and loss is shared.

One man I asked about the stone weirs shrugged.

"Who knows what else was once here that's forgotten?"

One day on the ferry that connects the island to mainland New Brunswick, I was watching out the window through fog as we neared Flagg Cove.

"Are we almost there?" I asked a kid, maybe ten years old, whose face was pressed to the window.

"Yeah. We are. See that fish thing?"

He pointed to the black stakes of the Cora Bell.

"That's a weir," I told him.

"Hunh?"

"It's for catching herring. Each one has a name. That's the Cora Bell."

It was news to him. How could a local kid not know such a basic fact about his home?

Many islanders complain that they're losing their heritage when yet another old house or sardine carrier is smashed apart to make way for progress. Something once necessary to the place is no longer. Traditional fisheries were owner-operated, small-scale, sustained with family labor and investment. "Traditional" fishery in Canada means owner-operated. And that means work that has dignity and meaning, shared responsibility for resources and shared suffering at their diminishment. Now fish stocks are depleted, waters warming, and salmon farming taking over the weir sites. Cooke Aquaculture runs the show, a corporation that operates fish farms in Canada, the United States, Chile, Scotland, and Spain. Cooke calls itself "a family of companies," a nod to the family-based fisheries heritage that it helps to erase.

"What's going to happen to us?" an island friend asked one day after we'd waded into these waters of lament. "We've always just lived our lives here. We've never had to think about it."

The lobsters didn't have to think about it either, when they moved north, drawn to colder waters. Their move was good news for the economy in the Gulf of Maine and Bay of Fundy, bad news for Massachusetts and Rhode Island. Current thinking says there are three reasons why lobsters are booming in the region. First, they like cold water and the habitat here remains hospitably cold. Second, many of the ground fish are gone from the bay—haddock and pollock and cod that were plentiful have been fished out. That means there is less predation on young lobsters, assuring greater reproductive success. Third, with the lobster industry booming, more and more traps are set loaded with bait, offering constantly replenished feed stations for the young ones, who enter the trap, have a meal, and exit through the opening left to allow youngsters to go free until they are legal size for capture. So, it's gold rush for lobsters in the northern waters and gold rush for the fishermen who catch them, millions of dollars' worth hauled up and stored in state-of-the-art tank houses to be sold when market conditions are optimal.

Tank houses, huge climate-controlled warehouses with metal siding, have replaced the old timber-built lobster pounds along the shore. Bigger and bigger lobster boats are laying out longer and longer trawl lines of traps. Digital marketing sends many of the biggest and best lobsters to China, which has an insatiable appetite for them. They use the giant ones, ten and twenty pounders that may be fifty years old, as centerpieces at banquets. Tank houses store hundreds of thousands of tubed lobsters in a grid of plastic condos flooded with seawater kept at temperatures just above freezing. In a torpid state, each lobster sleeps in its little tube, metabolism slowed down so that it will not molt, keeping the flesh firm and fresh for up to six months. Tank houses are crisp, clean facilities, the chemistry and temperature computer monitored and backup generators at the ready in the event of power failure. The old lobster pounds built in water along the shore led to more loss. The water grew polluted and lobsters tore into each other, as is their cannibalistic manner in confinement. Tank houses have turned what was basically a hunter-gatherer fishery into an agro-industrial business. Technology has risen to meet the voraciousness of the marketplace. Grand Mananers have always been wily and pragmatic about adapting to change and getting themselves a good perch in the commercial market.

After two years of a wildly high lobster ride, the island felt the catch slacken in 2017. And at the start of the 2018 season, the catch was down and the seas rougher than ever. Still crews go out in all weather conditions, hauling up the traps while the swell heaves the boat and waves slosh the deck. Twelve-, eighteen-, twenty-hour shifts. Many crew members stoke up their staying power with performance-enhancing drugs. Coffee. Weed. Speed. Cocaine. And when they get back home, their backs and shoulders and knees beat to hell from heaving the wire-mesh traps, there's beer or oxy or heroin. The fishermen, and now some women, work through the winter when waters rile. Plenty of them get seasick. That doesn't stop them.

"What do you do?" I ask.

"You puke and then haul another trap. You puke again. Then you haul."

Herring? There hasn't been much to celebrate for the past decade. There are plenty of herring in the North Atlantic, but no one seems sure where they are, even the deep-water seiners that can chase the fish down. A few islanders continue to build weirs. I think they do so out of love more than hope. Every day before sunrise a weirman motors out to check his weir. He goes with the tide, one day heading out at four in the morning, then an hour later each day. He heads out of the harbor, rounds the lighthouse, leaves the other boats behind, and motors along the wild and quiet backside of the island, basaltic cliffs shooting straight up to spruce forest. He knows the currents and eddies he will meet and just where he will meet them. The swell may be gentle, but always the sea is alive with motion, as if a breathing animal beneath the hull were carrying him along. It's the best part of his day, the morning's rosy glow spilling over the water like a blessing, gulls and shearwaters following his wake or perhaps ignoring him as they have other business to attend to.

"GO TO THE END OF SHILOH LANE AT LOW TIDE." THAT'S WHAT Russell Ingalls told me when I asked about stone weirs. He wasn't sure when they had been built or who built them, but the remnants remain. He and his brothers and their sons continue the family line of work, as does his father over ninety. Herring, lobsters, sea eggs (sea urchins sold at Christmas to the Japanese), scallops. Each in its season. Russell also runs whale-watching and bird-watching tours and tends the Bowdoin Scientific Station on nearby Kent Island.

I joined Russell and his brother David for a circumnavigation of the island. I wanted to look for weir sites that we could identify, checking against the list of the eighty-six weirs marked on a 1939 map made by Buchanan Charles as a fundraiser for the Grand Manan Historical Society. The Ingalls brothers knew just about every site listed, though mostly we saw empty water where the weirs had been. In a few sites we saw old weir stakes blackened by the sea slowly giving in to water's eroding force—ghost weirs, I call them. There used to be a herring weir every thousand feet all around the island. They told me that fishermen could navigate by weirs in dense fog.

There had been three just off the sand beach in Seal Cove: Seattle at the inside corner, Hawk further along, and Coon in the middle. A few water-blackened stakes from Coon are still standing. David remembers the Coon being built when he was eight or ten years old. He loved the sound of the driver setting stakes. The delay as the sound traveled fascinated him. Hawk, down by the Red Point geologic contact, has been gone since the 1960s. His grandfather built it. When he was in university, David wrote a paper and drew a map on the weirs. What I'd give to see that now—such a document of historical merit for this community.

"Coon wasn't a very good weir. Seattle would get all the fish."

I made hasty notes on the *Island Bound* as they talked me through the history, not wanting to miss any nugget of information. More than information, their knowledge was steeped in the experience of having worked for their whole lives on these waters.

They spoke of the good run in the 1940s and '50s, how it slowed during the war as men were taken overseas. They said 1954 had been a "hake year." Hake are aggressive feeders. Herring are terrified of them and run toward shore. That's good for the weirs. Hake are mostly gone now. They spoke of the Admiral Hector weir that had two "bunts"—the area encircled by the nets. It's only possible to build a weir that way where the bottom is flat. The inside bunt was abandoned first. The detail in Russell and David's memories was downright scholarly, though our tour was certainly a more felicitous introduction to the history than a university thesis project.

Turnip Patch lay just off the Long Pond sand beach. It was listed on our 1939 map, though it had been down for fifty years. It had been rebuilt in the last two, soon to fall to tatters after a few broken stakes followed by winter storms. Sonny had stood off Wood Island; the Goose close to the Good Luck.

"Good Luck gets the herring. We get shit."

We ticked the sites off on our map as we cruised. There had been twenty-five weirs in and around Seal Cove alone. Red Cross. Dolphin. Teaser. Admiral. Imperial. Bread and Butter. Nubble. Jack Tar. Pat's Cove. Toe Jam. King George. Hardwood Cover. Shag Rock. Oatmeal. There were so many weirs so close together that some guys just carried a watch, not a compass, or used "three cigarettes" as a measure of distance from weir to weir.

There were four weirs along the Ross Island shore. One at Three Islands until 1961. Two low-water weirs in Grand Harbour—one stone weir you can see at low tide.

"It's a square. Go down to the end of Shiloh Lane. That was the original method."

The people went in at low tide and gathered fish into carts. Or loaded an ox cart.

They spoke of super weirs—Mumps and Pat's Cove, Brown Bread & Beans. They could close off the whole of Pettes Cove and get a very large harvest. Used to be a weir below the campground in North Head. Gone. Another at the point. Gone. Hard keepers. Storms demolished them. Challenge was torn out by jellyfish. They drift in on the tide, block the twine until it collapses from their weight. Some guys tried to build a herring trap at Beal's Eddy, lugged rock all summer long. Was that eighty or a hundred years ago?

"They had herring scales in the eyes. They were brilliant just to survive."

Money Cove, a very lucrative weir with a pound, a "kingfisher." Some guys tried to build a steel weir. Pipe Dream. The steel pipes broke off. Couldn't take the weather. They rebuilt it with Doug fir stakes eighty feet long. That's what brought giant leopard slugs to the island from the Pacific Northwest. Actual name of that weir was Ladders, but the nickname stuck.

Weathered stakes leaning toward the water on the western side of Nantucket Island—Henclam.

By the end of the day circumnavigating Grand Manan, we counted eleven weirs operating in 2016:

Turnip Patch
Mumps
Iron Lady
Intruder
Gully
Star
Challenge
Money Cove
Sea Dream
Bradford Cove
Pat's Cove

AS WORD GOT OUT THAT I WAS INTERESTED IN STONE WEIRS, texts and Facebook messages rolled in.

"I think there's one on Nantucket," wrote Wayne, who'd gone there to pick periwinkles.

"Maybe there's one off the beach in Castalia," said Elton. "Could that be one in Whale Cove?"

Barry Russell reported, "They were all over Cow Passage. Used to be hard to get a boat through there, there were so many. They'd take out the dories, let them bottom out at low tide, fill them with fish and wait for the water to come back to row them ashore."

Once you started looking, the stone weirs were everywhere. And so were the Atlantic herring for two hundred years of the island's industry. Whether the herring swam into the weirs or not, their migratory urgency drove them into spawning grounds in the Bay of Fundy. This was their territory long before it had become a fishery.

IN JOHN HAY'S *THE RUN*, HIS BEAUTIFUL BOOK ON ALEWIVES, anadromous cousins of herring that ascend from ocean to river for spawning, he wrote that the sight of migrating shoals captivated the imagination of other species. Sometimes a little perch or sunfish would follow along the shoals of alewives: "These motions must be catching, communicating to other lives and races than those in which they originate. All have their way stations, or orbits, along a route that is being followed with primal grace and power." Alewives had even gotten into the water supply of New York City apartments after the Kensico Reservoir was built up the Hudson River. The New York Aquarium had investigated complaints of fish coming out of faucets. They found that landlocked alewives had spawned in the reservoir and their tiny offspring had been so eager to follow the migratory imperative of their ocean ancestors that they slipped through the five-eighths-inch mesh of screens at the reservoir outlet and shot through the pipes all the way to Manhattan.

"GO TO THE END OF SHILOH LANE AT LOW TIDE." ALDER AND hardhack scrub leaned into the lane, the smell of fallen apples, cidery ferment and funk, slipped into my car window. Maple and birch leaves still hung on, but crab apples were rotting to seed. Deer had come out of the woods at night to feast on pungent fruit, their hoof prints cut into muddy tire tracks. The lane dead-ended at the water, two sheds, one built onto a small pier, one planted on land. All quiet. Small pre-fab ranch house. No dogs in the yard. A van and pickup parked side by side in tall grass. Flat tires. A large rusted boiler had become a breakwater to sturdy the shore against tides, relic from the long-gone lobster canning factory in this harbor. The shore line on a fishing island is a landscape of work. Lobster traps made of plastic-clad wire were piled behind the shed, more stacked on the lip of the wharf. Like the vehicles, the gear looked like it had not been put to work for a season or two—none of the orderly care given to coiling ropes just so, tidying up the parlor and kitchen of the trap.

Grand Harbour is a wide and shallow bowl—more like a plate than bowl—in the middle of Grand Manan's eastern shore. It was a major port during the sailing ship era, though the larger vessels could not safely enter the harbor without grounding. They had to moor and launch smaller boats to come ashore. A hundred years ago the harbor would have been bustling with skiffs and dories, curing and smoking sheds, no end of work sheds and wharves stacked with wooden lobster traps, the lighthouse at Fish Fluke Point guiding mariners away from hazards obscured by fog. All of that industry is gone. Even the lighthouse has fallen to ruin. The quiet harbor stretches out, silky ripples stirring its surface.

The tide was low when I arrived—among the biggest tides of the year that happen when the moon is closest to Earth in its elliptical orbit and lined up with the sun, sun and moon pulling together on the seas. Spring tides. Mud flats ringed the harbor below the rockweed line, a slight slope extending where water had drained from the land. Mud, mud, mud. A few barnacled rocks. I stood at the shore, scanning, hand to forehead to shield the falling sun, scanning for any sign of a stone construction.

The red pickup slid up behind me—a monster truck like the ones most men on the island drive. Ford F-150 or Ram. Salty-haired driver, white T-shirt, window rolled down, gave me a quizzical look. I stepped up to the window.

"Sorry to barge in. I've been looking for the old weir sites. Russell Ingalls told me there was a stone weir around here. People look at me like I'm crazy when I say that. What do you think?"

"It's here." He nodded with a hint of a smile, introduced himself as Burtis Green, got out of the truck, and pointed southeastward down the shore.

"See that rock and line of rockweed? That's the fence. You can see the whole ring when the tide's out." He scanned the shoreline. "Coming flood now. Come back tomorrow at low tide and you'll see it. You can take some good pictures. I'll be down there picking wrinkles."

Rocks and rockweed. That's all I saw. But one ridge of rockweed seemed to run in too straight a line to be natural. Archaeologists say look for straight lines if you want to find something manmade. Nature doesn't do straight lines.

We settled into conversation. He'd sold his boat last year, wasn't feeling well and thought he'd better make provisions for his kids. He's better now, picking dulse and periwinkles. Periwinkles, known on the island as "wrinkles," are marine snails, smaller than escargots, but prized in some cuisines and ubiquitous in the rocky intertidal zone. I don't know why islanders call them "wrinkles," but they always seem to have a sparkle in the eye when they speak of them. It sounds like a silly name and everyone knows it. But knowing that everyone knows it is a sign of belonging in such a small place. Burt picks them, he says, not for the money. He just likes being out here. The sweep of an arm says where. Open water, open sky. Geese feeding in the eel grass. Gulls gathering for their talk.

He said, "The geese tell me when the tide's coming back in, tell me to get out of there." He laughs. "Of course, that's probably not what they're saying, but I like to think they are."

"Used to be a lobster factory here." He has a photo of it. "Ought to give it to the museum, but not ready to. I'll bring it down tomorrow, so you can take a picture of it."

He'd fallen off his roof one day. In a body cast for months. Doctor said he'd never fish again. Day the cast came off, he was fishing. Started working when he was twelve and a half. Worked at a fish stand, staking herring and loading them on the herring horse to carry to the spoke stand. Married at seventeen. He knew it sounded like a hard life, and I might look down on him for it.

"Wouldn't have wanted to do anything else."

The talk flowed. A man at peace with his life and his work and his place. Matters worth sharing with a stranger. He understood that such equanimity with one's fate was rare. He wore Black Watch plaid pajama pants and slippers. The clean white T-shirt thrown on to make himself presentable, I imagine. I'd disturbed him from a nap or TV while he was waiting for the tide to be right.

"I'll be back tomorrow. I won't bother you if you're working."

"I'll throw wrinkles at you if you do." Big smile. Warmth going both ways.

ACCORDING TO THE *DICTIONARY OF ARCHAEOLOGY*, THE EARLIEST fish traps date from 8,000 years ago in Denmark and the Netherlands. Others have turned up near Moscow dating from 7,500 years ago. A stonewalled fish trap for catching eels was built 6,600 years ago at Lake Condah in Australia, according to radiocarbon dates from the excavations. Japan's earliest weirs date back about 4,000 years, when hunter-gatherer society was becoming agrarian. A stone weir is part of the Band-e Dukhtar irrigation works of the Persian Empire from 2,500 years ago. In North America the oldest fish weir may be the Sebasticook Lake fish weir in central Maine, where sharpened stakes have been carbon-dated to about 8,000 years ago. In 2014, archaeologists used an unmanned robotic vehicle to explore what may be the earliest evidence of human habitation in Canada. Dating to 13,800 years ago, under four hundred feet of water in the Hecate Strait off the coast of British

Columbia, they found what appears to be a fish weir, probably for corralling salmon. The area would have been dry land 14,000 years ago when water was bound up during the last great Ice Age.

Maliseet and Passamaquoddy people along the Atlantic coast built fish traps on rivers and shut-off weirs in coves long before the European arrivals. They probably did so for thousands of years. The earliest written record I've found of the aboriginal weirs in the region comes from Captain William Pote, an Englishman commanding a merchant vessel heading from Boston to Nova Scotia. He was captured by an indigenous nation he called "herons" (historical records say Mi'kmaq and Maliseet) in 1745 during the third of four French and Indian (or "Intercolonial") Wars. England and France were fighting for supremacy in North America over who would gain the wealth to be had in furs and fish. Pote was held captive for two years, imprisoned and tortured until his release in 1747. When about to be freed, he gave his journal to a female prisoner "to carry under her petticoats" for safekeeping. On a forced march during his captivity, *The Journal of Captain William Pote, Jr.* recounts how the band set up a brush weir:

This day as we was padling up ye River we pased by a Small Cove and perceived at ye head of ye Cove, there was Sahnon playing in ye Cool water, at ye head of ye Cove, we Landed verey Carefully, and Cut Bushes and Brought them down to ye Entrance of ye Cove, and wile Some of us was Im-ployed, with perches and our paddles &c. thrashing in ye water, to hinder the fish from Coming out of ye Cove, Ye others built a ware across ye Entrance of ye Cove, with Bushes and our Blanketts &c. and we Caught In this Cove fifty four Salmo[n] which was So Exceptable to us at that time that I Shall never forget ye joy I was filled with.

The band was on the move, so they dried the salmon over fire and carried the jerky along for sustenance as they continued their prolonged march.

I would not want to have lived in those times, but what I'd give to know the manner in which Native and European populations learned from each other about how to reap a life from the land and water. Surely some fishing heritage came with the immigrants who crossed the Atlantic. Surely the indigenous had bountiful knowledge about the methods and materials best suited for fishing in the region. History gives us the woeful story of war, captivity, and violence. The stories that were lost in the blood and suffering are the stories of the makers. Surely men and women met on the northeast shores to discuss the migratory patterns of herring and salmon, the brush best suited for building weirs in the streams, how best to dry the fish in foggy weather. Surely such conversations have been ubiquitous in the human story—have been among the reasons to learn one another's language. I refuse to believe that human history has been made only in the story of conquest. The warmongers, the haters, the oppressors keep unmaking the world. I wish some anthropologist would write *A Maker's History of the World*. Such a history would necessarily be both a celebration and a lament. Lament not just for the unmaking but for the greed and excess that come hand in hand with human making.

MOSES HENRY PERLEY WAS A LAWYER, NATURALIST, ENTREPRE-neur, and surveyor in colonial New Brunswick who traveled extensively in the province to study ocean and river fisheries. He covered over nine hundred miles, five hundred of them by canoe. In 1851, he published his *Report upon the Fisheries of the Bay of Fundy*, with a section on Grand Manan that makes for lively reading. He circumnavigated the island, documenting fishing practices in remarkable detail and recounting a contentious meeting held with sixty fishermen to discuss his findings and make recommendations for improving the success of island fishermen. The Bay of Fundy, he wrote, was for fishes "a favorite place of resort where is food in abundance." Cod, pollack [his spelling], hake, and herring made up the bounty. He found in Cameron's

Cove (now Pettes Cove) one J. B. Pettes, an American citizen, who had set up a retail fish operation "purchasing green fish" and curing them on the premises. Perley didn't like what he saw.

At day-break, the fishing boats returned to shore, when the fish were thrown out upon the beach with a pitchfork. Soon after sunrise, the newly-caught Hake were lying on the gravel beach, sweltering under the heat. There were no splitting tables, as in a well-conducted establishment, but the fishermen set up pieces of board upon the open beach in a temporary manner, on which the fish were split; they could not be said to be cleaned, as no water was used in the operation. The heads and entrails were separated from the bodies of the fish, which, being split in a clumsy manner, with uncommonly bad knives, were thrown down on the gravel; thence they were carried off on hand barrows, upon which they were tossed in a heap, three or four at a time, with pitchforks. From the barrows the fish were pitchforked onto the scale to be weighed; from the scale they were again pitchforked upon the barrows; and being carried off to the pickling casks, were once more pitchforked into the pickle; by this time the fish were perforated in all directions, and looked little better than a mass of blood and dirt.

Perley reported boats off Long Island with torches flaring off their bows for driving herring. This small offshore island of Grand Manan had only one resident, a Mr. Ingersoll. About forty fishermen from Nova Scotia were encamped there with thirteen boats. What fish they caught were sold to Grand Manan for processing. At "Bencraft's Point," Perley found three large brush weirs and a fourth being built. Weirs so filled the channel, he wrote, that it was somewhat difficult to navigate among them. Tiny High Duck Island had a warehouse, two fish stores, and two large smokehouses. In 1849, they packed five thousand boxes of smoked herring. In 1850, only 175.

At the entrance to Grand Harbour, Perley learned, it was customary for two men to take seven or eight quintals (hundredweight) of cod in a day, but in 1851 there was no line fishing there. Perley concluded that the shoals of small herring, on which the ground fish feed, had been destroyed by brush weirs. Peaks and troughs, boom and bust. The rhythm of fishing. Lobsters were so plentiful in Grand Harbour that Perley's crew could take all they wanted with a gaff in two or four feet of water lying over the mud flats. All in all, Perley reported twenty-seven herring weirs around the island built in shallow water with several more under construction.

Perley found much to critique in the island's fishing practices. No regulations nor even the pretense of regulations. "Every man cured and packed his fish as he pleased." Dull knives. Filthy beaches and work sheds. Gurry thrown anywhere and everywhere fouling the waters. Fish put into the pickle with blood and dirt and slime and extra salt added—"a bushel of salt being used for each quintal of fish; every effort appears to be used to make the fish weigh as heavily as possible." He found the smokehouses insufficiently ventilated, the fires made too near the fish, locals at war with non-residents who came to fish, "usurping a privilege" that islanders saw properly belonging to themselves. In 1849, there were "one hundred or more" fishing vessels gill-netting off Southern Head. Boats with old scythes attached to their bottoms were rowed swiftly among the nets to destroy the competition.

Already in 1849, warnings rose among the island's settlers. Perley reported: "The fishery, they said, was continually falling off, and would eventually be destroyed, from the reckless manner in which it was prosecuted, and the place being over-fished." Within six weeks of publication, Perley's report spurred the New Brunswick legislature to pass a law banning fishing of herring on the Southern Head spawning grounds between the fifteenth of July and the fifteenth of October. Perley also introduced islanders to "excellent Sheffield knives used for splitting and dressing fish in the Bay of Chaleur" and "long-shanked hake-hooks used by Jersey fishermen, which are very superior, for that fishery."

❊

I WAITED ON THE ROCKY SHORE FOR THE TIDE TO EMPTY. SOME crows in conversation. Gull squawk. Gray immatures working the tideline. Not much to eat in the bay that summer. Some gulls starving. Puffins too on their nesting island. Few herring. Lots of butterfish, too big for the nestlings to eat.

Across the harbor, the collapsed lighthouse at Fish Fluke Point offered bleak testimony to the erasures of time and neglect. Underfoot, barnacled rock. Periwinkles scattered thick. Rockweed black-green at the base where attached to shore with longer fronds of greenish-gold swayed in high tide and lay flat at low. Three wrinklers had already begun picking on the far shore, though the tide had yet to hit low. They looked tiny clomping over the rocky shore to pluck snails into their buckets. Burtis arrived on his buggy to meet me. He too was on his way to go wrinkling. White T-shirt and jeans. Warm, tanned face of a man who works outdoors, a face that said something good about neighborliness.

He showed me where he used to work at the fish stand. Pointed across the harbor. Over there. No wheels on the herring horses in those days. Men were the horses. Men were the diesel engines. A weirman once told me that in those days it took six to eight men to work a pile driver, "running the whip" to raise the pig for pounding weir stakes into the ocean floor. It was, he said, "a hard day at the office."

"See that?" Burt pointed to a line of rockweed covered stones. "That's what we call the fence." He pointed to the high point on the beach, a seam of rocks sloping down off a ledge, low point descending into the water. It looked like Andy Goldsworthy's *Storm King Wall*, a sculpture disappearing into nothingness.

"That's the center fence. This one isn't in the center and the weir doesn't have a mouth. The fish swim in at high tide. Then they close the gap on the side and at low tide haul the fish out with carts."

He'd brought the photograph of the lobster canning factory that used to stand on this shore.

"It's on the front seat of the truck. Take a picture, then lock the truck."

Like most islanders, he loves the past, the hard work of his ancestors, shared memory that lends meaning to his days. People look to family history for a sense of continuity. Continuity sits in places. We shared that love.

"I wish the old people could take a spool of all they know out of their heads," he said, shaking his head at incomprehensible loss.

He headed off, four-wheeler jouncing along the weedy meadow at the top of the beach.

I stood waiting, squinting at the water's glare as tide receded. One minute a watery plate serves up its reflections. The next minute rock cobble and mud flats lie drying in the sun. Lowest tide for the year. Lowest tide in eighteen years. The seam of rock—each about the size a man could carry with effort in his arms—ran down toward the sea extending into a line that drew a square about the size of one-car garage. A two-foot gap stood on the seaward side. It was not really a stone wall, rather a collapsed rubble about three feet wide that defined the shape. The shape the stones made was like a flag on a flag pole. No nation to claim it but the nation of work, the nation of makers, who labored here in the days when herring, stemming the tide, raced into the harbor, a mass as numerous and unified as a murmuration of starlings.

Perley wrote about the kind of ballasted weirs he saw during his 1849 visit.

> The bottom of this weir is composed of framed timber of large size, sunk in about six feet of water at low tide, and ballasted with large stones of a ton or more in weight. Above the strong frame work which forms the bottom of the weir, there is the usual light wicker-work of poles with twigs interlaced, sufficient to retain the timid Herrings, but altogether unfit to retain other small fish of bolder character. The Herrings will not go out of a weir unless the opening is of large size, while all other fish will dash and

struggle through any opening sufficient for their passage, even with much squeezing.

This method of building weirs with woven brush served well in the early days of Grand Manan's herring fishery, before pile drivers made it possible to move the weirs into deeper water offshore and in places where the tide was so strong it would collapse the nets. The ghosts of these structures appear at the year's lowest tides: rings of stone with stories to tell. Historic engravings made from photographs by T. W. Smillie for the United States Commission on Fish and Fisheries are available through the Smithsonian Institution that show a variety of brush weir structures used near Eastport, Maine, in 1887. Smillie was the first photographer for the Smithsonian. It's safe to assume these images represent methods used on Grand Manan at the time. A crib-work of stout saplings holds the stones in place. Leafy brush, a material that sufficed for twine, was woven into two or three horizontal bands ringing the weir, top brush with leaves pointing upward and bottom brush with leaves pointing downward.

That's it. Stones, saplings, and brush, materials upon which a community was built that became the Sardine Capital of the World. It makes for a bizarre kind of joy to see the stones slowly reveal themselves as the tide recedes, like the unveiling of a lost work of art or the discovery of an archaeological ruin. I walk the perimeter of stones, filled with a bounty that has left us, but feeling its presence as an echo of the great inventive spirit of those makers and harvesters of the sea, feeling too their depth of learning from their place, reading the rhythm of tides and moon, the habits of hake and herring, and what the rocky forest might contribute without complaint.

10

✳

The Rise and Fall of the Crinoline

Fashion is not something that exists in dresses only.
Fashion is in the sky, in the street. Fashion has to do
with ideas, the way we live, what is happening.

COCO CHANEL

IN HIGH SCHOOL I WORE A CRINOLINE. MY CRINOLINE WAS
nothing like the cage crinoline made with steel hoops and whalebone and
linen strips of Empress Eugénie's renown. Mine was a half-slip with elas-
tic waistband, three tiers of nylon net, starched to stand out like a whirling
dervish skirt. I don't think I wore it very many times, but other girls in high
school kept talking about their crinolines with a tone of self-satisfaction, so
I guessed I had better step in line. Fashion at that time was not about fittings but about fitting in. *Seventeen* magazine groomed us to be perky, girl-
ish accessories to the times. Everly Brothers, Elvis, Connie Francis were the

soundtrack. Swing skirts and bobby sox were the style. I remember having great anxiety about how to dress, buying a black-and-white wool heathered straight skirt and pink crewneck sweater. It was an approximation of a style I had seen somewhere—perhaps *The New York Times*, which my grandmother had delivered daily to our home. The outfit did not suit my short body. I looked like a stump, not a willow. No one wore jeans or pants to school. Fashion defiance had not become an adolescent trope as yet. I was not at home in my body, though I felt beautiful inside.

I don't remember many of my clothes from this time. I think I wore the crinoline under the pink checkered shirtdress that had a skirt flared enough to accommodate the crinoline's breadth. The dress had a Peter Pan collar. It was a cute look, a bouncy look. I tried it out a few times, but it didn't really fit me. The crinoline embarrassed me—so poofy—and even then I felt an inner seriousness that led me to books rather than *Teen Beat*. A teenager holed up in her bedroom under the eaves reading *Crime and Punishment* may not be the best candidate for the pink and perky look. The crinoline announced a feminine silliness about my body that I did not feel. And it was awkward to wear, puffing up when I sat down, and when I stood keeping at a distance anyone I might want to come close. How inept the crinoline seemed then in conveying anything I actually felt about my body, suffering the first afflictions of sexual desire, which I dared not express. What garment could have conveyed that ambiguity? I wore the crinoline, I remember just now, under the yellow chiffon prom dress—another poor approximation of who I felt myself to be.

I'd been asked my sophomore year to the senior prom by the high school football star—handsome but built like a refrigerator. Fred Severni. I hardly knew the guy. We'd never spoken. Why did he ask me? I had no idea. That year I had played the ingénue Elaine in the high school play *Arsenic and Old Lace*. She was the sidekick to the protagonist, Mortimer, in the comedy about two charmingly murderous old women. I was on stage to be his date. I didn't much like the role, but I loved being on stage. In subsequent years, I played a series of women who had real agency. I think those characters too helped to raise me into the woman I have become. They shaped me. Lavinia, impassioned ally to the eponymous martyr in *Androcles and the Lion*; Annie Sullivan, the tutor who wrestled language into Helen Keller's hands, saving her from a fate of sensory exile; and the vamp Ilona Szabo in *The Play's the Thing*, a character who used wit and wiles to deceive her fiancé about her secondary dalliance. But Elaine was the role of the yellow prom dress year, the role that must have paraded me in front of the football player's gaze.

I guess I was the football player's prom date for the same reason I was onstage with Mortimer. Pretty accessory. For him to be seen, not for him to see me. Was it then that something clicked inside me insisting that I would never again be a mere accessory? But it was also the fashion statement of that yellow prom dress that made me feel inauthentic. My mother did not want to spend money on a new dress, so we went to the Clothes Horse in West Hartford, the consignment shop where she bought all of her chic clothes. How she managed to look so stylish wearing secondhand clothes is a mystery. Then again, this was Connecticut, the richest state in the union. Plenty of high-priced hand-me-downs. Fashion for her was the daily expression of self-love. She loved performing who she saw herself to be. She had felt emotionally abandoned in childhood by her mother. "My mother was a working woman. She had no time for me." Her father had literally abandoned the family when my mother was two years old. But love was always there in a dress. As a teenager, my mother would walk by a dress shop on Fifth Avenue, see a beaded flapper dress in the window, come home and tell her mother, "I must have that dress!" And her mother would see that it was done—beads, ruching, sashes, corsage, entire. Marie would cut the fabric without a pattern, and the staff of fourteen in the workroom, including the professional beader, would fit the job in among the dresses on order for paying clientele. My mother shunned her mother's business, experiencing it as the set of demands that took her mother's attention away from her. She preferred fantasies of Hollywood movie stars and Egyptian tomb robbers and Arctic adventurers. But when it came to her vanity, she knew how to get what she wanted. She knew the looks that worked on her hourglass body. V-necked décolleté, fitted bodice to the waist, full skirt. Strappy heels. She found feminine beauty easy to perform, having grown up in a salon of its performance.

We bought the yellow chiffon dress from the consignment store. It was too long and too plain. And yellow? I moped.

"Marnie will fix it for you."

My grandmother must have seen girls and women for decades with the same sad look of self-reproach that I wore modeling the thing. She stood me on the small upholstered stool she'd long used for clients' fittings. With tape measure in hand and straight pins in mouth, she took the matter to hand. She lopped off a foot from the bottom of the dress and fashioned of the remnant gauzy chiffon a gigantic flattened bow that she affixed to the bodice. The bow filled the space between my waist and breasts, making me look like a present to be unwrapped. The crinoline completed the look, making the skirt float on air, as if I might lift off with a slight gust of wind. The dress had become an artifice of attitude. I had become enlightened.

POP QUIZ: WHAT CAN BE MADE USING HORSE HAIR, WHALE BONE, linen, and steel from clock springs to enhance a woman's beauty? Answer: a crinoline. Or several crinolines, as they were constructed over the centuries. The crinoline that Empress Eugénie championed using steel hoops of increasing diameter descending from the waist and held together with linen strips was a technological advance over its predecessors. It meant women needed to wear only one petticoat to gird the girth of their gowns, rather than five, six, seven, eight layers of linen and flannel and homespun to bulk up their skirts. In the sixteenth century women wore farthingales to expand their skirts. These were made from hoops of rushes, wire, wood, and "whalebone"—stays made from baleen, the keratinous material that serves as strainer in the mouths of the mysticete whales. Materials varied, but effects were the same:

to elaborate upon female form, to establish substance and stature, to effect a seductive sway in a woman's passage. In the eighteenth century women wore panniers extending to the sides that made hips look like burden baskets—though no one wearing such a gown would be carrying much of anything but the weight of her garments. In the early nineteenth century, the crinoline widened the skirt's horizon and lightened the burden of wearing it. *Crin* means "horsehair" in French—the mane and tail hair being coarse enough to give structure. Weavers blended wool or linen with crin. Crin braid can still be purchased through Farthingales Corset Making Supply, an online retailer based in Ontario, though these days the weave is made primarily from polyester, not horsehair.

Materials. Methods. Makers.

The steel hoops favored by Empress Eugénie for the cage crinoline became popular in the 1850s and 1860s—and not only among the aristocracy. The steel proved strong enough to undergird gowns so grand they were said to have taken inspiration from the dome at St. Paul's Cathedral. In 1864 *The London Journal* reported that some twelve million kilograms of steel were "annually used for the fairer portion of the French people." Women of lesser means in rural areas made crinolines from wicker or, in one reported case, an overturned chicken roost. The cage crinoline had a run of about ten years, after which the empress wanted a "walking crinoline" cut shorter to make movement easier. A few years later, she favored narrowed skirts, and fashion followed her lead. The last to give up the big skirts were French prostitutes. Fashion is inherently neurotic: it must love the new and crave change. It must preserve female virtue and promote female allure. The industrial improvement of the female form is thus ever revivified as emblem of desire and unattainable beauty—though not without risk.

Skirts six feet in diameter with attached trains meant that a woman needed rehearsals in order to move with the grace expected of an aristocrat. As crinolines gained popularity across class lines, the higher one's stature, the wider the dress became. Anna Bicknell, British governess living at the

Tuileries, the French royal palace that stood next to the Louvre, described a dress worn by a young princess for a costume ball, the design taken from a historical portrait at the Louvre, a dress with such a circumference that the red velvet was spread "by her ladies" over three chairs. The emperor tried to dance with her, "but he was repeatedly obliged to stop because the velvet folds wound around him in such a manner as to paralyze his movements, until at last he was obliged to give up the attempt in despair, and to take her back to her seat with a bow and a smile."

Such dresses posed challenges for negotiating doorways, getting into carriages, avoiding open fireplaces, and even for sitting down. In the 1850s and '60s, according to a newspaper report, about three thousand women in England were killed in crinoline-related fires. For working women, the skirts could pose mortal danger. They were banned in some mills, where the threat of a woman being dragged by her petticoat under the wheels of industry was very real. In *Fashion Victims*, Alison Matthews David's chilling report on the high danger of high fashion, she writes that "Courtauld's cotton mills in Lancashire posted a sign in 1860 forbidding workpeople to wear 'the present ugly fashion of HOOPS, or CRINOLINE, as it is called' as 'quite unfitted for the work of our Factories.'" A print shop that banned the garments found the women showing up the next day "in full crinoline." The shop threatened to fire them "until they stripped off at the door when they arrived, making the office look like a secondhand clothing stall: 'one corner of the Printing Office looks like a decayed pawnbrokers shop with heaps of seedy bombazine.'"

Widespread derision of the crinoline dominated the press. In 1857 Honoré Daumier published a cartoon depicting a woman who uses her amply wired skirts to smuggle meat, alcohol, and tobacco past customs officers. The comedic image is immortalized as *De l'utilité de la crinoline pour frauder l'octroi* in the Achenbach Foundation for Graphic Arts of the Fine Arts Museums of San Francisco. Claims of the crinoline's virtue countered such calumny. Women saved from drowning by the buoyancy of their crinolines or saved from falling off cliffs by the parachutes of their skirts.

The feminist eye may construe such garments as instruments of oppression, but women liked the cage crinolines. They enabled a woman to glide more gracefully than when wearing six heavy petticoats. They enabled a woman to walk more freely without the added weight of underskirts as padded and heavy as a bed quilt. Cage crinolines kept sleazy men at an appropriate distance—even sweeping men aside as a pair of beskirted women strolled along a boardwalk. Fashion historian C. Willett Cunnington wrote in *The History of Underclothes* that the skirts "kept the wearer at arm's length from contact with the outer world. It was as though she had become petrified into a monument which, however impossible it might seem, continued to expand."

Partisans of the crinoline, such as the writer who penned the 1860s *Harper's Bazaar* column titled "The Rise and Fall of the Crinoline," had a more empathic understanding of what a woman might feel who enjoyed wearing the garment and her remorse at the fashion's demise. He wrote that sadly "after fourteen years' residence of earth, crinoline at length expired." Fine ladies were seen at balls "innocent of whalebone and steel supports." Many commentators celebrated the crinoline's demise. The column on March 28, 1868, posted this.

And how have the votaries of crinoline borne this somewhat sudden deprivation of their cherished ornament? Men can not place themselves at all in their position, and therefore can form no idea of their feelings under the trying circumstances. A young lady, however, bewailed her fate in the following remarks which describe pretty fairly the sentiments of a large number of her sex: "When I became obliged, owing to the change in fashion, to give up my crinoline entirely, I felt a kind of degradation. I was belittled. It was as if I had lost part of my body; for as I am only seventeen years of age, I was almost born to and brought up in crinoline. I can think of no better word than degradation; for it is no trifling matter for a young person of an ambitious turn of mind to melt away before every body's eyes like a heap of snow in the sun."

Fashion comments upon political history. There may be no more arresting example than one cited by historian Aileen Ribeiro of a craze that caught on in France in 1794 at the end of the Terror, when women wore a red ribbon around their necks, signifying the cut of the guillotine blade and cropped their hair *à la victime*. Fashion speaks to our obsession with change. Fashion expresses the ongoing challenge to dwell within our contradictions: mourn and celebrate, conceal and display, fit in and stand out, throw out the old and—wait, is this old or is this a classic?

In *Clothing Art*, Ribeiro writes of "the obvious sartorial excess of the 1850s and 1860s, the vast crinolines, very low necklines and bright aniline dyes, all of which could slide easily into the cloying sexuality and vulgarity for which the Second Empire was notorious." Empress Eugénie regularly hosted balls with one thousand guests. For hunting parties at Compiègne, hundreds of guests came and stayed for a month. It was understood that they were not to wear any dress more than once during their stay. Imagine the luggage. For the opening of the Suez Canal, the empress ordered 350 dresses. She "wished her court to be like that of Marie Antoinette." She "sometimes wore the diamonds that had belonged to her; on her desk she kept the queen's 1782 register of dress and fabric samples."

The Princess Metternich recalls in her memoirs an occasion when Eugénie was "attired in a white gown spangled with silver and dressed with her most beautiful diamonds. She had carelessly thrown over her shoulders a sort of burnous of white embroidered with gold, and the murmurs of admiration followed her like a trail of lighted gunpowder."

Somewhere in this morass of ribbon and chiffon and crepe de chine, perhaps my great-grandmother's hands labored, savoring the tactile liquidity of satin, the diaphanous drape of silk, the integrity lent by whalebone, the delicate intricacy of handmade lace.

✳

MY CRINOLINE CAME IN THE LATE FOSSIL FUEL AGE. THE WORLD was finished with using whales for energy and fashion. It was 1962. It was all about plastics. My crinoline was made of fine nylon mesh. Nylon, invented in 1935 and raising a commercial stir in 1939 when nylon stockings first were displayed at the New York World's Fair. DuPont announced "the first man-made organic textile fiber . . . derived from coal, water and air . . . strong as steel, as fine as the spider's web." The first year that nylon stockings went on the market, sixty-four million pairs were sold at twice the price of silk stockings. Then the war came and nylon was diverted for parachutes. But I was a postwar baby. Nylons were back. So were nylon slips and sweater sets and garter belts. And crinolines. No stays or hoops. Just crisp netted fabric gathered into tiers so that it radiated from the waist in the shape of a Christmas tree.

By the time I was a senior in high school I had found my own style: A-line wool camel-hair skirt, green-blue-heather crewneck cardigan with grosgrain ribbon trim lining the row of buttons, the elbows worn thin, brown loafers, baggy and worn until my big toe stuck out. I wore this get-up most days in defiance of what *Seventeen* magazine thought I should wear. Where did I get this idea of anti-fashion? I don't know. It had to do with not wanting to be considered second-rate because I was a girl. Not needing to prove my worth with clothes. Not wanting to be taken at face value. Wanting to be taken at mind value, talent value, character.

I remember feeling trivial when I dated a boy a couple of years older than I was, a boy who was in college when I was still in high school. He'd read everything James Baldwin had written and had traveled with the Student Nonviolent Coordinating Committee to Americus, Georgia, to register Black citizens for the vote. He'd been arrested. That was the first I learned of civil disobedience and the consequences it might demand. I felt that I knew nothing compared to him. And one day when I whined to him about my insecurity he tried to bolster me up by saying I knew a lot about Eugene O'Neill, my most recent art crush. But my knowledge was term paper knowledge and his was experiential. I knew the difference was significant.

I hung with the smart girls, the good girls. We looked down on those we saw as trashy girls, sexy ones, from the wrong side of town, until one of us—the prim Irish Catholic girl—dropped out from school with a mysterious sickness. As she disappeared from the cheerleading squad, from class, from Teen Club, quiet rumors flew. This was 1963. There was no Planned Parenthood. No women's health clinics. Abortion was illegal. So was birth control. It was not until 1965 that the Supreme Court ruled in *Griswold v. Connecticut* that married couples had the right to use birth control, protected by the Constitution under the right to privacy. Unmarried couples and unwitting teenagers—forget about it. Denial was the main contraceptive in our time. And its failure rate was high.

Surely this quiet, proper, devout Catholic girl was not the one among us first to be having sex. "Having sex." As if it could be a possession to have and hold. I went with two other girls to visit her after she dropped out of high school. Someone had called to ask her mother if it was okay. We walked into a staged performance. Our friend was lying on the living room couch, flowery pastel bathrobe up to her neck, blanket covering her body. She looked so frail, so diminished. The mother stayed in the room with us. We were under surveillance. No one had to tell us that for us to know the rules. No one knew what to say. Truth was not an option. We played along with the lie. We wished she would feel better. We missed her. We loved her. Would she be able to come back to school soon? We left feeling more confused and convicted than when we arrived.

A few days later the boy who had been dating her, a boy whose name was—so implausibly, so prophetically, that I cannot leave it out though even now, after half a century has passed and I have no idea if he is even alive and I worry that I may be violating his trust—Dick True, showed up at my house. My childhood home was built into a hillside so that the living room was on the second floor and the first floor was a small entry hall with a few chairs and a few paintings that had been given to my grandmother in trade by customers who could not afford their dressmaking bills—a couple of romantic Florida mangrove scenes and a portrait of Napoleon Bonaparte with his hand tucked into his military torso. The walls were dark green. It was a private and sheltering space away from family hearing. Dick came in, his face taut. He was handsome with a rectangular face and sandy hair. He was tall and fit. A boy I only knew through maybe a few parties and an awkward blind date I had with his roommate, who was less handsome, less fit, and of less interest to me than Dick. The date must have been a doubleheader with Dick and the Catholic girl. Why had he come to me that evening? So unlikely for him to just stop by. He began to weep, big gulping sobs that engulfed him. I had never seen a man (and this one only a boy) in such pain. "They won't let me see her." His whole body caved in to his anguish. "They're going to send her away." Did I hold him or did I stand awkwardly, stupidly humbled, not knowing how to meet the suffering of another? "They're going to make her give the baby away. But I *love* her." That "love" came out as animal cry, like the sound of the word "help" coming from a drowning man.

So it was in our youth. The falsehoods we were asked to live by and with which we largely complied were the fashion of the day and taught us that we had better to learn to speak our truths.

11

✳

The Paris Notebook

WHEN MY DAUGHTER WAS IN COLLEGE THERE WAS A STRETCH when she wore fishnet stockings. She painted her fingernails black and lived with a rocker who sang with screaming drop-to-his-knees intensity in an underground club—Geno's in Portland, Maine, for those who may remember the scene. They lived together and fed white rats to their pet boa constrictor. Lucinda played in an all-girl band named The Brood. They hoped to tour the punk clubs of Europe. That's when Mom exercised a little diplomatic authority. "Are you sure you don't want to go back to school?" The year off had become an open question for her. For me the scholarship to Skidmore was a gift not to be denied. I could not have gotten her through school without it. I had dropped out of university when I became pregnant with her. That detour had led to two decades of tough and improvised self-sufficiency as I raised her, ferrying past parental judgment, shotgun teenage marriage, divorce, poverty, and the good graces of a few wise older women, one of whom wrote to me, "The only time you've ever disappointed me was when you told me you didn't like field hockey." I have never forgotten her. Those were the decades I learned my strengths, when, through adversity and spite toward those who had judged me, I felt more deeply present to the responsibility of shaping my life, more deeply committed to finding truths worthy of sharing with the child entrusted to me by my youthful folly. I wished for her an easier road than the one I had taken.

The fishnets really got to me.

"You're wearing the vocabulary of porn."

I saw the sleazy deck of pornographic playing cards my teenage brother had kept hidden in his closet.

"It has nothing to do with that," she spat in all her independent glory.

She saw the punk scene—Siouxsie Sioux, a badass language of female power.

"I finally had a look," she tells me decades later, "for telling people to fuck off."

During the War on Poverty, when federal funds supported the launch of family planning clinics in underserved regions, I worked for over a decade for Planned Parenthood, trained as a para-professional sex educator and clinic organizer. I was not squeamish, as many parents are, about discussing sexuality with my daughter or about expressing my own as a source of pleasure and power in the pre-AIDS years. I wanted my daughter to feel empowered and pleasured by her sexuality. But I did not want her to be degraded or violated or fetishized. And I did not want her "look" to suggest she might invite that. Was I suggesting it would be her fault if she were mistreated because she had worn fishnet stockings? Not my intention, but that must be how she heard my complaint. I am sorry for that. Fishnets are a ubiquitous accessory among fashion models, Roller Derby stars, and at least one crime-fighting superhero, Black Canary. But at the time, my daughter's fishnets were for me a focal point of my maternal anxiety at knowing that just because she was a woman she faced vulnerabilities from which I could not protect her.

In recalling this, I began to wonder, when did fishnets enter the fashion lexicon? They were popular at the Moulin Rouge in 1900, cementing their association with strippers. But the erotic suggestion of fishnets, I have found, shows up much earlier in history. The Westcar Papyrus, a work written probably in ancient Egypt's Thirteenth Dynasty, offers five tales about miracles performed by magicians and priests as told to the Pharaoh Khufu (or Cheops) by his five sons. The tale told by Baufra takes place during the reign of his grandfather Sneferu, the first king of the Fourth Dynasty (circa 2500 B.C.E.). The pharaoh, suffering from royal ennui, wanders through his palace and can find no distraction to interest him. He calls to his high priest for help, who directs the pharaoh to go to the lake, where a boat will be fitted out "with all the beauties from inside the palace." The women rowing to and fro and the birds wading on the banks of the marshes will cheer him up. So Sneferu orders, according to the Westcar Papyrus, twenty oars made of ebony decorated with gold and "twenty virgin maidens with perfect bodies and well-developed bosoms, compassed with braided hair. Let them be draped in nets after they have disrobed their clothes."

And thus they row, these fishnetted nudes, and thus the king is cheered by his catch. But that is not the miracle. The "stroke maiden" runs her fingers through her braids and dislodges a malachite hair pendant in the shape of a fish. It falls into the water. She, aggrieved, falls silent and stops calling the pace to her rowers. The boat stops. Sneferu urges the stroke maiden on, telling her not to worry, he has the means to replace the pendant. "Row!" he orders. No. She'd prefer to have back her own property. The king calls again to his high priest, who casts a spell that makes one half side of the lake rest on the other half—like an omelet flipped sideways in the pan. The priest walks out on the lake's dry ground, picks up the lost fish pendant, returns it to the stroke maiden, and flips the waters back to their original position. The maiden resumes her beat. The boat resumes its task. Sneferu spends the rest of the day celebrating the miracle and the powers of his priest. But the stroke maiden deserves some credit for sticking up for her desires. She is more than an instrument for soothing the pharaoh's ennui. A woman in fishnets is the catalyst for invoking supernatural powers that turn out to be more powerful than the king's own authority in bringing him pleasure.

Now, decades after my daughter's punk phase, when she is an accomplished visual artist and academic, a woman who can throw onto her runner's body a cheap faux-tapestry skirt and black tee and look like a hipster model, then give a brilliant lecture on kinetic landscape representation in her work, I have nothing but admiration for her fashion sense. In fact, I often defer to her for advice on my own style, which seems perpetually to elude me. I could think of no better travel companion for a research trip to Paris seeking traces of my maternal great-grandmother, Louisa de St. Isle Bregny.

How do I tell a story when there is so little story to tell? I have looked for my great-grandmother in New York, knowing she had lived and run a dressmaking business there for thirty or forty years. I did not find her at Castle Garden, the old concert hall turned into immigrant station during the flood of arrivals from Europe to the United States in the mid-1800s, when she would have arrived. I did not find her on ship manifests or immigration and naturalization documents. I did not find her at the Tenement Museum on the Lower East Side, though I took a tour of the home-based sweatshop to understand how those less fortunate than Louisa had found sustenance in the garment trades. I did not find her at the Cosmopolitan Hotel in Tribeca when I arrived at one in the morning, the hallway sooty from street construction. But the room was so small it conjured the old New York of Louisa's time, a dense and crowded city growing so fast it had to cram more and more people into less and less space.

I did not find her at 272 West Eleventh Street, the five-story redbrick walk-up where she lived in 1880. The building is gone. One of only two houses on the block demolished to make way for an apartment building the size of two former brick walk-ups. I did not find her at the Eleventh Street café where I stopped for coffee, though in that narrow space, brick walls maybe ten feet wide, pressed tin ceiling, I again felt the compressed scale of places in old New York. I sat beside a young Japanese couple, he with an open notebook, characters indecipherable to me, and she with spiked leather boots and faux fur vest, hair streaked with blond wisps sweeping her cheek, the two talking fiercely. I was about to apologize for sitting two inches from them at the only table space available. Outside the wind had jacked up the ten-degree cold, so cold I had chilblains on my thighs from walking from Tribeca to Chelsea. Who wouldn't be glad for a warm table no matter how cramped on such a day? The spiked-boots woman instead apologized. "We're just talking, not fighting." She translated this to him and we all laughed. She was explaining to him how to fill out a W-4 form that he kept protected in a clear plastic sleeve.

Louisa would have had an experience like this—tucked into a homey and crowded space for warmth, cold backlit clouds adrift above the brownstones, someone translating for her the necessary forms for the new life. Did she speak English when she arrived? French remained her first language. I know this because I found among my grandmother Marie's things a letter that Louisa had written to Marie on the day my mother was born, celebrating the birth. The handwriting is French—still Louisa's language of intimate conveyance forty years after her immigration.

I did not find Louisa in the history of fashion or the memoirs of women who had lived when she lived, though I fell in love with her contemporary Louise Michel, who wrote of growing up with wolves wandering into the courtyard of her childhood home. Louise Michel, a woman born of a mother who was a servant in the home and a father who was the son of the household head, the young man hightailing out of France after knocking up the maid, but his father, honorably, taking the child in as if his own daughter and educating her and setting the stage for her dynamic life. Michel became a teacher, an orator, a revolutionary leader during the Paris Commune, a prisoner and exile in New Caledonia. That was a life worth remembering, but it could not speak for Louisa de St. Isle Bregny, dressmaker to Empress Eugénie, proprietor of "Bregny & Cie." "private house" in New York City, daughter of unknowns (did my mother once say Louisa's parents had been bakers?), mother of my grandmother, anchor to the matrilineal line I seek to know if only to honor the truth that I have received more than mitochondrial DNA from my female ancestors. Needlework has long been a skill of women in every social class, their "work." Custom dressmakers, as labor historian Helen Sumner wrote in 1910, "have always been aristocrats among clothing makers." Surely there must be a trace of her.

When Lucinda and I arrived in Paris, we agreed to walk off our jet lag. We would plan but we would also wander, taking in the immutable aspects of the city—placid Seine, lofty Montmartre, refuge of the Bois de Boulogne, plane trees in the Jardin des Plantes. We stayed in a small boutique hotel on the Rue des Gobelins near the eponymous tapestry factory—the Gobelin brothers, master dyers, who had crafted grand tapestries in the time of Henry XIV and where weaving continues on looms working with seventeenth-century techniques. At first my American eyes had seen the name through the taxi window and thought "goblins"—as if this place were some kind of Disneyland of cute icons. Pay attention. Pay attention. I told myself again and again. You know nothing about this place.

We made our way through Le Mouffetard, the medieval cobblestone street quiet on a Monday, stopping for a bite of gruyere crepe, sitting for espresso, then sloping down toward the Seine and finding ourselves staring up at Notre-Dame. No choice but to go in, be humbled by the grandeur of a space devoted to reverie. I lit a candle for our ancestor. Had Louisa worshipped here? The cathedral had been sacked during the Revolution, religious icons smashed, the space turned into a warehouse. It was restored during Louisa's youth, part of the reconstruction of Paris led by Napoleon III in the Second Empire. She may have lit a candle in prayer in the exact alcove where I stood lighting mine, heard the massive organ pipes fill the cavernous nave, billowing the walls against the flying buttresses.

We climbed the winding and worn stone staircase up to the Chimera Gallery, added during Louisa's childhood. Designed by architect Viollet-le-Duc, the hybrid creatures joined the gargoyle gutter spouts that had stood there for centuries. I remember learning in Prague that the Vatican had a special office for approving what chimeras were allowed on cathedrals. The intent is to say to demons, "Don't try entering these premises. The demons are already here." We lingered beside the stryga, most contemplative of the beasts, head in hands, wings and horns aloft, tongue protruding, as if to say that a thinking animal is itself a demonic presence. Or perhaps that there is no room here for mockery of lofty pretense. That tongue-splayed irreverence is already here.

Louisa must have felt that she was on the right side of history, a time in which the wealth of empire meant huge investments in beauty and civic pride. Her youth had been a time of suffering and turmoil in France—riots spurred by harvest failure and food shortage, cholera and smallpox, coup after coup, war after war. She was a teenager when Louis-Napoleon staged the coup to proclaim himself emperor. He'd served one term as president, and the law did not allow a second term by election. During his 1851 coup hundreds of his opponents were killed on the street, tens of thousands arrested, thousands sent to penal colonies in Algeria or Guyana or into exile. Newspapers were not allowed to print political news without permission of the government. After three warnings, a paper could be shut down. He believed that his fate was to rule. As a child, he had visited his uncle Napoleon Bonaparte at the Tuileries, an experience that ignited his ambition. He was one of those men, he later wrote, "whom I call volunteers of providence, in whose hands are placed the destiny of their countries." It was a hard road for him to get there. Before his presidency, he served time in prison and exile in England for his earlier attempts at a coup. He had written in prison a book widely celebrated by socialists on the elimination of poverty through assistance to the working and farming class. *L'Extinction du Pauperisme* was published in 1844 and raised hopes that he would champion the working class. He wrote, "They have no other wealth than their own labor . . . they are without rights and without a future." These sympathies helped him win his place in public office. But it's hard to get a grasp on the man. Once in power, he seemed to want both monarchy and republicanism. Perhaps these two forces were at war within him.

From 1815 until the time Louis-Napoleon attained the stature of emperor as Napoleon III in 1851, the population of Paris grew by more than 60 percent with no expansion of its area. As emperor he annexed eleven surrounding municipalities, displacing hundreds of thousands of citizens and increasing the number of arrondissements from twelve to twenty. In the city center, hundreds of buildings were torn down, new avenues lined with gas lights, the buildings all faced with cream-colored stone. The poor suffered in the advance of this progress. Citizens were angry over lost streets and being moved to outlying slums, tradesmen lost shops, and new workers came in from provinces to compete for the new jobs. Napoleon III was hated for turning away from the ideals he had espoused in his writing, for neglecting the poor to realize his goal of making Paris into "the capital of capitals."

Louisa would have come of age as the empire did. She would have known the city's reconstruction as a tempo of life, a filthy and dark medieval city becoming a showpiece with broad tree-lined streets, new railways and new shipping lines, hygienic water and sewer systems. The Bois de Boulogne was constructed, modeled on Hyde Park in London. The Palais Garnier Opera House went up, the largest theater in the world, and the Luxembourg Gardens were replanted as part of a plan to create "green and flowering salons" in each of the city's neighborhoods.

Empress Eugénie was an impresario of high fashion. She made Charles Frederick Worth, the first name-brand designer, a celebrity. Before him, the dressmaker's art was that of women, in part because of the physical intimacy of the dressmaker's relationship to her customer's body. Stripping, measuring, fitting, corseting, trying on the toile, stripping, measuring, fitting, hands guiding the fabric along the client's frame. Louisa was a performer of the dressmaker's art, bringing the *femmes élégantes* onto the stage of life. Anna Bicknell, a governess in the Palace Tuileries in those years, wrote that "there was a sort of intoxication in the very atmosphere of Paris, a fever of enjoyment—a passion for constant amusement, for constant excitement, and, amongst women, for extravagance of dress." She wrote that Eugénie "had the art of constantly choosing something new and unusual, which attracted attention, so that, instead of being satisfied with conventional types of silks and satins, which formerly had been considered sufficient for all occasions, every one tried to invent something different from the others, and to improve upon what had been seen before." There was a constant struggle "to reach a higher degree of splendor, and extravagance became universal."

At the Tuileries the empress had several rooms lined with oak wardrobes with sliding panels. Four manikins were stationed there for preparing the dresses for the day. Dresses tiered and pouffed, shirred into gathers and festoons, decked with paillettes and gorgettes, garments more florid than royal wedding cakes, sequined and beaded, beribboned and braided with gold, corsaged and feathered, dresses that require a lexicon of lost words to describe: leg-of-mutton sleeves, chinoiserie roundels and foulard des Indes, organza and tulle, polonaise and paletot, pin tucks and welt tucks, vandyke and passamenterie, casaque and aigrette, selvage and bias.

When Lucinda and I returned from our first walk in Paris to Hotel Henriette, we found a fashion shoot happening in the lobby so small we had to thread our way through electrical wires vining the floor and monstrous cameras bolted to tripods. The room was dark with an island of intense white light focused on the perfect braceleted arms of a model pale as a hospital sheet. The bracelet was a chunky circle of ivory-colored plastic that wound round and round her wrist. She held the arms elbow down on a pedestal, wrists up and slightly crossed. Lucinda described the stillness in the room as "a tomb of fashion seriousness." We blundered through, apologizing for our intrusion, slipped into the elevator just large enough for two, and found our way to sleep.

At breakfast Lucinda was reading a history of Paris fashion—how the dresses got so low cut in the early 1800s, the nipples showed. The English, fearing French licentiousness, raised the neckline. No more nipples in public. Lucinda planned to head off on a twelve-mile run—her method for reconnoitering a new place. I would meet my research assistant to look for birth records circa 1838, passenger lists circa 1864, historical records of a coterie of French dressmakers and tailors leaving Paris to settle in the French Empire in Mexico circa 1865. I was looking for someone who lived after Victor Hugo's *Les Miserables* and before Ivan Turgenev's "The Execution of Tropmann." In the case of either literary example, this was a time from which a woman would have many reasons to want to escape.

My great-grandmother did not intend to move to New York City. She was bound from Paris for Mexico sometime in the mid-1860s. By the time her ship got to New York, it was no longer safe for her to continue her journey. Had Napoleon III sponsored her trip, part of his plan to send European immigrants to populate the nation? The pretense for the war and occupation was Mexico's unpaid debt to France. But the "Mexican Adventure" had more to do with economic power derived from resources. The American Civil War meant a decline in imports of cotton from the Confederate states. The cotton shortage devastated the Lyon textile mills. The Confederate government had offered Napoleon twenty-two thousand tons of raw cotton in 1862, but to obtain it France would have to sail through a U.S. blockade. Napoleon was unwilling to risk war with the Union, so he declined. To complicate matters, France had turned to India for cotton, and they demanded payment in silver. As France ran low on the precious metal, the silver mines in Sonora added further appeal to the exploit.

History remembers how many French troops went to Mexico in December 1861 (six thousand), how many in January 1862 (twenty-six hundred, including six hundred mercenaries from North Africa, who were thought to tolerate Mexico's heat and tropical diseases better than the French). But who stitched the britches and mended the shoes of these thousands? Who made and mended the dresses of the officers' consorts? Who brought French fashion to Mexico? For it too had arrived. When one prominent French woman, as described by M. M. McAllen in *Maximilian and Carlota: Europe's Last Empire in Mexico*, "arrived at mass wearing the latest in French fashion (meaning a hoop skirt, décolletage, bare arms, and Parisian hat), the officiating priest became offended that she was not wearing the black mantilla customary for most women supplicants. The priest made a rude gesture to her husband, who in reply complained to the priest's superior." It was decided that the priest was within his right to excuse her from church, which prompted "an angry letter that the French were good Catholics, just as reverent as the Mexicans, and French women should be allowed the right to attend mass in the attire of their homeland." Surely all of a woman's finery could not have come with her in a sea chest. Who made that dress? So many skilled and accomplished and specialized artisans stand behind history's performance of wealth and power: the dressmakers, beaders, sleevers, pressers, tailors, shoemakers, tool makers, saddle makers, carriage makers—that vast class of artisans who served the European ruling class, last gasp of the *ancien régime*, as they roved from chateau to palace to royal hunting grounds in sumptuous ostentation. History does not care about the makers, only the overtakers.

"De St. Isle?" queried the woman who keeps the records. "That would be a very unusual name in France." My great-grandmother Louisa de St. Isle Bregny appears not to have existed.

I can almost hear her laughing at the endless erasure of women, this accomplished woman who established a business in New York City and ran it right into the twentieth century. At that time, though, a woman and her children, I've been told, might be included on her husband's passport. No need to have one of her own. But her birth? Should there not be at least a record of that fact? She knew a Paris where women were fighting for the right to divorce, the right to a secular education, an end to the distinction between married women and concubines, between legitimate and illegitimate children. She knew a nation of worker revolts in the silk mills, a nation ruled by an autocrat who failed at every one of his military ventures and compensated for his failures by engaging in obscene sexual mores.

Napoleon III was a systematic philanderer. At the Palace Tuileries, a staircase led from his imperial study to a bedroom above. The Goncourt Journal, written by two brothers who seemed to have thrived on café gossip, recorded details of the emperor's seamier behaviors. Potential candidates for liaison were presented to the emperor in his study. If he was not attracted to a candidate, he announced, "I am summoned by my papers." If he was attracted, the woman was taken to a room to undress, then led naked to the bedroom where the naked emperor waited. "You may kiss His Majesty on any part of his person except his face," she was told. One woman said he wore a mauve silk nightshirt. She reported that "his performance in bed lacked distinction." And then there was the two-year affair beginning in 1863 with his young *cocodette,* "The Laughing Margot," whom he set up in two homes. There was no question of discretion; indiscretion was the turn-on. Her place became a party scene for the sophisticates. "The gravest and most frivolous persons flocked thither," writes Fenton Bresler in his biography of the emperor. "Ministers, senators, equerries, chamberlains, diplomats, tenors, soldiers and buffoons."

Eugénie was fully aware of her husband's cocking around. Of the ladies presented in court, she said, "I'd like to know which one of them hasn't slept with the emperor." Her compensation for these indignities was to become increasingly influential in political decisions. She sat in on cabinet meetings, served as regent when the emperor was on military ventures, and had her own diplomatic discussions with ambassadors to Paris during the 1860s, among them Bismarck, who called her "the only man in Paris." She was the most powerful woman in Europe and a philanthropist. When the city of Paris offered her a diamond necklace worth six hundred thousand francs, she asked that the money be used to fund an orphanage for girls. She held huge receptions at Fontainebleau and Compiègne, to which she invited Flaubert, Dumas, Berlioz, Verdi, and Delacroix for conversation.

"DE ST. ISLE? I FIND NO ONE BY THAT NAME," SAID THE WOMAN who keeps the records. Was Louisa a "first hand" or one of the *"petit mains"* in a couture house? Did she work for Worth or in competition, one of the hold-outs against the turning of the tide in fashion toward male couturiers? Was she an *entrepreneuse* who had more work than she could do by herself and hired less-skilled seamstresses and skirt hands and embroiderers to work for her? How did she pass from modest origin into the empyrean of dressmaking in Paris and then in New York? Imagine the silks that passed through her hands, the crepe de chine, the chiffon, the fine lace saved from the finest dresses to be employed on a new creation.

After giving up on another day of archival dead-ends, I decided to take the train to Compiègne to seek some atmospherics of the place where Napoleon had courted Eugénie and that became their autumn palace during his reign. For the Royal Hunt, a forest had been built in a series of octagons. Horses trotted out from the palace under a grand canopy laced over with vines and sculpted plane trees. The hunt is immortalized in nine massive eighteenth-century tapestries woven at Gobelins, designed by Jean-Baptiste Oudry, known for his paintings of dogs, that hang on palace walls. The grand chase in the forest. Over a dozen dogs. Men on horseback. Women sidesaddle. A forest of trees and stags and foxes and rabbits. A melee of wildness and genteel ritualized killing. A tiny figure in the lower right-hand corner of one tapestry shows the artist, leaning over his sketch pad, sentinel to the act of witness.

On such a hunt, Napoleon sought to bed the vivacious Spanish beauty Eugénie de Montijo. He'd given her a horse on a previous visit to Fontaine-bleau. At Compiègne he rode with her into the forest, passion doubly roused, but she denied him. I like to imagine a coterie of seamstresses hanging out in some dark recess of the palace grounds, making bawdy hay of the erotic escapade.

The emperor has split his pants again.

Yes, he was so hard he split his pants, and still she would not let him have her.

He blamed the tear on a feint executed by his mount at the sight of a rabbit, but we had all seen the bulge in his pantaloons grow more desperate as the week bore on.

That pansy ass.

And when she came to our salon to be dressed for the ball, she told us what she'd told him. Make me empress and I'll make you a man.

Then she acted all the virgin at the ball, that spirited huntress who knew her prey.

ON THE RETURN TRAIN TO PARIS A SMALL, LEAN WOMAN WITH a narrow Mohawk on a shaved head asked me in French, "Is this the train to Paris?"

I'd already noticed her, attractive, Black, silver earrings (were they skulls or razor blades?), black leather femme-stylized biker jacket and jeans all pocked with fashion tears.

"Yes, I think so."

We joked.

"Then we will be lost together."

"Let me ask someone in my bad French."

Her accent was very thick in English. Somewhat English, somewhat French. Maybe North African.

"Can I sit with you?"

I was worried she wanted to hit on me for money, but I said yes.

Slowly our stories unfolded. She had grown up in London. Her mother died there of AIDS. She went back to Kenya to see her father for the funeral. She has a half-sister there. They didn't want to know her. She said she was trying to get back to Somalia.

Somalia, where forty years of drought and a collapsed government have led to war, poverty, disease, and starvation, where AIDS burns like a wildfire, young women and girls hit hardest through transactional or sugar-daddy or violent sex, where people living with AIDS suffer such stigma that their families want nothing to do with them, where al-Shabaab terrorists siphon off the food and drugs targeted for humanitarian aid, where to become a displaced person may be the only way to survive. How hard must a person's life be in order for her to long for a return to this homeland?

I told my traveling companion some stories from my life, but they didn't sound very hard anymore.

"You've had a hard life," I said. "I'm sorry."

"You don't need to be sorry," she said.

We rode quietly while the train passed through wooded hills, then a spindly plantation of trees, then a vast field of something that looked like cabbages. We were hurtling out of the past toward the Paris not of the Tuileries and Montmartre but of the *banlieues* and *cités*, those Brutalist projects where immigrants from Algeria, Tunisia, Mali, Syria—many of them Arabs—were stacked twenty stories high. They mixed with earlier immigrants from Poland and Italy and Portugal. Christian, Muslim, and Jew thrown together by their disadvantage, without a vocabulary for bridging distance in a secular nation and lacking a community to embrace them. These neighborhoods on the Paris outskirts are beds of the poverty and social isolation. Crime, drug use, and violence are high in alienated communities where a sense of belonging is absent.

I might have come to Paris in search of the past, but I found in the present moment lament beyond my imagining.

"Because of what we've talked about," my companion said, "I want to tell you."

"Yes?" She paused, as if embarrassed to continue. To what extent could she entrust me with her story?

"I am a stripper." But she said "strippah" in that British way that sounds so beautiful. "Don't judge me. I'm sorry."

"You don't need to be sorry." I thought then of the woman's vulnerability and power all clothed in the economy of her body and how she had used it to survive. Her body unclothed signified her survival.

Then we arrived at the Gare du Nord.

We embraced. Gone.

12

✳

At the Seining

Salt fish were stacked up on the wharves, looking like
corded wood, maple and yellow birch with the bark
left on. I mistook them for this at first, and such in one
sense they were,—fuel to maintain our vital fires,—an
eastern wood which grew on the Grand Banks.

HENRY DAVID THOREAU, *Cape Cod*, 1851

SINCE I WAS A CHILD ON GRAND MANAN WHEN I FIRST SAW THE
seining of a herring weir, the image of that bounty has never left me. I will
be talking with students about the ecology of metaphor or scanning photos
of absurdly elaborate ball gowns from the Gilded Age, and suddenly I will
picture the graceful twine draped over birch top-poles, the poles lashed side-
to-side with manila wrapped just so, the gauzy light softened by sea mist
filtering through nets, the little squares and rectangles of netting that have
been stitched in place to repair tears, the team of men pulling together, all
hands leaning over the gunwale, hauling and hauling to bring up the catch

that will fuel their vital fires. I will picture water sieving out of the seine net and the mass of fish rising until nothing remains but herring, a thrashing mass of glistening energy fighting against its fate. I will hear the soft growl of the carrier as its pump labors, and the loud rush of water sluicing through the scuppers as the fish are parted from the sea and ride down the chute into the carrier's hold. Deeper and deeper they pile up, and, yes, it is not a beautiful thing for the herring, as they smother in the fish-heavy hold.

I sometimes wonder what it is about the weir that makes me think of it at times when I might have thought about Christo and Jeanne-Claude's *Running Fence*. A herring weir has always looked more like art than work to me, the shape so pleasing to the eye, but hard to take in at a glance, requiring a second look and a third and a few questions about how the mechanism works. It's a thing that can't be understood without understanding the thing it was made to catch. The Atlantic herring, the silver darlings of the sea, the most abundant fish in the North Atlantic, that come to shore in massive shoals at night in pursuit of zooplankton, being specialized to forage on the *Calanus finmarchicus*, a rice-sized fatty copepod vastly abundant in the region, that supports the food web from herring and shrimp all the way up to whales. But waters are warming, currents are changing. *Calanus* likes cold water. A simple way to put the situation is this: no copepods, no herring. According to Graham Sherwood, self-described as a "jack-of-all-trades" fish ecologist at the Gulf of Maine Research Institute, if copepods move north for cooler waters, herring won't make it in the Bay of Fundy.

In 2018, a summer of surprising abundance when the bay is full of life again after nearly a decade of quiet years, when whales are breaching near shore and porpoises are entertaining everyone and herring are swimming into just about everyone's weir, the story once again is bounty. The herring with their tinsel flash scatter the light. Silver is their camouflage. They are nearly transparent in the water. The sea has made them, and they wear its colors: silver, blue, gray. They move as one, the shift, the swerve, the underwater flight. If you move, I will move with you. They all say that together.

But it's not just bounty that moves me about the herring harvest. It's also the quiet accord among men working together, a syncopation in which everyone knows his role, knowledge passed from father to son, father to son, father to son. The cooperation, skill, and stamina. On the day I write this, Junior Ingalls at age ninety stands on a skiff in Pat's Cove to seine his weir. It's not unusual to go out on a seine boat and find three generations of men are working side by side. I hear their voices all commingling now, in the eternal present of memory, after a few years of listening to words that have new meanings because of the weirs: wings, bunts, pounds, shut-off weirs, bar weirs, ballasted weirs, stop seines. Of the hard work of those who came before them: "They had herring scales in their eyes. They were brilliant just to survive." Respect for their elders is founded in understanding the meaning of work in such a place. I hear their voices rise and fall on the swells of memory.

Any herring in Pat's Cove?

Just enough to keep the shags. (The locals' word for cormorants.)

But then the weir is full, the seine net mended, the seine rings lined up on deck to fall just so along the weir's perimeter so that the diver can fix it to the bottom.

OK, let's go fishing!

Get your oil pants on, boys. We're all gonna get wet!

And then there is the waiting.

Too much tide yet—still running.

And then the tide has slackened.

Take your time—just creep that thing around.

Not too fast. It's hard on the boys' hands.

And then it's all ropes and twine and diesel thrum as the carrier enters the weir, the skiff just kissing the larger boat's bow at a right angle to help it thread the needle into the weir.

Gonna drum them out of this hook.

The skiff wheels in a fast spin to get the herring where they need to be.

And then the pumper takes its haul, silver fish spewing in a torrent into the *Andrew and Deane*'s belly, and the carrier rides lower and lower in the water and night has come on and no one has really noticed.

A herring weir all dressed and empty is nothing but a hope and a prayer. A herring weir all dressed and full of fish is an exaltation. "This is a gift," says the weirman. "This is a gift," he repeats, when one carrier is full and another is required.

No moon.

Stars fill up the sky, the Milky Way so dense the milk has spilled everywhere. The Dipper shines in the northern sky. Abundance above and abundance below and here in the middle we find our way in the dark. Someone stirs the water and it glows.

See the water fire? That's what they're eating.

It's a long wait for the second carrier to make its way from North Head. The *Andrew and Deane* is loaded and ready to go.

We can stay until the other carrier gets here. So you have light.

Dark night, skiffs bobbing, seals snorting on the perimeter.

We don't need light.

The *Andrew and Deane* on the last night of summer rides low and full out into the night.

13

※

Seal Skin Coat

Let me sing to you now about how people turn into
other things.

OVID, *Metamorphoses*

THE MOST BEAUTIFUL GARMENT I EVER OWNED WAS A SEAL SKIN
coat given to me by my grandmother Marnie. I don't know where she got
the coat. She may have bought it in the city when she was flush from her
dressmaking business. She may have had it custom-made by a friend in the
business. It fit her short, stout frame perfectly. She may have gotten it in trade
from a customer who could not afford her bill. My guess is it had been with
her since the 1920s, the Jazz Age, when seal coats were the rage. The fur was
dark brown, silky fine, and short-haired. The coat had a brown satin lining.
The long narrow pelts had been hand-stitched together vertically with waxed
thread, the stitches visible only underneath the lining. Dozens of seals to
make one human coat. The cut was princess style, fitted in the bodice, then
flowing gracefully out in gentle A-line to reach mid-calf. Small Chinese col-

lar like a Coco Chanel suit. Front closures were large hook-and-eye pairings hidden under fur, the wire covered with a chain-stitch of heavy-gauge brown thread. It was a very strange sensation, wearing the seal skin coat. It was heavy. It was dense. It was embracingly warm. Wind and cold could not penetrate the seal skin. It was elegant. Too elegant for me, I thought at nineteen. But the pelt invited touch. I could not stop myself from stroking it, enamored with the animal life I had taken on. There, there, my beauty, I soothed, as if beauty itself were a frightened animal.

Marnie was a vibrant ninety-one when she gave me the coat. She had lived with us in Connecticut throughout my childhood, my mother taking her in, though she had never much liked her mother. That accommodation to her mother's aging was a blow for my mother, who'd had ten years of childless marriage to frolic with her beloved—driving across country, my father making 8 mm movies of their encounter with Navajo vendors in Santa Fe, the Firefall at Yosemite, their Irish setter tongue-lapping the air as the Plymouth convertible rolled along on their great American road trip. They had boarded a freighter to cruise to Trinidad and Tobago, becoming lifelong friends with the ship's Norwegian captain. They were like that young martini-drinking couple on the old *Topper* television show. Beautiful, witty, oblivious to suffering, helping each other feel that joy alone was the purpose of life. Once they had settled down, Marnie arrived, her savings gone. They took her in. From 1945 until Marnie's death in 1971, my mother gave the mother she didn't love a home. They danced their chilly dance, leaving enough space between them to thrive. They were like forest trees that grow leaves in a cooperatively avoidant pattern, allowing each other to get to the light.

Marnie preferred her black Persian lamb over her seal skin coat. The karakul had a matching hat in the shape of an army private's garrison hat that could be folded flat to slip into pocket, belt, or rucksack. The hat was a parody, as is so much fashion, boasting a story of luxury while confessing a story of strife. High feminine style saluting masculine sacrifice in those days before women went to war and after men had been to too many. Marnie was cleaning out her closet in preparation for a move. My parents, preparing for retirement, were moving back to Redding, Connecticut, where my father had grown up. They had never liked Avon, being theater people who did not cotton to the suburbs taking over the farmland outside Hartford, the Insurance Capital of the World and the home of Colt Firearms, a city spawning amoeboid sprawl. They had made a good life there—my father in radio, television, and theater, my mother writing and directing for the stage. They had made a peaceful home in woods bountiful with mountain laurel and copperheads. Yes, beauty and danger were our surround. Marnie established territory in her room at a dignified remove from our busy days. But my parents longed for my father's family home ground, a place where three other family members lived into very old age, playing tennis, growing gardens, building trails. A place where the family held a rural beachhead against commercial development for nearly a century.

My father's family was given to storytelling and playacting and naturalist excursions. As children, my father's cohort of five siblings had listened rapt to tales of the old Mohawk ways from men who had traveled among the tribes. The children thought of the woods in their town as harboring those ancient spirits. They were tutored by their eccentric Harvard-educated uncle, part-hermit, part-artist, part-intellectual, and an aspiring pedophile. He had exposed himself to the girls. Chased them screaming until they hid in a closet. I'm not sure how far his perversion extended. Such matters were not discussed. The cohort remained close.

When the children were young adults, family members who worked in the city came out by train for the weekend. Uncle Michael, editor of the *Architectural Record* in New York City, set them to work on a short story contest. Everyone had to write a story about, say, the old barn. On Sunday evening Uncle Michael would pick the winner and read it aloud. Siblings and cousins, aunts and uncles, they were fiercely bonded as a clan. The fierceness increasing with the consumption of gin at Christmas gatherings or summer tennis parties. They argued about politics or the rules of croquet. They argued about family stories. Was it true that Hal had gone fishing and hooked a heron? That he brought the bird back to the barn and clipped its wings to keep it as a pet? That one brother had asked his sister, "Is it true that the Negroes are like children that could never grow up?" "Of course not," she had argued. "They're just like you and me!" Well, of course, Julian was innocent, took up with the wrong people, should never have gone to prison. Was it Uncle Jack who bellowed, "Why have you brought me this quail?" when asked to carve the Thanksgiving turkey? Coming of age in this family felt like walking into a movie halfway through, trying to discern the plot, and knowing at best I played a bit part. Their personalities loomed larger than their accomplishments, though among them were statesmen and journalists and town council members, library and land trust presidents and trailblazers. But before their professional identities registered in those of us growing up among them, they were the celebrities of our lives.

My mother's family, by contrast, was sparse on story. No script or storyboard. She had been an only child. Her father had split, harboring desires incompatible with family life. Marnie was busy with work—cutting fabric on the dining table, hiring seamstresses and finishers who labored in the workroom downstairs, conducting fittings in the parlor. My mother as a girl lived in her head. Marnie provided for her—private school, summer at the beach, piano lessons—but my mother felt alone and unsafe. Even the summer trips to the beach were frightening. After my mother's death, I found among the memorabilia a note she had written as a child.

Dear Mother,
I am at Islip and there is no bathing down here, mother to-night I am so homesick I am crying for you—please please please please come for me so I can come home I do not like here . . .

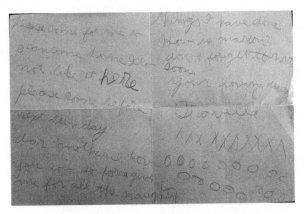

"Dear Mother." *Photo courtesy of the author.*

When she was eleven, Marnie said, "You should know your father." She sent the girl alone by train to North Carolina. A stranger in an off-white linen suit met her at the station. They stayed in a hotel. At breakfast the man read his newspaper. He held it up so that it obscured his face. All the girl could see were his blackened fingernails. She remembered vividly the suit, the fingernails, the silence at the table. A scene from an unfinished movie. Most footage has fallen to the cutting room floor. But the child's letter is tangible and clear. When Marnie received it, she may have been too busy to bring the child back home, too preoccupied with work to feel the child's desperation, or too bent on creating opportunity for her daughter to have the child hanging around all day with nothing to do.

"Did you ever help out in the business," I asked my mother.

"She tried to teach me, but I was hopeless. Too nervous."

Marnie may have kept the letter for its evidence of the child's love without feeling the intensity of the child's anguish. Perhaps she felt both, love and anguish, as the working mother's lot.

I was nineteen when Marnie gave me the seal skin coat. I think again of what Roland Barthes describes as the ways fashion creates meaning. Protection. Yes. What could serve better as shelter from the cold and wet than the skin of a marine mammal? Wearing skins makes one feel how helplessly thin-skinned humans are among mammals, how basically inadequate our bodies are to the demands of the environment. Without clothes we easily wound, freeze, and burn. A seal can swim in arctic waters, slip itself onto rocks or ice for a sunbath and nap in the broad daylight. To wear a seal skin coat is to wear the mantle of the animal's utter suitability to its time and place. No worries, the coat might say, you belong here. You are safe.

Modesty. Clothes follow or defy social codes. How much ankle, how much breast, how much face shall a woman expose? *Harper's Bazaar* gives helpful tips on suitable leg exposure for a girl in 1868. As a child, knee-length is fine. Every two years the skirt must cover more until by puberty nothing shows but the spats on her boots. Not sure if this guidance is about protection or modesty. Perhaps modesty is an imagined form of protection from the leers and assaults of men.

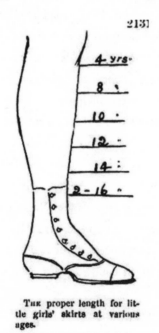

THE proper length for little girls' skirts at various ages.

Photo from Harper's Bazaar, *1868.*

And now? We know modesty protects no one. So, Madonna, Rihanna, let it all hang out and sing yourself a klieg-lit sphere of protection right up there on the stadium stage. Modesty has to do with norms of time and place. A seal skin coat is nothing if not modest. Fur may be form-fitting on the animal. On the human, fur turns an hourglass figure into a refrigerator box. However, no matter the shape, these days in the diminished and diminishing animal world, a human wearing fur is an exaggeration and a fraud. Modesty means free from exaggeration, self-effacing, keeping measure. In this sense, the seal skin coat was immodest. It was boastful. An arrogant coat. I admired it, but I was embarrassed by its ostentation. I may have worn it once or twice. It was old when it came to me and shortly the skins began to split, so that little gaps, like cuts from a paring knife, popped out all over the pelts. Beyond modest, the coat began to look mangy. I threw it out. Of all the garments I have lost and given away—most I could not care less about. But I wish I'd had the presence of mind and the resources to find a way to repair the seal skin coat, to wrap myself in the largesse of the gift, to keep it as talisman of protection.

Decoration. People may be decorated for valor. For ceremony. For power. For magic. For pleasure. Purple Heart. Wedding dress. Power suit or crown or military uniform. Cowrie shell beads or shark's tooth necklace or deer dancer's headdress. Toreador pants—my latest pleasure, because the black leggings with a red stripe down each leg and a cluster of camellias at the ankle make my friends laugh. Leather now is the skin of democratic choice for body decoration. Cow or lamb or goat or polyurethane. We get to choose. Leather jacket, kid gloves, biker pants, faux suede vest.

Some of the old animistic magic of clothes still walks in the world. When the Yaqui people in Tucson celebrate Easter, the most sacred moment is when the deer dancer straps the deer's head on top of his human head, binding his human eyes with a white cotton cloth so that the deer's glass eyes may see. The eyes dart, watchful for danger, ready to startle, stunned at the world's beauty, legs lifting precise and slow so as not to disturb the ground beneath his hooves. Decoration in the deer dancer is transformation. When no one is watching, the dancer becomes the deer.

The seal skin coat did not have such a power. I was raised into a world that has largely forgotten how people could change into other things, a world that sees magic as a game, not a truth of spirit. I might wear the seal skin coat for pleasure, but I would never become a selkie, the shapeshifter of Scottish lore who could transform herself from seal to human and back again.

Signification. Clothes are a sign. I belong here or I am stranger here. I love myself or I want to hide myself. I am wealthy enough to buy jeans with manufactured tears or I am poor enough to never wear a pair of jeans that have not been patched. What did the seal skin coat mean? The coat meant love. To be seen wearing the coat might mean to others wealth. It might have meant wealth—or the striving toward it—for Marnie when she acquired it in that last decade of her enterprise in New York, the decade heading into the Great Depression when the custom dressmaking trade was outrivaled by department stores. Clothes were Marnie's vocabulary. They meant stature. They meant beauty. And they meant love. The camel hair coat she made me when I was four, the red polka dot dress when I was ten, the garish yellow prom dress remade into a confection. The beaded dress my mother had seen in a shop window—Oh, mother, I must have that dress.

Marnie's greatest gesture of sartorial love came when my mother had radical surgery for premenopausal breast cancer. These women—mother and daughter—moved through the house as if boats paddling separate streams in order to avoid one another. Oh, there were the Sunday dinners when everyone sat at formal table for leg of lamb and apple brown Betty. But I recall no easy banter, no joyful sharing of stories, no embraces, no comforting when one of them was sick. No mothering. There might be soup, there might be toast, and a bell to ring to call for help. But theirs was a strange kind of love, steady yet remote. Marnie had a home with us and that remained unquestioned. But love seemed a matter of duty, not of devotion.

In the last New York City home my mother had shared with her mother—a five-story townhouse on West Seventy-Eighth Street—the work-room was on the bottom floor, the parlor and fitting room and bedroom on the second floor. Rooms on the upper floors were rented out. It was the way Marnie could afford to live in a brownstone respectable enough to attract her high-class clientele. Mostly the rooms went to single men. Marnie preferred male tenants, she said, because the women, no matter how severe the warn-ing, always cooked in their rooms, frying something that made the whole house smell like a tenement. Men had the sense to eat somewhere else. My mother recalled among the tenants the embittered veteran with a shriveled arm, the violist who played with Alfred Newman's orchestra in a Broadway production, the Italian dock worker, the piano teacher who played for si-lent films in the nearby movie house. It was by and large a dignified house. Men kept to their rooms. A few befriended mother and daughter, including the tenant who helped Marnie make gin in the bathtub during Prohibition. Some of her customers enjoyed an offering of gin and grapefruit juice.

At least one man stalked my mother. She begged Marnie to make him move out. Marnie said she couldn't because he had invested some of her money for her. This was around the time that Marnie's friend and neighbor, an elegant Chinese woman, was arrested for running a house of prostitution. The neighbor was sent to prison and my mother adopted the woman's Sia-mese cat named Blue. My brother, given to salacious views of most people, used to joke that our grandmother wasn't really a dressmaker. That her "girls" were engaged in that older profession of female renown. That's unlikely, as it is that single men boarding next door to a whorehouse is an accident. The women running these two businesses were friends. Successful entrepreneurs.

My mother resented her mother's working life. Whatever Marnie was able to provide fell short in my mother's perception. The distance between them never closed.

"I know I was supposed to love my mother," she told me in her old age. "But I couldn't."

"But you took her in. You gave her a home."

"I had no choice," she complained.

My mother's disdain for Marnie reached its apotheosis one morning after a dinner party at our house. Marnie, as was her custom, had been a sparkling conversationalist with the guests. She had things to say about the New York City news, her travels in Vienna in 1935, the Annual Flower and Garden Show in Hartford, the Metropolitan Opera. She was an enthusiastic aesthete. The guests were charmed by this elegant and worldly old woman, short and stout, blue eyes lit with curiosity, diamonds glittering on her hands and breast. My mother, in competition for the attention of her guests, was not charmed. The next morning, she made her edict.

"You are not welcome at our parties any longer. You dominate the conversation. You will take your dinners in your room."

There was no fight. This was an instruction from the sergeant at arms, and Marnie with quiet dignity obeyed. My mother was good at inflicting this type of emotional exile on those closest to her.

My mother's breast cancer diagnosis in 1957 led to surgical removal of her right breast, underlying chest muscle, lymph nodes, and muscle under her right arm. It was a mutilating surgery. It left my mother feeling ravaged, red gash running across her ribs, the bones rising in skeletal proximity to the skin, the blade's violence leaving a wasteland in its wake. Her chest looked like a corduroy road. My mother had always been a vain woman. She knew what worked on her body—fitted to the waist and flared below—and she could pull off chic as if dressed by a stylist. V-necks that showed just enough décolleté to suit her theatrical style. Bare arms—her skin an alabaster white— for evening wear and sundresses for summer travel. After the surgery, she stopped getting up to make breakfast for the family, staying in her room long past the time my brother and I had gone to school. She enclosed herself in the privacy of her grief. No one spoke of this. My father just quietly assumed the duties of preparing our breakfast.

Marnie set to work, pulling dresses from the closet, trimming some fabric from the hem to fashion a dickey for the V-neck, a cap sleeve for the sundress, a bit of lace for the dress cut too low—whatever was necessary to disguise the hollows and scars, restoring my mother to her performance of beauty. Love performed as labor. Love performed as duty. Love performed as an exercise of skill. Didn't a therapist once tell me, pretend you care until you do? Empathy was an acting job that might penetrate to the level of character, given practice. The relationship between my mother and her mother was emotionally lacking throughout their shared lives, and yet in the vocabulary of material care they met.

I loved the seal skin coat for its beauty. It was a legacy gift. Its beauty made me feel loved.

SHOULD THERE BE ANOTHER QUESTION? YES. IN THIS AGE OF injury and diminishment, there is always another question. Fur is a question. Fur is a matter of moral and legal debate. Who gets to wear it? Who gets to harvest it? The Canadian Sealers Association oversees the hunt on behalf of sealers in Newfoundland, Quebec's North Shore, and the Magdalen Islands. There are about six thousand professional sealers licensed by the Canadian government. The details of regulation are gruesome, prescribing the precise method of clubbing the seal's cranium and bleeding it to assure that it is dead before skinning.

In the United States the Marine Mammal Protection Act of 1972 bans seal hunting except among Alaskan Natives and for scientific research. It is illegal to transport, purchase, sell, or offer to sell marine mammals in the United States. The European Parliament banned trade in seal products in 2010, allowing an exemption for seals taken by traditional indigenous hunters where the animals contribute to the community's subsistence. According to Nunavut premier Eva Aariak, the ban felt like an attack on the Inuit way of life. The European market for seal products tanked. Even seals killed to protect fish stocks went to waste.

Fishermen hate seals. Most fishermen. Seals are assholes. They hunt for the fun of it. Rip nets. Take bites out of fish they don't eat. Invade the herring weirs and rob a family of its livelihood. From shore, we say, Oh, they are so cute. They are so curious. The little beady-eyed heads pop up and the seals tread water, staring at the humans on shore. Perhaps they listen to our conversation as a kind of landward music, like the cadence a child hears from her bedroom when the adults are talking just out of range, that rippling of sound that says, You are not alone, even though you can't understand a word of what's being said. When I hear a rifle shot in summer outside my island home, I know a fisherman has claimed his stake in the sea. I understand the imperative. And the law allows it, given specific parameters. It seems impossible to live without causing harm. That is why I was so charmed recently to see a Facebook post celebrating an uncharacteristically bountiful herring season, a carrier fully loaded and setting sail for market and a harbor seal resting on a nearby ledge, taking its time to let the men finish their work before diving in for feeding. My neighbor captioned the photo "A shareholder watching."

FASHION IS LOCATED IN TIME AND PLACE. FASHION IS DEVOTED to change. Wearing a seal skin coat if you are an Inuit living in Nunavut sends a message of resilience and gratitude to the animal world for granting subsistence to those possessing the wits to live in a brutally cold environment. It also means peril, as climate change melts the ice on which the seal hunt depends. Gretel Ehrlich writes eloquently of the depth of this loss, a way of life sinking into the melting sea ice. Wearing a seal skin coat today means privilege being blind to cruelty and invites a commentary written in spray paint on the back of the wearer. Melania Trump's famous mean-meme jacket ("I really don't care. Do U?") may be the inverse of the impulse. Fashion statements carry moral weight. This is nothing new, though ecological consciousness is rising in the fashion industry as every profession asks itself,

How am I implicated in the diminishment of the future? Fashion statements are simplistic glosses of complex moral questions. For whom do I care? For whom should I care?

Today cotton signifies purity, the shunning of artificial and irreducible manufactured fabrics in favor of embracing "organic" nature. For Ralph Waldo Emerson, writing to advocate for abolition, cotton meant slavery. "The American flag was sewn with cotton threads," he wrote, insisting that to know ourselves as Americans was to know the brutality embedded into the very weave of the nation. And now, I, in the early twenty-first century, wishing to no longer enslave Earth to our insatiable human desires, have the privilege to purchase new carpet for my home that is made out of recycled plastic water bottles. Purity? Nature? Sure.

Frances Corner, head of London College of Fashion, in *Why Fashion Matters*, calls for the fashion industry to heed the ecological and social costs of its practices. For what injury am I responsible? That question drives us to soul-searching—and a good deal of pigheaded denial—as society sinks into the morass of knowing more than it ever wanted to know about the injury people have caused to one another and the planet. To paraphrase Corner's most salient points:

The majority of new clothes are manufactured in Asian factories. Bangladesh has a minimum wage of thirty-eight dollars a month. Eighty percent of its garment workers are women.

It takes twenty-seven hundred liters of water to produce one cotton T-shirt from "crop to shop."

White fabrics, often associated with cleanliness, even godliness, rely on optical brighteners for their whiteness. Optical brighteners are made using stilbenes, which are toxic to fish.

The clothes of an average British household have produced carbon emissions equivalent to driving the average modern car some six thousand miles and have consumed enough water to fill a thousand bathtubs to capacity. Yet 30 percent of these clothes are rarely, if ever, worn.

IF I WORE MY SEAL SKIN COAT TODAY, SAVORING THE EMBRACE of my grandmother and her wish to love and protect me, others would see me as a hypocrite: she writes about how much she loves animals and grieves their fate, then she flaunts the pelts of clubbed baby seals. Both readings of my fashion choice would be true.

The seal skin coat is long gone and I am sorry for that. I can still feel its embrace, still lament the stitches that no longer hold.

14

*

The Lacemaker

UNTIL WE STOOD BEFORE THE SMALL FRAME OF VERMEER'S MAS-
terpiece hanging in a quiet corner of the Louvre, we had remained distracted,
Lucinda and I, alert to surroundings, unable to focus, uncertain how close at
hand risk might be. On the night of the attacks we'd had dinner at Olio Pane
Vino, a small restaurant on the Rue de Coquillière run by an Italian chef, a
friend of one of Lucinda's art colleagues. The place was buzzing. The meal
superb and simple. The chef coming out to talk with us, lingering, as if he
had nowhere else in the world to be. I snapped a photo of Lucinda standing
beside him. Tall and lean. Rugged handsome. White shirt and jeans. They
looked like old pals. He told us about a customer who had complained that
the food in the establishment was not real Italian. He laughed and shrugged
with the pride of a man who knows he's right. *"I'm Italian."* Did he mention
the town he came from? I think so. It was a memorably warm evening. The
human warmth of companionship and pleasure in breaking bread. Savoring.

We had walked a few blocks in the cool evening and caught the Metro
at Rivoli, so we would not have to make a change, still unsure of our bearings
in the city. We crossed under the Seine and emerged to exit at Les Gobelins.

After celebrating our purchases of the day—my black leather tote made in London and her sexy taupe leather boots—we parted for our respective hotel rooms at opposite ends of the narrow hall. Every detail of the day seems now rarefied in retrospect. The news was waiting on our screens. Soccer stadium. Concert hall. Café. Six attacks in all. While we had been underground, Paris had changed into an open wound. It would be days before the details would become clear, but the scope of violence, the sense of anticipation that more was to come, gripped us. There was talk of bio-suits gone missing. Would there be anthrax in the Metro? Chemical weapons? Would the bombs be topped off with random knife attacks? Would the airport shut down? London's Gatwick was closed—a suspicious article found in the north terminal. Officials had found a weapons stash including a rocket launcher in Lyon. Brussels had closed its Metro. Was something ever bigger in the wings? So much for researching birth and immigration records. So much for scanning archives advertising corsets named La Sirène and Jeanne d'Arc, a dress named Fauvette. Fashion no longer looked very seductive.

We spent a day in the hotel, trying to figure out whether we should stay in Paris or try to leave. The hotel breakfast room and lobby were crammed. Avoid large crowds, the State Department warned. Stay indoors. A state of emergency had been declared. Search and seizure—168 in Paris alone. Cultural institutions were all shut down. Louvre, libraries, theaters, and opera. The Eiffel Tower remained blackened. To live on the edge of violence is nothing new in the world. Certainly, nothing new for Paris after surviving countless coups, occupations, revolutions, sieges, and world wars. Pick a day. September 3, 1792: massacre of priests and prisoners held at the Saint-Germain-des-Prés Abbey, one of the oldest in France, hacked to death by mobs who went on a four-day spree killing hundreds, the "First Terror" of the French Revolution. It is an old, old story, this violence that lurks on the edge of the city, on the edge of the nation, on the edge of the psyche. Centuries of longing for a higher way.

This was not even the first time that Lucinda and I had felt the cold wind of terrorism rattle our bones. The year Lucinda graduated from Skidmore, she had traveled alone to Europe to meet a friend. They bummed around for a couple of weeks, eager to feel their freedom on a grander scale. She flew from London back to New York on the night that Pan Am Flight 103 from London to New York was blown apart in the air over Lockerbie, Scotland. I did not know what plane she was on. She had purchased one of those budget flights, which in those years did not let you know until the last minute what airline you'd be flying on. Silent hours of pre–cell phone anxiety passed until I reached her friend, still in London, and confirmed Lucinda had not been on that flight. When she landed at JFK, the place teemed with keening and confusion. Lucinda's second terrorist near-miss came on the day of the bomb attacks at the Boston Marathon. She and her teenage sons had been watching the race from separate vantages. They had texted "Meet you at the finish!" back and forth. She did not know where they were in the crowd, and they didn't get it together in time for the finish. But they could have. Which is what we all think when these attacks are announced: It could have been me. It could have been my child.

Her third frisson was Paris. That afternoon we had set out with her GPS tracking our path. Late afternoon we walked from our hotel in a straight line across the Seine heading toward the Place de la République. Lucky for us, I got tired and hungry. She remembered Olio Pane Vino—a tip from an artist friend—and we checked the map. We were close, a short loop back away from what would soon be ground zero of the Bataclan and café attacks. We had a lovely dinner. Easy conversation with the chef. A quiet walk. A metro ride. Then the hotel and the news.

"I would have gone to the concert if I'd known that band was playing."

"What kind of band was it?"

"Eagles of Death Metal," she laughed at the name. "They're ironic, not metal. I kept thinking, Wouldn't it be a blast to hear some live music in Paris? I kept looking online but didn't see that concert."

If she had wanted to go, I would have said, "Sure, let's do it!" just to be a part of her life.

"THEY SHOT AT US LIKE WE WERE BIRDS," SAID ONE SURVIVOR
at the Bataclan.

Soft targets.

"I met a man. Spoke with him, exited, stepping over his corpse."

DAY THREE OF THE NATIONAL EMERGENCY. WE STOOD IN THE
rain, hundreds of strangers, in rope lines outside the Louvre, waiting for the
museum to reopen. Dogs played in the park—a dozen chasing a Frisbee—
one man orchestrating. One little fox dog sitting it out. Gulls dropped down
into the moat. The Louvre Palace was built to be a fortress for royalty. And
now this—a fortress for art, the best of what humans can make, what portion
of it survives fires, floods, and war.

Police and soldiers in body armor paced the plaza, long guns ready, riot
helmets strapped to waist, finger on trigger. One guy seemed a bit lax. The
barrel of his rifle pointed out from his thigh as he patrolled. One little startle,
one little slip of the finger ... The thought became a nervous joke. And what
about these people standing with us in the snaking rope line? Which one
might be wearing a suicide vest? What would they care about the police? The
attackers wanted to die. The line inched and inched for an hour. No telling
where anyone was from in the crowd, the global reach of art drawing us together. Every one of us had made the decision not to give in to fear. That did
not mean we were oblivious. I noticed a man in the rope line reaching inside
his coat. Suicide vest? Ah, no, only a copy of André Breton's *Nadja* shielded
from the light rain drizzling upon the cobblestones.

THE LOUVRE WAS EERILY QUIET AS THE FIRST FLOW OF VISITORS
entered after the two-day closure. We found it hard to shed the tension that
had become part of the deal in deciding to stay in Paris. Not until we found
The Lacemaker in a darkened corner did we become transported into art space
and time. Lucinda fell quiet and stared. "It's a perfect painting," she said. I
was not sure what she saw, her eye more trained than mine to read visual cues.
She loves Vermeer, she tells me, for his balanced compositions, the tension
between representational depiction and speaking beyond representation.

The young woman, dressed in a lemon-yellow dress with lace trimming,
hair in loose pipe curls beside her temples, bends over her work. Her eyes are
cast downward, absorbed in lacing threads around the pins that describe the
pattern to be constructed. It looks as if her eyes are closed, but they are not.
Her focus excludes anything but the work. The only element in the painting
that reaches out to the viewer are the threads, red and white, that spill like
thin streams of blood and milk from her sewing cushion, all vitality lodged
in their potential.

She is making bobbin lace, the pattern laid out first on paper, then
pricked with pins onto the sewing cushion, then thread laced around the
pins to shape the holes making the delicate filigree. A thick book lies on the
table beside the lacemaker. Some art historians claim the book is a Bible,
representing the virtue in her work. I prefer the view that the book is a com-
pendium of patterns against which she checks her accuracy. This view places
her virtue in her hands and the hands of those that have preceded her in this
work rather than in the amorphous hands of God. She looks too well dressed
to be a workshop laborer, too attentive to detail to be a dilettante. She is
simply herself.

A woman's "work" for so much of history was embodied in her basket
of sewing, knitting, embroidery, lace. Drawing rooms in nineteenth-century
novels are populated by women with their "work" in their laps. Button, embroidery, hem, knitted cloche. A modest bit of needlework was a virtue and

a comfort. But the threads that pass through a woman's hands signify more than thrift and utility. For the ancient Greeks, one's destiny at birth was measured out in thread by the three Fates—one to spin the fiber, one to measure the allotment, and one to make the cut at its end. Sometimes men work with thread—fishermen working on their nets and some, in the lacemaker's time, working on bobbin lace during the off-season. I once knew an old Vermont farmer who made tatted lace on the cold winter nights of the north. But the Fates are female deities, vestiges of the old earth religions in which the female body is seen for its true wealth in relieving the impoverishment of our mortality.

Vermeer's painting was made around 1670. It lived mostly in Holland until moving to the Louvre in 1870. Another thing about the painting that I find compelling is the light. It spills gently over the left side of the lacemaker's face and her hands, like a spotlight focused on her working fingers, the tension as she places the pins, allots the thread, and winds the bobbins. Where does it come from, this light? There are no windows, no lamps or candles. It has the glow of sunlight, but the lacemaker is posed in front of a whitewashed wall. The painting is so unlike Vermeer's *Geographer* or *Astronomer*, men posed at their work, each beside a huge, many-lighted window. The astronomer gazes outward, the geographer gazes at the globe. The window connects them to the world outside their chamber. Theirs is an outward-facing agency. But the lacemaker has no such vantage. What lights her world remains out of the picture's frame. Hers is an interior life, her agency earned in privacy where she too has the freedom to be absorbed in thought. Vermeer exalted her with his attention. Is it necessary to know any more about her life than this one moment? Narrative detail is not the only way to get to the essence of an individual life. She must have posed for many hours, many days. Did she work while the painter worked? Did she complete one lace and begin another while posing, in order for the painter to create this illusion, a moment held as eternal, the work of art transcending its time and living still in ours? Be present with me, *The Lacemaker* says, across three and a half centuries.

✳

A WEEK AFTER THE PARIS ATTACKS, LUCINDA AND I, STILL A BIT raw about what constituted risk and what did not, ginned up our courage to visit the Bataclan and pay our respects. The Paris Metro had remained open, though it was easy to feel alarm riding through those ghostly tunnels—especially when we rode through stations where not a soul was in sight. Did others know something we did not? Outside the concert hall with its chinoiserie of red and yellow paint, makeshift memorials bloomed along the sidewalk: long-stemmed white lilies stuck through the slats in a wrought-iron fence, a purple bicycle locked to the slats with a bouquet of white roses exploding through the spokes, a roughly lettered sign JE SUIS MUSULMANE ET CONTRE LE TERRORISME!!!!! planted in a field of cheap prayer candles. "I am a Muslim and against terrorism," though I got a laugh misreading, "I am a muscleman and against terrorism." Mounds of flowers still in their plastic wrapping, as if to protect them from the pain in the air, had been laid along the sidewalk. We added ours to the mass. The street hosted a tent city of world news media outlets, each tent fitted with satellite dish, generator, editing bay, and teleprompter. Days before, mortuary vans had lined the street. Ninety killed at the Bataclan. Hundreds wounded. One media van had its back doors wide open. There was something comforting in seeing the lovely yellow and red lights blinking, lights of communication. The passionate need of people to connect was twice embodied at the site. In memorial gifts—tacky bouquets and candles and a rain-drenched handmade poster shouting RAGE AGAINST THE MACHINE!—and in the global storytelling we call news. Gifts that felt like the mobilization of the social body's immune response.

At one café that had been attacked, we saw chairs, black with gold trim, stacked on the sidewalk, the whole place cleared out and freshly power-washed. Carnations pushed through the bullet holes in glass.

Paris was defiant. The icon of the Eiffel Tower morphed into a graphic of the peace sign and popped up in café windows with the caption reading

"Not Afraid." Cafés reopened. We found joy and warmth and conversation. People did not seem nervous or hypervigilant. Parisian friends said they only thought about the attacks if they turned on the news. "Otherwise, I go to work. I go to bars." But fireworks one night in the Place de la République set off a panic. Hundreds of mourners racing for their lives. Sirens again sliced the city. When our host at a dinner party served a gorgeous homemade apple tart, all the apples exquisitely lined up like overlapping quarter moons, someone joked, "This is what they want to kill us for."

RUNNING IS THE WAY LUCINDA SEES A CITY. SHE WEARS A GPS unit and comes home with a map. The map becomes a drawing. The drawing becomes an interrogation of borders and boundaries in nature. The run becomes a documentary of the female body as an element in the landscape. One of her projects led her to remote stretches on the border of the northeastern United States and Canada. She invited conversational partners to join her: Passamaquoddy elder, geologist, border patrol agent, an environmental scientist who works for big oil. It's place-based work, a digitally enhanced enactment of the land. Landscape is not an object to possess or idealize, but an instrument for interrogating how you know what you know about the land. How you understand it depends upon the eyes through which you see. Historical circumstances give context. The cultural moment gives shape to experience. Then *I* is never a solitary thing, but an expression of these inscrutable continuities. "It is the soul of the world," wrote James Hillman, "by which my soul is afflicted."

I did not want her to run in the days right after the attacks, my maternal anxiety at a high pitch. But running is a physical and intellectual need for her, and besides I had no agency to stop her. The weird thing about Lucinda's first post-attack run in Paris was that when she pulled up the graphic mapping the ground she had covered, we saw a map in the shape of a Glock. There it was—

the city superimposed with a semi-automatic pistol made to fit in the palm of your hand, one of the world's most popular weapons. It was a circumstantial detail, but it made us recoil in surprise, clenching down on the knowledge of how close either one of us might be to the wrong end of a gun.

"How do you like our city of abomination and perversity?" asked the hotel clerk. "That's what they called us."

"We still love Paris."

"Good. Paris needs your love."

She held up a selfie. She was posed with her Muslim friend, the two encircled by a red heart.

"It won't work, what they are trying to do. They're trying to start a civil war."

She had been in Bayonne visiting her mother when the attacks came.

Her mother said, "Stay."

"No," she said. "Paris is home. I need to be there."

She said that a woman who loved Paris had called from Boston after the attacks. "I need to be there," she said and booked a room.

LUCINDA'S RUNNING SPURRED ME TO RETURN TO MY URBAN habit of walking, so I made my way to the Jardin des Plantes, stopping at the entrance to visit the bronze statue of Buffon made in 1908. The naturalist was draped in an overcoat so grandiose it threatened to swallow him, his hair coiled into three horizontal pipes on either side of his head, a bird in his hand about to take flight. It was the visage of a master, as Buffon, the father of natural history in France, surely was. Born George-Louis Leclerc in 1707 into a family of civil servants, he became an aristocrat thanks to an inheritance with which his father purchased an estate that included the village of Buffon. As a young man, he took a year-and-a-half grand tour with his friend the English Duke of Kensington. During the trip, he gave himself the title Comte de Buffon. What makes him memorable is not his achievement of transcending the rigidity of European class, but the revolutionary work in science that led him to challenge two thousand years of dogma about the origin of species and the age of Earth. One hundred years before Darwin, Buffon penned his thirty-six volume *Histoire Naturelle*, works read as widely as those of his contemporary Voltaire. Buffon studied law, mathematics, and medicine with Jesuits. He made an extended study of the properties of wood used in ship construction. He tested more than one thousand small specimens of wood. Then he realized he could not learn what he needed to know without studying large pieces. A master of scientific patience and attention, he realigned the research and pressed on.

In 1739 Buffon was appointed keeper of the Jardin du Roi (now known as the Jardin des Plantes), his job to catalog the royal collection of medicinal plants. The garden had been opened to the public in 1645—a garden older than the United States. A garden situated in history, made necessary by history, land tended with care for centuries. Robert Pogue Harrison, in his inspired *Gardens: An Essay on the Human Condition*, writes:

> Human beings are not made to look too intently at the Medusa head of history—its rage, death, and endless suffering. This is not a shortcoming on our part; on the contrary, our reluctance to let history's realities petrify us underlies much of what makes human life bearable: our religious impulses, our poetic and utopian imagination, our moral ideals, our metaphysical projections, our storytelling, our aesthetic transfigurations of the real, our passion for games, our delight in nature.

We move through, he writes, "relatively permanent worlds that precede our birth and outlast our death ... These worlds, with their transgenerational things, houses, cities, institutions, and artworks, are brought into being by work." These transgenerational gifts feed the human need for continuity and belonging in ways that transcend the political sphere.

Buffon's work far exceeded his job description of cataloging the king's medicinal plants. He aimed to catalog the whole natural world, studying minerals and animals and plants. He grew the garden into a major natural history museum, gathering specimens of flora and fauna from around the world. Buffon disagreed with church dogma that Earth was six thousand years old. He thought it much older. He disagreed with Linnaeus's idea of classifying species with clear borders. He saw gradations between species and individuals that made the definitions less clear. He was curious that similar environments in different regions spawned different plants and animals—the idea behind the contemporary science of biogeography. He believed that life, like Earth, had a history—the idea behind the science of evolution that would advance over the next century. So prized was his work that his cerebellum is sequestered in the base of a marble sculpture made by Augustin Pajou in 1776. The young Buffon stands beside a globe, lion and snake at his feet. The scientist is dressed in a toga, one bare leg exposed to the thigh, folds of cloth draping over the globe, as if he were unveiling its secrets, his chest bare and virile, his locks long, curly, and spilling onto his shoulders. Science has rarely looked so sexy.

In the Jardin des Plantes, I walked past an old woman doing tai chi beside the garden of medicinal plants. Foxglove for the heart, aloe vera for burns, chamomile for the gut, willow for pain, ginger for inflammation. Walkways lined with bare-limbed plane trees scraped the gray sky. It was a marvel to see such beauty built with living plants, given a few hundred years of tending. I lingered at the Dodo Manège where children circled round and round riding on the backs of dodo, tortoise, panda, gorilla, glyptodon, and Tasmanian wolf—extant and extinct brought together and animated for the delight of children. I walked past Aristotle, his shoulders warmed with a gray patina growing over the stone. Nature seems to have grown him a shawl. Seated he was contemplating the egg held in his left hand, the hand resting on his left thigh. He was lost in thought. Which came first? The little egg had become almost too heavy to hold. Scrolls of completed manuscripts were rolled up and tucked behind his chair. No matter how much wisdom he accrued, he would be forever lost in curiosity at the mystery of existence. How perfect that he could hold that pose in the garden, seated beneath the silence of the arboreal ancients.

I entered the Grand Gallery of Evolution, stepping up worn marble stairs to encounter the spectacle of ghostly animal force. The stampede of pristine skeletons galloped head-on toward me, horses and zebras with leading hoof raised and head leaning forward in flight, gators and crocs floating in their glass cases of air with jaws wide, herons and cranes, sturgeons and hares, cats and catfish, all posed and poised as dancers in a macabre celebration of fixed movement. Hearts and inner ears floated in formalin vases. You must take life apart to understand it, the relics said. Here is the lining of a giraffe's esophagus, the terrain of the tissue bearing the same irregular pattern of the plaid on its pelt. Here are a set of brains attached to their stalks and spines, standing upright in narrow vases with a blue glass backing to accentuate detail. Here we creatures are, all just lilies with brains above ground and our feet wading in the sea. And the brains, shocking, like so much tubing packed into the skull. Here is the sine wave of a python skeleton suspended in space, here the arteries of a human brain teased out and spread like a flower—everywhere deltas and tributaries, ripples and waves. Hearts and their piping—the masters of flow.

Even the monsters are represented—cyclops cat, faceless fish, pig fetus with one head and two bodies, two lambs joined at the chest. And the thing is that everyone looks happy here among the dead in the Père Lachaise of the world's fauna. The Grand Gallery of Evolution exists to serve science, to catalog and detail and define our fellow creatures and to learn how we all got to be the creatures we are. Yet the visitors to this place are not making scientific illustrations or gathering data. They are staring in astonishment, telling one another, Look at this! Did you see this! They are feasting on the wonder of life, filling themselves with nutrients they did not realize they lacked. They are like the deer who come out of forest in winter and go to the beach to lick salt off the rocks at low tide, then dance in the waves. Here is the heron's neck, bones like the links on a bicycle chain. People are being reunited with their distant relatives, all these beings that have lived a life of movement, appetite, decisions, and daydreams and like us improvised their way through the forests and plains and waters and deserts where predators might leap, but most days they did not.

In *Invisible Cities*, Italo Calvino offers this wisdom—a quote I've held in my heart for decades without remembering its source and only just rediscovered thanks to Harrison's book on gardens—for finding sanity in times of madness, advice spoken by Marco Polo in his last words to Kublai Khan.

> There are two ways to escape suffering from the inferno where we live every day, that we form by being together. [The first is] to accept the inferno and become such a part of it that you can no longer see it. [The second] is risky and demands constant vigilance and apprehension: seek and learn to recognize who and what, in the midst of inferno, are not inferno, then make them endure, give them space.

I had not come to Paris to learn about natural history, nor had I come to learn about terrorism. But terrorism sent me on an errand into a new wilderness, one where the opulence of the nineteenth-century court, the theater of aristocracy that artisans such as my great-grandmother served, faded into the startled apprehension of the present moment. I became animal in those days, tense to the environment, knowing someone or something might kill me just because I was alive, knowing that all these wonders were on display in the Jardin des Plantes because people had killed them, then lovingly restored their bones. Life, the work of so many hands, became as delicate and precious as lace.

15

✳

Invasive Beauty

No other creature holds the same romance in the minds
of Icelanders as herring.

ANITA ELEFSEN, historian, Herring Era Museum

I SIT AT A TINY COFFEEHOUSE NESTLED ON THE SOUTHERN
rocky coast of Iceland's Snaefellsnes Peninsula, a finger of jagged volcanic
rock that juts out from the western shore. An abandoned concrete pier leads
out from that shore, angling a shelter against stormy seas. A rusted steel lad-
der runs down the side of the pier to the tidal swirl, but no boats are tied, no
fishermen are cleaning fish or mending nets. I spoon savory fish soup into
my mouth. Tiny twigs of broccoli and toothpicks of carrot swim on the surface, the broth, milky and light, laden with chunks of sea wolf, tiny Atlantic
shrimp, and flakes of chili for heat. The soup is nothing like the rich New
England fish chowder of my childhood: potato, onion, haddock, cream, and
butter. There is no end to the inventiveness expressed in kitchens.

The fishermen's icehouse has become a coffeehouse with a tiny deck where bundled tourists gaggle and joke their way into friendships as they pursue their Ring Road adventure. They have come from Norway, Canada, China, the United States, and Germany to sip beer or coffee. At least that is what I glean from eavesdropping on their conversations. They have come to watch black-legged kittiwakes whirl and then settle onto nests tucked into black basaltic cliffs. They have come to eat cod cheeks and oatmeal cakes with rhubarb jam. They have come to walk through lichen-covered lava fields on a path from one village to the next.

As a child, I played alone in our rural yard, an archaeologist of the ordinary, digging sticks into the dirt, so richly brown and mica-flecked beneath the pelt of grass and dandelions. Occasionally I would visit a classmate in her neighborhood, the suburban developments that were taking over the dairy farms, and the corn and tobacco fields of our town in the 1950s. Kids gathered in sandlots to play tag or hopscotch, or just to walk and talk beyond the gaze of adults. They were mostly good kids, plus a few bullies—but that bunch mostly hung around together to reinforce their badass credentials and left the rest of us alone. I found all of this hard to understand, how bands of kids in aimless pleasure played together. How they parted themselves into good kids and bad kids, kids to play with and kids to be scared of. It seemed there were rules—norms at least—but I did not know them. My family, artistic and egotistical, held itself aloof from the town. I knew about theater and show tunes and literature. I knew the names of trees and wildflowers. I did not know the games the other kids played. I hung back, stuck in the strange, unshakable feeling that I wanted to belong and did not know how. I didn't feel better or worse than others. I just felt like myself, as I do sitting at a table for one on the deck of the icehouse café.

I'm headed for Siglufjörður, one of the northernmost villages in Iceland, located less than twenty-five miles from the Arctic Circle, to visit the Herring Era Museum. The village was named the herring capital of the world in 1903. I am not sure who did the naming, though certainly not the same authority that named Blacks Harbour, New Brunswick, Canada, the sardine capital of the world. A sardine is a juvenile herring put in a can, so the two designations are synonymous. Among the cities that have earned such sardine renown are Lagos, Portugal; Essaouira, Morocco; and Monterey, California. Perhaps the one truth is that wherever herring show up, they mean abundance to the people who fish them, and often as not a spike-and-collapse economy. Such is the rhythm between fishermen and herring.

I take my time driving from cosmopolitan Reykjavík to head north, avoiding the tourist thicket of the southern region. I digress by foot to find waterfalls and cinder cones and village pathways and interpretive signs marking the landscape with ancient Viking sagas that still have a voice in Iceland. The terrain is as unstable as it can be, dotted with hundreds of volcanoes, prone to rifts and quakes, teeming with voluminous rivers and streams and waterfalls of glacial melt, featuring water as pure as it comes. Grass thrives on the lower slopes of the volcanic hills, with meadows sprawling out at the base of steep inclines—a vibrant green hospitality fronting the island's stark and stony interior. People live along the green perimeter that rings the coast. It seems a tentative way of life, farmhouses tucked at the base of looming volcanic cliffs. The scale is unsettling, human habitations like little Monopoly houses on the game board of tectonic unrest.

During my weeklong visit in June 2017, five hundred earthquakes shook Iceland. No big deal for the locals. Thirty or forty volcanoes have erupted within the past few centuries. Another hundred volcanoes rest on the central plateau but have kindly not erupted in the past thousand years. Sometimes a volcano that has long been dead erupts and swallows a village in lava and ash, all of this unrest strewn like a broken necklace on land that teeters on the Mid-Atlantic Ridge. The North American and European plates are going through a prolonged breakup, cracking the island open and inviting lava to rise. Geothermal geysers shoot from Earth's furnace at temperatures that can exceed three hundred degrees. Even on a calm summer day, the wind inspires car rental companies to direct customers to check wind direction and force before opening a car door and to "always keep a firm grip on the door when it is open."

Perhaps tentative is not the best word to describe life in these challenging environs. During my visit, a tour guide built like a lumberjack, in response to a tourist's question about whether life was harder during the settlement times when Vikings hacked a life out of the land, said with a wry smile, "Life in Iceland is always either hard or harder." He laid out slices of smoked lamb and buttered flatbread cooked underground from geothermal heat. "This is what we eat when we go on a hike. None of that trail mix stuff."

Heading north, I find a waystation in the tiny town of Hellnar. One hotel, one coffee house, one café, one defunct nineteenth-century church, originally built with peat walls that have been replaced by wood. The church's historical marker tells the story of Johannes Helgason Fanndal, born in this village in 1887, craftsman and carver, the first Icelandic artist to win a scholarship from the parliament. As a young man, he became engaged to a woman who lived in the village of Hellissandur thirty kilometers to the north. Walking from his village to hers in a snowstorm, carrying a rucksack "full of masterpieces" including a "carved casket," he died. The little jewelry box was engraved with the name of his betrothed: Kristen.

I pass meadow after meadow of grazing horses, milling lambs and sheep, dandelions and bright grass illuminating the gentler slopes—grass, grass, grass, that saint among plants so quickly does it ascend miraculous from the dead. Black lambs, white lambs, lambs inside their fences, lambs outside their fences, lambs in the road, lambs oblivious to boundaries. Farmers have built wind blocks of bushy birch trees to shelter their fields, but even these stalwart defenders of domesticity lean from the constant torment of wind. The lupines are blooming, sprawling meadows of indigo that look like great spilled bouquets. Lupines are an invasive species, the plants brought to control erosion. They have taken over vast stretches of scenic roadways, crowding out native plants and habitat. Some people want to get rid of the invasive beauty, whose blooming is an ecstasy of blue, the tiniest sliver of the lupine's year.

Their beauty and its abundance make it hard to accept they might be a threat. Largely the lupine's days are about endurance through cold, wind, snow, and months of unmitigated darkness in the far north. Then comes the bloom, abundance drowning out privation.

"Beauty is the form under which the intellect prefers to study the world," Emerson wrote.

What did he mean? Beauty calls one outward to the things of the world and to people. Beauty relieves one of the error, Elaine Scarry writes, of thinking, "I am the center." Beauty is not truth. Beauty can subvert truth. The tourist visiting the seaside town finds the harbor seal a thing of beauty. The local fishermen see them as varmints—competitors and troublemakers that harass fish for pleasure. The Gospel of St. John warns, "Love not the world, neither the things that are in the world." John Donne's Sermon XXI counters, "All things that are, are equally removed from being nothing." William Wordsworth enters the ring: "The world is too much with us." Denise Levertov puts on her gloves: "The world is not with us enough."

If ever there was a time in history to see the world and the things thereof as the very locus of our moral and spiritual evolution, it is now. The anguish over globalization and the mind-boggling challenge of climate change have ignited a conflagration of rage, denial, and argument, when what's needed are reflection, evidence-based thinking, and new alliances.

Czech novelist Arnost Lustig, who survived Auschwitz and Buchenwald, used to give daily writing exercises to his students at the Prague Summer Seminars, where I too have had the pleasure of teaching. *Write about something beautiful that has happened to you. Write about something morally beautiful. Write about something ugly that has happened to you. Something morally ugly.* Lustig had plenty of opportunity to till this ground, having been taken to Auschwitz as a teenager in 1942. He was later transported to Buchenwald. In 1945 he escaped from a train carrying him to Dachau when the engine was destroyed by an American fighter-bomber. He wrote novels of aching beauty about characters who are forced to make morally impossible decisions: a Jew-ish woman who passes as Gentile and survives the Holocaust by prostituting herself to Nazi officers, and that's just the beginning of the moral quagmire that besets her.

What's happening in America is a different kind of moral ugliness; borders between good and evil are less clearly defined when truth is subverted. And something morally ugly is happening to the planet; borders are obsolete when the sea and the sky are imperiled.

These days I think about the beauty of herring, their spangled, silver, dancing bodies, their jumbo eyes that take up most of their heads, the flicker of their tinfoil luminescence as they dart through the water. When I think about herring, I think about abundance, about patterns of migration and return, about the wealth and wile of small means that kept so many northern villages from Holland to Scotland to Iceland to the Canadian Maritimes alive through brutal winters.

In the Hellnar coffeehouse that was once an icehouse on a sunny afternoon in June the wind beats down, nothing to stop the weather that blasts over the Atlantic, but travelers are warmed by companionship, Gull beer, fish soup, rye bread. Everyone branded for adventure wearing their Marmot and North Face and Arc'teryx, the Scandinavians wearing Scandinavian sweaters with snowflake yokes. They remind me that when I first moved to Tucson from New England, I was surprised to see that cowboys actually wore cowboy boots and rodeo belts and hats. At first, I'd thought it was an affectation, until I met the cowboy poet electrician who made me see authenticity where I least expected it, the brand of place still genuine in fashion decisions.

The Hellnar cove may have been worked by five or six boats, no room for more. A rusted winch lies abandoned at the head of the pier, wild grass and buttercups climbing over the casing. The fishermen may have rowed out to trawl for cod, torsk, lumpfish. They used seines and dip nets for herring. Without herring, Iceland may not have survived, such is the abundance of the fish and the hardship of the people. Herring travel in enormous schools, so when they are near they are easy to catch in large quantities, easy to salt in wooden barrels and hang over the spars of a fish shed for drying. Near the coffeehouse that was once an icehouse is the foundation of a shelter built into a concavity in rock, large enough only for one man to sit hunched over on the small rock shelf. Stones have been piled on either side of the entrance to form an entryway, and a few nails have been pounded into the overhang of stone. A canvas or sheepskin perhaps was extended to create shelter against storms. It has long been out of use. Perhaps turf walls and roof extended the hut beyond the rock. The path that leads from the village of Hellnar to adjacent Arnarstapi crosses in front of the hut's absent door, a path that was for centuries the main road for traveling five kilometers on foot or horseback, winding through sharp hardened lava, over rills, and down dips. Remnants of other peat huts and stone sheds lie under the pelt of grass, dandelions, and buttercups, rims of basaltic stone marking grids—the straight lines in the jagged jumble of lava that are the mark of human hands. A mire of fish scales must have muddied the hut's ground, a cup of chicory brew heated over a peat fire—cold comfort.

I imagine a child in those times, knowing no other place, watching Father mending nets, the shuttle weaving grid by grid, knot by knot, or splitting the fish to hang over wooden splines for drying, a man never at rest and rarely having anything to say. Watching Mother salting down the cod in summer and in winter gathering a stiffened fish from the icehouse to cook in the fish pot over the open hearth. Watching her knitting socks or caps or sweaters from the wool she'd spun without a wheel, the wile of her hands twirling the wool just so and just so until the limitless strand took shape, and dyeing the yarn with brambleberries or goldenrod, an exuberance of color to enhance the wool's warmth.

Life could go wrong in such a place at any moment. A child watching the sea break on the protruding ledge offshore knew from an early age that the stormier the sea became the harder it was to see the peril above the white spume. Only the gulls and terns and gannets seemed truly at home on the water. Fishermen's nets were holy. Mending nets was a prayer, the shuttle passing back and forth like a rosary in the hands of a penitent, head bowed to his work. The child's mind was continuous with the land, continuous with the sea and all the craft of living in ceremonial rhythm with the seasons.

Halldór Laxness, Iceland's Nobel Prize–winning author, in his novel *The Fish Can Sing* (1957), ennobles the hard lives of turf cottage dwellers, and the way such a child might find her own path. I'm reading the novel as I write, disturbing myself from the desk by falling into the reverie of his storytelling. "Many have died trying to reach a neighbor in need who lived two kilometers away," Laxness writes. "Ours was not the first village to close shop." Many villages are gone now that tourism is Iceland's largest industry. In place of fish huts and icehouses are hotels, coffeehouses, a theater in a former frozen fish factory, Eider Duck Museum, Mineral Museum, Whale Museum, Folk Museum, Phallological Museum (yes, a penis museum), Arctic Fox Museum, Punk Music Museum, Saga Museum, Library of Water, Museum of War and Peace. Iceland's small museum culture is a brilliant smorgasbord of curiosities. Of course, there are the larger institutional museums for art and history, but I favor the inventive genius of making a small town a destination for something other than T-shirt and postcard acquisitions, honoring cultural memories in a place while squarely facing the future.

A family that harvests eider down from remote nesting colonies, as did their ancestors in a fifteenth-century tradition, has built a tiny museum to the eider duck. The ducks pull out their own feathers to line their nests, so harvesters can gather the down when the ducks are off the nest, replacing the feathers with soft grass, without perturbing the nesting fowl. A visitor can view on video every step from nest to down duvet while sipping gourmet coffee from a handmade ceramic cup, and then sink her fingers into a large ball of tiny gray feathers soft as air.

Surely Laxness had a role in helping the Icelandic people to love themselves and their history enough not to sell it out to the nullity of an ahistorical tourist trade. The Eider Duck Museum sits in neighborly relationship with the Norwegian House (a historical recreation of a settler family's lifestyle) and the Library of Water (an art installation where glass towers filled with melted glacial ice have replaced the books) in the village of Stykkishólmur, a trade port since the 1550s. These village homes retrofitted into small museums nourish the tourist's hunger for a continuity between past and present. Invasive beauty.

A painting hangs over the mantel in the dining room at Hellnar where the travelers (we who want for almost nothing and will die from our ceaseless want for more) gather for our ample breakfast buffet—scrambled eggs, cheeses, ham, bacon, salami, sardines, pickled herring, sliced English cucumber, sliced tomatoes, chunks of kiwi, watermelon, pineapple, croissants, seeded bread fresh on wood block for cutting, muesli, hard-boiled egg, pitchers of yogurt plain and strawberry.

The painting's background is icy blue, a storehouse built of stones covered with ice, a wall of ice stones with a low open doorway, a wooden barrel beside the door, and, just departing after gathering her stores, a woman dressed in a skirt of seal skins, thin shoes made of skins with lacing round the ankles, black leggings made from the wool of black sheep, loose lavender knitted wool bodice, russet scarf covering her head enveloping as a hijab—but this last for protection from the weather, not from her condition of being a woman. She carries a stiff splayed cod, salted and frozen, in one hand. The fish is so ample it reaches to her ankle and is split open with the skin intact to keep the flesh whole. In the other hand, she carries a wooden bucket—perhaps some pickled herring scooped from the barrel. Her gaze reaches past her left shoulder, nothing warm in her face nor fearful, maybe apprehension or just alertness to whatever might be coming in a place where a blasting wind can rouse a widow-making wave. The pelts of the fishwife's skirt are splitting apart from wear and dryness; her fashion is built on need and materials at hand. She will wear it through many repairs, stitching and restitching, a danger to fail. In the time of the stone and turf huts, money wasn't a thought. Payment was a fish, a lamb, a calf, a pelt. Now, money runs through everyone's mind, a flow unstoppable as glacial melt; then, a stitch that mended a skirt or net was life.

A few stray sheep outside the window call to each other. They do not want to be alone in the barren heath. My god, how to make a life—whether woman, man, or sheep—out of this hard ground where grass can barely disguise the jagged lava and the wind bites into everything without rest. Invasive beauty: the lupines, the fishwife, the bleating, the grass, the white farmhouses with red roofs tucked at the feet of volcanic cones, the persistence in making life work.

Karl Ove Knausgaard, whose work I had not loved until I heard him speak in Reykjavík, says that the use of literature is not to recover history but to be in the moment of uncertainty, to sit in the knowingness that sits in the middle of unknowing and find a door latch, an openness to the world, a certitude that within uncertainty lies a narrative. Will she live through another winter, the fishwife? How long will I be given this gift of language with which to parse out beauty? Such questions would be unbearable if one required certainty in the answers.

The Icelandic sagas written in the thirteenth century tell of events taking place during the settlement times of the ninth and tenth centuries. The sagas run all over this landscape like the ubiquitous glacial melt, stories of heroism, hauntings, and violence of neighbor upon neighbor. They fought over property, firewood, sheep, horses. A man killed a shepherd to gain grazing for his sheep. Men were hurled out into "the pit of sacrifice" to satisfy Thor. The settlers had fled the "unpeace" of warring kings in Norway and created their version as warring subjects on the new land before settling into the rule of law. The Eyrbyggja saga sprang from the Snaefellsnes Peninsula, telling of some chieftains' exile from Norway. They tore down their ceremonial halls, carried the timbers on ships to reassemble in Iceland. To find out where to land, the chieftain threw a pillar off the ship and chose his "land-take" based upon where the timber came ashore. It might take years to find such a timber, given the roiling sea. One account tells of a lost pillar, the chieftain settling where he could. Ten years later, when he found the pillar, he moved a great distance to resettle under the auspicious sign. A chief might give land to his sailors. Some women, too, held land, captained ships, and conducted trade, some as brutally as the men. People bloodied the fields over territorial disputes. To know the land was to make it holy, its defense a "duty of honor," and blood violence a ritual of sacred belief. The sagas display a cordial embrace of lawfulness, while violence reigns.

"We are seeking horses stolen from me in autumn, therefore we claim to ransack your house."

"Is this ransacking taken up according to law; or have ye called any lawful law-seers to search into this case?"

Most often it seems the law was enacted with a "door-doom" and slaying with axe, adze, or sword. Sometimes a mere amputation.

There were many accounts of "ride-by-nights," troll women riding wolves with snakes for reins and troll ghosts riding oxen.

A man drowned at sea returned each evening to sit dripping wet by his fire and drink his own "burial ale."

In a fire-hall, a ghost emerged as a seal's head rising up through the floor. Struck again and again, it kept rising up to its flippers. A man hit it with a sledge-hammer, blow after blow, as if "knocking down a peg," until the seal was gone.

A brutal man refused to die. After he was buried, cattle nearing his grave went mad. A herdsman was found dead, "coal-blue and every bone in him was broked" near the grave. Birds died when they landed on the grave. The undead man walked through the country killing things. All winter people were afraid to walk outside and do errands. Come spring they dug him up. He was undecayed. They laid him on a sledge and yoked up two oxen. The oxen died. Another team put under the yoke went mad and ran out to sea. Finally, they dragged him to Halt-foot's Head, buried him, and built a wall of "three-man-heights' tall" on the landward side, the front and sides being guarded by cliffs. He did not trouble them again.

A woman of strong mind, falling ill and anticipating her death, asked that she be buried in a certain place, a holy place, where "priests would sing over her." Her body was swathed in linen but not sewn up. She was laid in a cart. "Trusty men" and "good horses" carried her over the heath on the burial journey, the cart upsetting many times on rough ground. The party stopped for the night seeking board, but were denied. They agreed to "abide unfed" in a great hall and went to bed by daylight. The corpse and cart lay outside the inner door. In the night, the party awoke to hear clattering in the "buttery" and found the naked dead woman preparing a meal for them. She set it out on the table. They could not doubt the food was real, and so they blessed the meat with holy water and ate. They slept well. The journey continued to the woman's desired resting place. She never troubled nor fed them again, having had one last chance to feed her beloveds when they least expected it.

I WAS SURPRISED HOW GOOD THE FOOD WAS IN ICELAND. WOLF fish with a velvety tarragon sauce so vibrant green it might have been moss growing out of my plate. A swirl of parsnip puree on the side. Cod cheeks cooked in lemon and garlic, with fried-crisp surface and jelly-soft centers, presented in an iron skillet with roasted new potatoes and tomatoes. An undressed spinach and arugula salad. Rhubarb-and-currant tea. And everywhere the earthy rye bread loaded with flax and sunflower seeds, with a shot of Björk, birch twig in the bottle for flavor, to top it off.

When the New Nordic Food Manifesto came out in 2004, culinary tradition became a site of reinvention. Herring, which has been traditionally served pickled on rye bread, remained popular mostly with the older generation. (Chef Gunnar Karl Gíslason's restaurant Dill offered herring ice cream served on fresh greens and rye bread.) The manifesto advocates for principles of "purity, season, ethics, health, sustainability and quality." The blending of local cookery with influences from abroad evolved in concert with the growth of Icelandic tourism, but it was not merely a touristic ploy. In 2013, New Nordic Food also launched the Nordic Children's Kitchen Manifesto advocating that "every Nordic child has the right to learn how to cook good healthy food." These efforts are backed by the Nordic Council of Ministers.

Will herring rise to celebrity status in new wave cuisine? In too many regions the fish are harvested to be turned into fertilizer and aquaculture feed, and they are prized as bait fish in the lobster fishery. These uses help conservationists argue for the protection of herring, which are essential to the marine food web and to local economies. I wish they were more highly prized as food. Fresh herring are sweet to the palate, delicate in texture, a good source of calcium, and, when canned as sardines, offer the weird pleasure and soft crunch of tiny tenderized bones. Living low in the food chain, herring do not concentrate heavy metals such as mercury the way larger fish do.

Herring have made a comeback in Iceland's coastal waters after the overfishing of the 1960s. In the first half of the twentieth century, they accounted for 30 percent of the nation's export income, but by 1968 herring had disappeared. After a twenty-five-year moratorium on fishing, herring stocks are in good condition, though fishing them is heavily regulated. Only 20 percent of the stock can be fished out each year.

The abundance of herring is a survival strategy for the species—those massive shoals and fish balls of flickering, undulating light racing through the sea confuse predators. Abundance can also mean peril, as I learned driving along the edge of volcanic hills in northern Iceland. In December 2012 and again in February 2013, mass mortality struck Kolgrafafjörður. Herring had been wintering in the area in vast numbers. They peaked in 2008 at nine hundred thousand tons of herring, many more than had been seen for seventy years. A shoal of three hundred thousand came into the shallow broad cove, so many that they depleted the water of oxygen. In 2012, twenty-two tons of herring died of oxygen deprivation; in 2013, thirty thousand tons. The entire quota for the landing of summer-spawning herring was only sixty-seven thousand tons. Mass mortality of herring on this scale had not previously been documented anywhere in the world. Thousands and thousands of gulls, cormorants, gannets, and sea eagles assembled to prey on the fish. Decaying fat covered the shores and surface of the bay, an oil spill dangerous to birds. The next winter, dozers and loaders came to bury thousands of tons of stinking rotted fish.

Siglufjörður's herring spike ran from 1903 to 1968. Fish were caught near shore using nets to close off fjords and lowering huge dip nets into the teeming seine. What had been a small village expanded to become the fifth-largest town in Iceland, with twenty-three salting stations and five rendering factories processing the fish, thousands of tons of fish per day, into meal and oil for export—half of Iceland's national income in those years. The Herring Era Museum commemorates that history:

> This period resembles the gold rush in North America in many ways. Many people risked everything they possessed and grew stinking rich and others lost everything. During bad weather spells, many hundreds of fishing vessels sought shelter in the harbour and all the streets were congested like in a big city.

> Herring brought relief from a thousand years of oppression. *Herring* was the magic word. Through the herring industries Icelanders became independent people, the village became independent of the city, and poor fishermen became rich men.

Siglufjörður's bustling harbor, circa 1930s. Over four hundred ships fished for herring that was later processed into barrels or smelted into meal or oil in local herring factories. *Photo courtesy of the Herring Era Museum Archive.*

Tens of thousands of workers came to Siglo, as the town is nicknamed, during its peak productivity. They salted and barreled herring; they sat at the boning tables, knives flying in skilled hands. Women came to work from distant villages and bunked in dormitories, knitting or crocheting finger cots for protection from the blades. Workers ground herring into meal for pet food and fertilizer, stuffed the meal into burlap sacks, then sewed the sacks shut. They spun fish oil out of water to make soap. They built bigger and faster boats that hunted herring in deeper and more distant waters. They invented and built the tools they needed to do the work. They built dip nets six feet in diameter, the frames made from lean birch saplings steam-heated and bent into a circle. They built a dam and power station to fuel the work. They built a laboratory to test the quality of their products, assaying water, fat, and minerals.

In 1948, Arni Fridriksson began tagging herring to study their migratory path. He proved that north Iceland's summer herring and Norwegian spring herring were the same. The town built bigger and faster boats. People say that Amsterdam was built on herring bones. Siglufjörður was as well. And how many other towns and cities share this legacy within the migratory ranges of herring and their family—menhaden, shad, alewives, and, all told, more than two hundred of the world's fish species? Civilization was built on herring bones.

During the years of the heaviest fishing, the herring began to move from northern Iceland to the east. By 1965 the fishing communities in the east were thriving. Siglo was beginning to fade. It's a herring thing to change migratory routes that have appeared stable for decades. Researchers are not clear about why the fish make these changes; it probably has to do with movement of plankton, their primary food source. But overfishing was also to blame, as technologies improved fishing in deeper waters. By 1969 the herring were gone from eastern Iceland as well—but by the 1990s, given that mandate's reprieve from being fished, the stocks rebounded. The Norwegian-Icelandic herring stocks are the largest in the world, and they are so far sustainable:

even as technologies improve for fishing in deeper waters, the herring can go deeper.

Many tropical fish species have already perceived climate change and are moving away from the equator at the rate of fifty kilometers per decade, heading toward more ideal conditions for their feeding and spawning. As temperatures and currents and prey species change, the herring change too. They like cold water, so as water warms it is safe to assume they will favor the north. Common lore says that the species has changed little since the time of the dinosaurs; better said, they have been wise about adapting to change.

In Siglo a couple of pubs and an oversized resort hotel occupy the piers where once the barrels of salted fish were stacked like cord wood. There's an Icelandic Folk Music Centre, the Seagull craft brewery, an artist's residency, and the Herring House B and B. One pub has created a scrubbed patio staged with benches made from barrel end-plates, and stools made from barrels cut in half and topped with faux leather. The barrel heads boast in stenciled letters ICELAND CUT HERRING, SIGLUFJÖRÐUR, two arcs of black letters rounding the top and bottom of the barrel head's circumference, and wood varnished to glow in the gloom of a foggy afternoon. Only a handful of tourists meander about town, stopping in for beer and *plotfiskur*, traditional stew of haddock, potato, and leek. The town had no road until 1940, so it was accessible only by boat or horse trail. Now it has roads and an airport.

The museum has a cheery front, but less shine inside. After all, it commemorates work, none of it easy. Five bright buildings, once part of the industry, have been decked out with multicolored sheet-metal siding and boardwalks to connect them. The boathouse harbors eleven boats: a thirty-eight-ton lapstrake oak fishing vessel, two purse seiners, a dory rigged with drift nets, a dinghy, another dory—all relics, set here in the grimy semi-dark, with the wheelhouse lights on the biggest ship shining like the eyes of history that cannot close.

For decades "herring girls" came by the dozens for summer employment. The meal plant is a careful display of machinery, lab, machine shop. The behemoth industrial grinder is a reconstruction, since Siglo's was long gone when this exhibit was built in 2003. Parts were painstakingly dismantled from other villages, brought here, and reconstructed, yet the place feels as if the work stopped just yesterday. A heavy smell of metal shavings and oil permeates the wood, and everything that can't be seen calls the mind back to those who are gone. Is this love, the obsession to feel lives one cannot know? The herring girls who have come for summer work are still sleeping upstairs in their bunk beds, in the hard sleep that comes after the ache of long labor. I don't want to wake them, only to say I hear the softness of their breathing, the tidal soughing of their breath.

The great oak vessel grounded inside the boathouse—a carrier, perhaps, from the look of her capacious hold and upswept bow with the wheelhouse well near the stern—has a double-ended dory tied at her side. The lines are graceful, with centuries of Viking knowledge in every plank and fastening. The building is dark, as winter days are when one is so close to the Arctic Circle. The museum lights are sparse, bright white—no red and green needed now for port and starboard. The ghost ship is not going anywhere.

In the times before the gods and monsters had all moved inside our heads, the times when they still lived in landscape and household, haunting was not uncommon. What is a ghost story? Something in us needs to feel that the material world can transmit communications from the spirit world, that we are meant to know our dead, even if they were monsters in life, even if they suffered and failed and died unloved, we are meant to know them. And if we fail to know them, they will rise up through the floorboards to haunt us until we set them free. In the old time, death demanded careful attention, according to the sagas, given the peril of ghosts with malign intent. A hole must be cut in the wall of the house closest to where the corpse lies, the body removed through the hole. If taken out through the front door, the ghost would re-member how to enter, returning to haunt. Better to set the dead free through an exit that can be barred against reentry; better to return the dead to the homeless night, sip the burial ale, and spin stories by the fire with the living.

16

*

Two-Tone Satin Dress

Many creatures must
make, but only one must seek

within itself what to make
FRANK BIDART, "Lament for the Makers"

THE DRESS WAS A WOMAN SAWED IN HALF. I HAD STIFFENED
the cranberry satin skirt with heavyweight interfacing to make it hold the bell
shape. I had folded the broad paired pleats into the waist to give the fabric its
body. The sleeveless bodice was pale pink satin, lined with thinner Bemberg
rayon. Featherweight interfacing gave structure to the armholes and mod-
estly scooped neckline. The satin dress was the most demanding garment I
had ever made. The design was simple but required finesse. The piping meant
to run between bodice and skirt gave me the most trouble. There was no
room to hide mistakes in the glistening sheen of satin, where a needle might
pull a silk thread loose, marring the slick perfection of the weave. The bodice

needed to fit like upholstery while the skirt needed to bring its own idea of shape to the whole. I loved the elegance of the design, the two-tone panache. After the disappointment of the earlier prom dress, a tawdry thrift store find remade by my gifted grandmother into something serviceable, I was determined to make my own statement. I wanted a Grace Kelly look, sophisticated and sleek.

Throughout my teenager years I had been in competition with the girls at the elite Ethel Walker School, where my mother taught speech and dramatics. Some days I hung out in the back of the school gym during her rehearsals for the annual play, pretending to do my homework. Goddess, she was impressive, leaping to the stage with her notes and clipboard to transform her students into Kate and Petruchio in an all-girl production of *Taming of the Shrew*. One year they performed a play my mother had written, a knock-off of the musical *Brigadoon*. She had imagined an island populated by beautiful young women lost in the fog. Romance of course was the problem, as a shipwrecked sailor washes up on shore, driving all the women to their worst behavior and ending of course with the redemptive power of romantic love. The play was thin and imitative, as were most of the thirty or so plays my mother wrote. Quite a fall from the great bard. But she understood play structure and loved the theater and modeled artistic discipline for me. At Walker's she took under her wing the girls she felt sorry for—parents roiled in a mean divorce or too many European holidays sans offspring. At home she would speak with disdain about such parents—she loved to hate those she saw as standing above her in class or privilege. She would speak of their daughters as if they were poor little match girls. The wealthy especially offended her, because she wanted most to be wealthy. Well, perhaps she did not want wealth as much as she wanted fame as a playwright. She never accomplished either of those goals. But she wrote and wrote. And how she whipped those girls of privilege into acolytes of the *theah-tah*. She invited the ones with neglectful parents to our home for Thanksgiving dinners. They became surrogate daughters whom she mentored in the ways of family love. I always felt she loved them more than she loved me, that she wished they had been her daughters rather than me. But I understood my role was to help her perform the happy family she wished those girls to have.

The school required the girls to put away their fashionable wardrobes and wear uniforms as a nod to egalitarianism. Simple dresses of a silky rayon for every day. Pink or pistachio green. Certainly pastels. Sensible oxford shoes. For dressy occasions the dresses were ivory white shirtwaists, topped with unstructured black velvet blazers. Black ballet pumps. Classic. Flare without flair. I was a townie nerd by comparison. What on earth was I wearing? A-line camel wool skirt and heathered cardigan and loafers. Invisible. Worse for me was the envy I felt each spring when the Ethel Walker yearbook came home with its professional photos and brags about the girls heading to Wellesley, Radcliffe, Vassar, and Smith. How could it be that these girls were both more beautiful and smarter than I was? Who knew then about legacy or transactional admissions for the rich and famous? Certainly not a public school girl who burned with envy.

I was stunned when I beat a New York sophisticate from Miss Walker's to win the starring role of Ilona Szabo in *The Play's the Thing* at the nearby Westminster School for boys. The director was my mother's friend from theater circles. That must be how I was invited to read for the part, though the role seemed earmarked for a Walker's student. I was hardly the sexy vamp of Molnár's farce. I have no idea why I was chosen. I think the chic one was too cold, too angular. I was beautiful enough but wanted to be chosen for my talent—about which I was deeply insecure. The play was vastly inappropriate for high school students. The central scene had to do with the fiancé overhearing a conversation when another man fondles Szabo's breast in the next room. She and her buddy concoct a plan to convince him that the beautiful orb about which the lover rhapsodized was a peach, the encounter therefore totally innocent. That's how I remember the plot. Desire is the game and the best deceiver wins. In a twisted way, the role taught me something about female agency over desire.

Once I had the top and bottom halves of the satin prom dress constructed, the pattern called for joining them at the waist with piping inserted into the seam. I bought the yardage necessary, woven cotton cord, then folded a strip of pink satin around its length, stitching the two sides of the folded fabric tight against the cord. This left plenty of edge material to stitch into the seam, allowing the piping to serve its function of accentuating the waistline. It made for a lot of fabric that had to be bunched into the seam without lumping up the sleek style lines. If I could manage that, then the back zipper had to traverse through the piped waistline and stiffened skirt, the sewing machine's feed dogs pulling all those layers as one, the foot compressing at the waist two layers of satin plus rayon lining plus two more layers of satin that had folded around the piping plus the piping too, so that the rising and falling needle could slip through without breaking against so much obstinacy or without pulling threads loose from the fabric's delicate weave.

I had made other dresses. And skirts. Nothing as complicated as the two-tone satin prom dress. Or with such high expectations. Unlike my grandmother, who made clothes with no pattern, cutting and fitting to the manikin, I used patterns. I had learned about them in school, a compulsory class in home ec, where the girls made a series of insipid items about which they cared not a whit. Potholder. Apron. Maybe a simple gathered skirt? I hated the class, but I learned to use patterns, and that sent me down the road of making my own clothes. I used Simplicity patterns mostly. I tried Vogue, but their patterns were too complicated, like recipes from *Gourmet* magazine. Still, I loved the ritual elements of dressmaking, the problem-solving that had gone into the pattern-making. In the fabric department of Myrtle Mills department store, I flipped through the oversized pattern books, scanning style after style, trying to see myself in the paper doll drawings that filled the pages. And the fabrics—that was the great confounding joy. Bolt after bolt of color, texture, pattern—all available to touch and imagine into garments. I remember egging myself on to make more and more difficult pieces. I remember one dress in particular that I was proud of having made in the high school years. The fabric was poplin with an imbrication of dense forest greens, finely detailed, a dark and calm print. The dress had a boat neck, three-quarter-length sleeves, gently gathered skirt. The bodice fit like skin from neck to waist. I made a fabric covered belt, amazed to find a kit for this in the fabric store.

I wore the forest dress to school—maybe this was junior year of high school—aglow with amazement that I'd made this thing. A friend at school—a girl much more domestically inclined than I—complimented me on the dress.

"Where did you get it?"

"I made it!"

"Oh, I'm sorry, but I can't believe that."

"Well, if you see the inside of the belt, you'd believe it."

We went to the girls' room. I took off the belt. I hadn't enough fabric to properly tuck the edges under for hemming. The belt looked great when I was wearing it but take it off and the slapdash craft revealed crookedly cut fabric with unraveling threads. The belt was flawed and therefore proof of being handmade and therefore a thing to be admired.

I found pleasure in each stage of dressmaking. I had always loved puzzles. Even as teenager I found Nancy Drew mysteries, quadratic equations, and diagramming sentences equally engaging. Activities that focused the mind and engaged the hands. Dressmaking patterns came in an envelope the size of a paperback. The tissue paper templates were printed akimbo so that the large rectangular sheets unfolded to show all the dismembered body parts of the finished product inked as close together as possible. Right arm, left arm. Right back, left back. Collar facing. Back facing. Front skirt, back skirt. Place the tissues over the yardage, pin and cut. Cutting one sleeve shape out of a doubled-over fabric meant that the body's symmetry was matched in the two sleeve parts. Each pattern sheet showed the cut lines for several sizes—take your pick—and the marks for detailing. Darts to give fullness to the bust. Pleats to shape the upper skirt. Tiny I-beams for buttonholes.

Transferring the marks to the fabric required slipping a sheet of colored tracing paper between pattern and cloth, then scoring with a tracing wheel that perforated pattern and tracing sheet to leave a chalk line of colored dots on the fabric. Perilous on delicate cloth. My grandmother used no patterns, no tracing wheel, instead marked each cut, detail, or alteration using a matchbook-sized block of tailor's chalk. I recently found a chunk of sky-blue tailor's chalk in a plastic box of straight pins that had been kicking around the Grand Manan cottage for fifty years. I realized these must have been my grandmother's sewing accessories. Perhaps I used these very pins and chalk on the cranberry satin for my two-tone dress. My grandmother's DNA must have been embedded in the little block that fit so perfectly between my forefinger and thumb. The sweat of decades and decades, a body memory held in the chalk. I felt close to her in such a material way that she did not feel lost to me. Then again, some unzipped portion of her DNA is in my cells, so it is ridiculous to think that she is lost.

Often a dress pattern's instructions seemed to make no sense, but if I tried to shortcut and skip an inscrutable stage, I paid the price in a redo. Difficult sections like sleeves and collars and waistlines often asked for basting. I did not have the patience for hand-stitching a loose draft of the final version to test if I'd gotten it right before finishing the seam with machine stitching. I did not like the assumption that I might get it wrong. Basting leads to a rough draft—the toile in haute couture—refined in subsequent renderings. It assumes error and imprecision and makes allowances for correction. I always skipped basting, wanting to feel that perfection was within easy reach. When I, perplexed, brought my woman-cut-in-half dress parts to my grandmother's room, I got the message. Basting. One step at a time. Piping to bodice. Piped bodice to skirt. As a bonus, she showed me how to do an invisible slip stitch for the hem. An expert incorporates the allowance for error into her process. Perfection is not expected, rather labored toward.

What does it matter that I remember in such detail the making of that dress? There was a prom. There must have been a prom committee and a prom theme and prom crepe paper shaped into waves and mermaids painted on half-shells. I don't remember. There was a boy. Handsome, baseball pitcher, trout fisherman, son of the local doctor, the whole family handsome and private school special, and the boy randy and cocksure about his sexual abilities. I remember as a child fantasizing about the boy. His father would come in an ambulance to our house to save me and the boy would ride with me, sitting beside the stretcher all the way to the hospital. But that was when I believed in being saved. Or needing to be. But the boy had become something new in my eyes. I had come to feel desire as an end in itself, felt the inexplicable force in me reaching out to be dissolved in sensation and connection.

I had battled with my mother that last year of high school. She had been fiercely opposed to my first love, a boy I'd met in a summer Transition to College program at Trinity College in Hartford after my junior year in high school. She feared his politics and that I'd be hanging out in mixed-race company. It had never occurred to me before this time that she might be racist. I had gone to Trinity to study Latin poetry and theater in what we would now call a gifted-and-talented program. I'd wanted to study psychology or sociology, but the school offered a scholarship if I went for Latin. That turned out to be fortuitous, as intensive language study and close reading of classical poetry and plays turned on my literary sensibility. The other turn-on was Jack.

He was a few years older, already a college student. He'd taken time off from school to work for the Student Nonviolent Coordinating Committee canvasing in the South to register Black citizens for the vote. Jack had been arrested in Americus, Georgia, and survived some rough treatment. This was the year before the murders of Schwerner, Goodman, and Chaney, the year before the Civil Rights Act was passed in 1964. Violence was erupting, as was the insistence on change. In contrast, my high school life felt trivial. Were the civil rights struggles even discussed in our classes? Jack turned me on to the work of James Baldwin, which I read in a fever of rising conscience. I suffered that other adolescent fever with Jack, aroused and terrified, playing the edges of sexual intimacy, unbearably aroused and wanting more. We spent hours tumbling in the heat of desire. I always stopped us short, which, I understood only after we broke up, he grew tired of. By the time I lost him, my mother gloated as if she had made it happen, but I was ready by then to follow desire when it showed up at the door.

What I remember about the prom is the two-tone satin dress more than anything. What was the image that led me to make the two-tone satin dress? Most girls would buy fluffy organza frocks in pastel colors for the prom. They looked as if they could blow away in the wind. Not the look for me. When I scan for pop women of the time, looking for the fashion gravitas the dress suggested, I come up empty. Connie Francis? Too sugary. Joan Baez, yes, possible. But would she even go to prom? The overt sexuality of Marilyn Monroe in *Some Like It Hot* embarrassed me. I liked the style of Grace Kelly in *To Catch a Thief*. Elegant, headstrong, ambiguously seductive. I was ten years old when Kelly abdicated filmdom to marry the Prince of Monaco. She was a study in contradictions, giving up a career to become a princess—not a cutesy Disneyesque princess but one who acquired titles and wealth associated with her husband's lineage—whose *peau de soie* and lace wedding dress required, some say, thirty-five seamstresses working for six weeks, who became a philanthropist to the arts and a tragic heroine when she died in a car crash. The sheen of her self-confidence was like, well, grace. I can see now the importance of my choosing the dress and fabric and look. Coming out of the wound of losing love, I chose fabric in two shades of desire. Half of me was an innocent; the other half aflame.

17

∗

From Calvary to the Subway on Fifty-Eighth Street

So things evolved, and out of blind confusion
each found its place, bound in eternal order.

OVID, *Metamorphoses*

THE 7 TRAIN TRUNDLES UNDER THE HUDSON RIVER TO EMERGE at Calvary. I get off at the elevated station on Fifty-Second Street and Queens Boulevard, disoriented in the industrial roar. Earlier in the day I had visited the Egyptian room at the Metropolitan Museum to see what the ancients had made of their dead. Since childhood I have been transfixed by Egyptian funerary art, work that insisted death would not have the last word over life. I had walked among the mummies in their glass cases, bodies wrapped in symmetrically crisscrossed ribbons of linen interwoven so the intersections form little diamonds, a painted panel affixed over the face so the spirit could introduce itself to the afterlife with the face the deceased had been known by in life. Even the inside of the sarcophagus wears the will to transcendence: painted lilies, the jackal-headed god Anubis, the winged beetle heart scarab, the walking owl. Come, let the scavengers that would consume your flesh lift you so that you step lightly into the dark.

But I walk in America. The democracy of the dead is where my great-grandmother Louisa de St. Isle Bregny—the one who emigrated from France—is buried along with three million other bodies marked with orderly rows of white stone. Calvary Cemetery is a vast urban sprawl of closely set graves, surrounded by mechanized sprawl, the Long Island Expressway and Queens Boulevard concussing the air with a nonstop bassline. In the near distance, Manhattan rises like a pleasant dream. Calvary Cemetery was established in the mid-nineteenth century when this was farmland belonging to the Alsop family. They had a small family graveyard on their land—seed corn for what was to follow. Waves of cholera epidemics had come through the city in the 1800s. Manhattan was filling up with the dead, many of them poor Irish who had lived in the squalid Lower East Side. In 1845, the Trustees of St. Patrick's Cathedral purchased the Alsop farm in Queens, several hundred peaceful acres where the dead could be honored by their kin. The first burial in Calvary came in 1848. During one week in 1854, a wave of cholera brought 226 bodies to Calvary. One Irishman wrote that "men were sleeping four deep in Calvary." Many of the deaths were children under seven years of age. At least the deaths were marked, the lives verified, the losses mourned. Too many leave this world without a trace. Gone missing in war, thrown from the slave ship, drowned struggling to cross the Mediterranean, dehydrated trying to cross the Arizona desert, neglected having suffered disease or poverty or exile or madness, or left nameless simply due to the anguishes of family life.

I had been haunted to learn that my grandmother Marie Bregny was buried in an unmarked grave. She died in our family home. "I went upstairs one morning to bring her breakfast and she was dead," my mother reported weeks after the death—as if an incidental bit of news conveyed in a phone call to me in northern Vermont, where I was living with my young daughter. This was a period of self-exile for me after the shunning my mother had subjected me to when I confessed to being five months pregnant—yes, the ambulance/ prom boy—during my freshman year of college. "Take her away," my mother had told the undertaker. She wanted no more to do with the dead than that small bit of business.

Decades later I visited Valhalla, where Marie had been buried a year after her ashes had been delivered without ceremony or instructions. It shook me to see such concrete evidence of my mother's disdain toward her mother. Hadn't she given the woman a home for a quarter century? Hadn't we known her to be part of us, the maker of crepes and childhood dresses and French songs and DIY opera karaoke and lively repartee?

John Bowlby, the British psychoanalyst who pioneered attachment theory, proposed that early attachment to a primary caregiver—most commonly a mother—shaped later development of emotional and mental well-being. Human beings are not like giraffes, who can stand on their own just minutes after birth. We come into the world dependent on the care of others for survival. Infants have inherent methods to stimulate caregiving. Smiling and crying draw the caregiver near to reciprocate the smile and comfort the crying. If the caregiver is unable to respond for whatever reasons, the child is deprived of important lessons on the trustworthiness of her caregiver and herself as inherently valuable. She may become insecure, anxious, or avoidant in social interactions. Extreme deprivation can result in what Bowlby termed "affectionless psychopathy," an individual unable to consider the consequences of her actions or feel guilt for her antisocial behavior. When a child intuitively senses that a primary relationship is endangered, she feels anxiety. Bowlby observed that the child also feels anger, and thus the seeds are sown for what he describes as "the stark nakedness and simplicity of the conflict with which humanity is oppressed—that of getting angry with and wishing to hurt the very person who is most loved."

I remember vividly the confusion of such feelings in my childhood. I sleep in my narrow bed under the slanted ceiling upstairs in my childhood home. It is the room into which I have hurled myself in rage a hundred times, slamming the door to announce my fury, plunging into the bed. Screaming and crying into the pillow until my throat is raw, my eyes too swollen to close, my body limp and empty. When the rage has passed and I have stopped gulping for air, I get up and walk to the window, stare out past the clothesline that hangs at the lawn's edge, sinking my gaze into the chokecherry scrub beyond, the green lace of the woods where light pours through the gaps.

My childhood rage felt righteous, though I could not say what caused it. Can I remember a single incident? Not one. Only the emotion endures. This must have been the feeling I had as an infant. My mother said I was inconsolable for the first three years of my life. I have no memory of that time, no words to describe the mind of the baby, but this feeling of desperation, of crying out with no expectation of comfort, of expelling from my body the force that had overtaken it, remains close and real. Sometimes something in me I do not recognize as my own longs to feel that intensity again, and I pick a fight with someone I love for no reason that makes sense after the fact. After the spasm comes the return to the ordinary, to the dining table, to the creaking house, the shame of the outburst, the wound of having wounded others.

Sometimes I think that the places where I grew up mothered me, the living room perched on the second floor, bay windows overlooking wooded hillsides where my father cut ski trails by hand, finding his refuge in physical work and nature. He built fieldstone walls and stairways in the yard, transplanted mountain laurels from the woods, sharpened his axe in the dirt-floored shed. He used a grindstone spun with his foot pumping a rickety treadle. I can smell the dirt floor and oiled stone, the funk of firewood stacked against the shed wall, bark rotting, fungus steeping in the air, smells of Earth reducing itself to the elements that foster growth. I knew this wisdom of the land very early in life, father digging up humus from the forest to lace into the soil of his transplants, the forest always at work nursing seedlings from the particles of its decay.

My mother too, though a New Yorker, found intimacy in our woods. When I was small, we'd go up the pathway to where the thick mosses and red-headed soldiers and rattlesnake plantain and chains of ground pine thrived. If we were lucky we would find some ripe red partridge berries. Sometimes a tiny fern. We'd clip and pluck all we wanted, then haul the take back to the dining room table, spread them out on newspaper, and arrange the plants in a giant brandy snifter. The smell was an embarrassment of deciduous richness. Downright sexy in its overt promise of fertility. I remember tasting leaves and berries from the partridge plant, its gentle bitterness so much closer to the wild than domesticated berries. We covered the snifter with cellophane and watched our micro-world grow and sleep all winter in our living room. The terrarium created its own rain, droplets condensing on the cellophane roof and dropping down to keep the moss plush and green. Eventually the glass container became too small a world for our captives. They wilted, desiccated, faded. So back they went into the land.

What is a self and how do we come to know it? Surely it is nothing fixed like a hand or a spleen or a parietal lobe or a dendritic delta of neurons. Why do we feel the need to know the self, to become more authentically the self, to have the self be known, seen, verified by others, and yet distinct from them? What is the real self and, if we ever found it, if we ever became the perfect embodiment of the real self toward which we feel we are progressing, what would that mean? The self is not part of identity that can be described, in the way that cultural heritage and genetic predisposition can be described. The self is the process of seeking for a way of being that transcends the impaired self as we have known it, the wounded and suffering self. The self is an aspiration and yet too a fact.

The pattern of detachment between mother and daughter has dogged two generations in my matrilineal line (my mother and her mother, my mother and me), and this has led me to wonder how far back it might have begun. The detachment meant that family story had been logjammed from my grandmother to my mother and my mother to me. I wanted to make something of the lack, find the frayed places and weave in some missing threads, so that I could pass on a more robust story of these accomplished women than had been passed on to me. I felt a bond with Louisa and Marie that defied the gaps in the story. I wanted to tease a path back into a sense of cultural belonging and continuity as mothering forces that grounded me, despite what I felt I had lacked.

I remember conversations with my mother in the last of her one-hundred-and-two years, when I was bringing her homemade soup and flowers and pastry every week, knowing it was not enough to compensate her losses and fear. I remember her saying that her mother never touched her, held her, kissed her. She felt something was missing but did not know what it was. And while Marie had been occupied running the couture business, my mother as a teenager had to fend off the boarders who lived in rooms Marie rented out in their brownstone. One man wanted to teach her "how to handle his penis." Marie had had her struggles. Abused by her priest, left a widow by her first husband, abandoned by her second husband to raise her daughter on her own, losing her savings when she invested in the *Titanic*, and again when the Depression erased what remained of her bank accounts.

"Why didn't she ask my father for money?" my aged mother said. "Only when I was sixteen did he start to send her fifty dollars a month."

"I did the same thing with Lucinda's father," I replied. "Stubborn pride. I needed to prove I could survive and take care of this child on my own. Do you think Marnie was like that?"

"Yes, she had that—a survivor. You have. I have it. We're not really women. I mean, we are, and we can dress up like that. But there's a lot that's male in us."

Bowlby also wrote that "the human psyche, like human bones, is strongly inclined towards self-healing." Will and determination contribute. Yet the psyche comprises forces not really subject to will. Fate, if you will. "The sanctity of the soul," as one artificial intelligence expert termed those aspects of the human mind that make it impossible for AI ever to match it.

That sanctity may show up as twists in the plot that look tragic but end up being the comic relief or even the heroic transcendence when seen from some distance in the lives of women who might have been broken by their circumstances, but who remade themselves. Hannah Gadsby says in her stand-up performance, "There is nothing stronger than a broken woman who has rebuilt herself." Yes. We are the Fates, the Furies, the Muses, the peasants who become soothsayers at Delphi.

As I write this, I can't help but feel there is something fateful too in the act of creation. Yes, it takes so much will to sit down at the desk and stay there. But fate has a hand too. I am surprised at how things turn out, as they fall from my head to the page, surprised that psyche, which may be fate's refugium in the forest of mind, wakes me in the middle of the night to deliver a word or a phrase that will drive the next day's work. Last night: "I am pagan; this process is my god."

I found a letter from Celestine, one of Marie's sisters, among a paltry stack of memorabilia that came to me from a cousin-in-law. If I extrapolate from this letter, my guess is that Louisa and her three daughters felt a secure attachment that went beyond their sharing of work in the couture business. Maybe the shared work helped them to realize a spirit of connection and reciprocity in the emotional arena. Celestine writes of her mother's decline:

> Mother is gone to-day to Lillie's but I don't know if she will be able to stay there as she wasn't able to walk to the car, I had to get her a cab. It was so pittible to see her go away. I wanted her to come back but she wouldn't.—I feel now if she is not better and needs more care I shall care for her even if I lose every earthly thing I care for. Now is the time she needs care when she can't help herself. She stood by me when I was once in the same condition, and sooner than live with the memory that I hadn't done all I could for her I would rather die than suffer the ungratitude—

"My great-grandmother is buried here," I tell the woman who is the keeper of records at Calvary Cemetery.

"Do you know when she was buried?" The tone suggests she doesn't think I do. But this isn't my first rodeo with the dead. I read from the death certificate for Louisa Bregny. Nothing is as definitive as a death certificate.

Long silence.

"Are you *sure* she's buried here ... Oh ... October first ... I was looking at eleventh. She's in Section Fourteen, Range Thirty-Three, Quad A Apple, Grave Five."

I make my way section by section, passing the statue of Rachel weeping for her children, passing winged angels, a Jesus with lilies, a Jesus in a nave, crosses of granite, crosses of marble, a handmade cross of red and white stone. A dove is perched on a cross. A groundsman passes. A jogger passes. Jets slice the sky. There is no monument like the one named Bregny that stands under the shade of a broad maple tree at the edge of Section 14, Range 33, Quad A Apple. It's phallic. A slightly squared turret, whiter, simpler than the others. Six letters engraved on the pedestal: BREGNY. En-graved. Lichen cracked and scored, a slight indentation on the top where an ornament or cross might once have been fixed. Breeze stirring. I sit on her grave, the fragrant swell of cut grass filling my head. So many stones, the weight of which taken together would equal a pyramid built for an Egyptian queen. A plastic bag drifts down from the sky like a shiny bit of protoplasm and lands on the east edge of Section 14. Grackles chatter as I head back toward the Chrysler Building and One World Trade Center, inviting on the skyline.

I believe in the power of place. Place is an essential aspect of identity. I believe that something inheres of all that has transpired in a place—the whole story held in the present moment. Objects become vessels for meaning. Aristotle said that place is a vessel that holds us. Place creates a sense of belonging. It is, Merleau-Ponty wrote, "the primary condition of all living perception." Place links the individual with others, with history, with nature, with the future. Place is continuity and connection. But place is an imaginary vessel. New York City is not a boat. Paris is not a soup bowl.

The quest for Louisa's past led me to sleuth out the addresses where she'd lived and worked from 1878 to 1909—the years for which I'd found her listed in the Trow Business Directory of Manhattan. The quest began with erasure and ended with absurdity.

On September 11, 2017, I walked her addresses, heading from Fourteenth Street down Greenwich Avenue to Eleventh, turning onto the quiet residential street. A well-heeled man was tending his wrought iron trimmed pocket garden. I snapped photos of the block, tidy redbrick rowhouses with tiny gardens. He noticed me. I'm not stalking you, I said. And I told him the story—how his house with its half-basement, windows facing the street, had been where my great-grandmother lived, the workshop on the lower level and the family living above, renting out rooms above to make it work. Would these be the houses that were there at that time? Yes, he said, this one was built in 1834. Bregny & Cie. lived and worked here from 1878 to 1889. I was breathless with enthusiasm, feeling some vestige of Louisa still hovering. I thanked him in earnest, walked on, then noticed the house numbers were not what I'd thought. I had given him a false narrative of his home. Perhaps he tells that story now when friends come to visit. It is almost true. The whole block is lined with redbrick identical rowhouses. Narrow three-story houses. The Village, we call it. Except the actual address where Louisa lived and worked, 272 West Eleventh, just a half block east of Bleecker Street (once named Herring Street, but after a man not a fish). That house is gone, replaced by a double-wide six-story apartment building at 270 named Tudor Arms, its façade heavily mortared, the bricks rough and burnt with black smudges. Going for a British look of coal dust? Number 272 is the only redbrick rowhouse missing on the block. Did the family and business move because their building was to be torn down? Who knows. Their place is long gone to rubble.

I stopped on a concrete ledge to write in my notebook. A young Black woman with hair bunned up under her ball cap stopped to ask, "Are you here for the Oscar Wilde press conference?" Might as well be.

From there I hiked north on Seventh Avenue, five lanes of traffic flow and caterwauling attempts to park where a little over a century ago would have been vendors' pushcarts, jammed carriages and trolleys, and horseshit ankle deep. The rivers are still here flanking the island, just as they did a thousand years ago. Ten thousand. Think of that quiet. The blue sky on a warm September is still here, though this day happened to be 9/11, so even the sky was imprinted with a human stain. Those planes. Those falling bodies. The crushing weight of history.

"Family is water," writes Colum McCann, "it has a memory of what it once filled, always trying to get back to the original stream."

From 1890 to 1894, the Bregny family and business lived at 211 West Forty-Eighth Street. They had flowed northward with the city as it grew. The area has been known as Hell's Kitchen since 1881, so named by a reporter researching multiple murders at a notorious tenement on Thirty-Ninth Street. But the area also overlapped the garment district, which must have been an incentive for the Bregnys. Now the neighborhood sits on the edge of fast and bright Times Square: *Springsteen on Broadway*, the Soup Nazi, Actors Studio. The Crowne Plaza Times Square basically eats most of the block. Not a sign of whatever might have been the Bregnys' place. No soup for me.

For the next five years, during which Marie was living in Mexico City, the business and home were located at 244 West Fifty-Third, an address just west of Seventh Avenue. I was in canyon country attempting to find a geocache—a scale shift from residential valleys to the towering cliffs of Sheraton and Hilton and Coming Soon. All signs of domestic life obliterated.

When Marie returned from Mexico in 1900 after her husband had died of consumption (as now it seems we all will, if we take the word back to its roots), Bregny & Cie. moved to 314 West Fifty-Eighth Street. Census records show a mortgage in her name (then Marie del Valle). Louisa is still at the address, the family business still a family business, though the hand-off to the next generation had begun. I suspect Marie had a legacy from her husband Antonio del Valle, who was a man of significant means, that helped this transition.

I hoofed up Eighth Avenue heading toward Columbus Circle, one of those circular moments in Manhattan that offers visual relief from the hurtling grid. I thought, no way am I going to find their building, after this smorgasbord of urban erasure that has been their history. I walked, eyes down on the GPS, until approaching the corner of Fifty-Eighth, where a guy hawked bike rentals and a Duane Reade Rx occupied the real estate. Eyes up, I saw a guy I almost did not see, insignificant it seemed until I saw. Darkish khakis, blue ball jacket and cap, he stood holding a PVC pipe topped with a green "SUBWAY Wow 10% OFF" sign, arrow pointing to the left and the address right smack there before me: 314 West Fifty-Eighth Street. Exhibit A, below, because who would believe this Fellini movie in which I suddenly found myself without also seeing some evidence.

Subway, New York City. *Photo courtesy of the author.*

I caught my breath and made the turn; the north side of the street had been swallowed up by the Time Warner Center and CNN, the Columbus Circle shops towering over the street like *Game of Thrones* Night Kings with their cold glass faces. The last of the block's four-story redbrick rowhouses stood facing the colossus of progress, sandwiched in between other giants.

Building number 314 housed on its first floor Subway and Coliseum Restaurant, two businesses twinned with one slab of concrete lying a few steps up from the sidewalk. "No sitting on steps."

From here, the business floated north to the Upper West Side, but those were the years of Marie's dominion over the enterprise. The Subway shop marks the end of Louisa's half century as a Manhattan couturiere. The Subway shop stands as actual virtual reality. Here the women came responding to ads for "Expert Corset Markers" and "Skirt Finishers." Here they arrived, "Prepared to Work," as Louisa's ads stipulated. Here the "impoverished counts" of my mother's memory came to pick up gowns for delivery to the customers. Here Louisa directed the action of the script that was her life. Hear, hear, we say like brandy-snifter-wielding parliamentarians. Here, here.

18

✳

Some of the Ghosts

IN AUGUST 2018, I TOOK A CHARTER FLIGHT IN A SINGLE-ENGINE plane over the waters surrounding Grand Manan Island. I had been researching the origins of the weir-based herring fishery in the region for several years and finding sketchy rings of stone in offshore waters that appeared only at the year's lowest tides, hinting at the ballasted weirs they once anchored. I found it hard to draw conclusions from the evidence, though it was a thrill to discover traces of a legacy that had nearly fallen from the island's memory. Many knowledgeable islanders had scoffed at the notion that undiscovered treasure lay off our shores. I'm not talking about the legend that Captain Kidd had buried gold in Money Cove on the western side of island. Legend has it that Captain Kidd buried treasure on innumerable islands along the eastern seaboard. I am talking about the treasure of a shared sense of place and history, of ruins that are a monument to community and the dignity of work.

Our flight was not exactly rigged for high-tech reconnaissance. One pilot, one poet, one photographer leaning out the window, one fisherman, all crammed into the Seahawk. We lifted over the island's interior bogs and spruce forest and ponds glinting with morning light. The plane lofted light as a red-tail. Our spirits matched the brightness. Peter Cunningham, our pho-tographer, rode shotgun beside the pilot. Peter is, like me, an island convert since childhood. His father, Robert Cunningham, a cloud physicist based at MIT, conducted fog studies on nearby Kent Island, beginning in the 1930s. His work continued there for sixty years, providing evidence that industrial effluent from the Midwest was falling as acid rain on the Northeast. His work helped lead to the 1970 U.S. Clean Air Act.

Peter spent summers as a kid hanging out with island families, and they are still among his kin. As a photographer, he apprenticed with Henri Cartier-Bresson. Peter's work bears witness to rock musicians (Bowie to Springsteen to Laurie Anderson), the fall of the Twin Towers, Zen practice with Peter Matthiessen in Japan, and sitting for witness at Auschwitz. His images make him a world citizen. One obsession of his work is to document "The Rock" and its people—fishermen, clamdiggers, dulse pickers, worship-pers, toddlers, centenarians, ship builders and ship wreckers, quilters and bakers. He understands the island's situation, as it emerges from a history wed to the sea onto the uncertain waters of climate change—which inevitably means culture change.

We've clomped around some shorelines together in pursuit of stone weir ruins. After the clear message of the ring of rock in Grand Harbour, our minds became magnetized to objects emerging at low tides. It became easy to imagine a ruin wherever a sliver of stone peaked out of the water looking suspiciously linear and well-placed. I say ruins, but there was something vital about the sightings, something so present and actual that the word seems wrong. The rocks that draw the shape of work once done in these waters are a cultural heritage. To see them, record them, are acts of preservation. To hold them in photograph or writing is to participate emotionally with place and community.

J. B. Jackson writes, in *The Necessity for Ruins*, that "a traditional mon-ument ... is an object which is supposed to remind us of something impor-tant. That is to say it exists to put people in mind of some obligation that they have incurred: a great public figure, a great public event, a great public declaration which the group had pledged itself to honor." That can backfire. Saddam Hussein's statue is toppled and everyone cheers. General Robert E. Lee is toppled and ghosts of the Confederacy send up smoke signals of rancor and hatred. Pledging oneself to the wrong side of history is poison. A monument to seventeenth-century British slave trader Edward Colston was recently toppled and dumped into Bristol Harbour as Black Lives Matter protestors acted to detoxify their environment. But ruins marking the labor of forgotten makers, the millions whose hands crafted civilizations, can be monuments worth honoring. Jackson writes, "Many of us know the joy and excitement not so much of creating the new as of redeeming what has been neglected."

Russell Ingalls and his family have been fishing these waters for four or five generations. Their Pat's Cove weir has been dressed with twine each summer for one hundred years. He works all the local fisheries from herring weir to lobster trap, scalloping to sea-egg dragging. I have learned a great deal from him and appreciate his generosity in sharing his knowledge. I admire this kind of knowledge, won through work and careful observation over a lifetime. Russell is a pious and thoughtful man. He speaks with the sparkle of island wit, a judicious coping mechanism on an island of twenty-five hundred souls where no one escapes another's scrutiny. I ask how the herring season has been, and he shakes his head in discouragement, then lights up with a smile. "Just enough to feed the seals."

I was tasked with holding open Peter's window so that he could lean out and focus his lens on the tidal flats in Cow Passage, that shallow reach that separates Cheney and White Head Islands. I reached over his shoulder with a metal pole we'd found behind our seats—something like a long-handled engine crank. I braced the pole against my knees to gain the proper angle. It was an awkward matter. Russell was leaning into me to catch shots out the window over my shoulder. No one cared how awkward it got because we were on a mission. My cap flew off as soon as the window opened, hair blowing wild as rockweed in a high tide surge. How'd your pictures come out, I later asked Russell. "Pretty good, except your hair's in most of them."

Our pilot was Peter Sonnenberg, a young man whose father had launched Atlantic Charters, the flight service connecting island to mainland with air ambulance and charter flight services. Peter's father had died a few years earlier in a plane crash just shy of the island's runway. He was returning from a hospital run to Saint John late in the middle of a foggy night. Russell, as first responder and fireman, had been first to arrive at the crash. It could not have been an easy thing for him to board a small plane in the aftermath of that crash, to fly right over the ground where two people he'd known for decades had died. Stories were still percolating about how things had gone wrong. An intimacy with death fuels a small community. The island is fifty-five square miles of rock, balsam fir, black spruce, and collective memory as keen as a spotting scope. Islanders know their landscape as marked by those of their own who have died, when and how.

Islanders carry the spirits of the dead in story. No death is anonymous in such a place. Every death is a shared lamentation and cause to bind more closely together with the living. It's as if those who have gone before us into the long night are still watching us and we are watching them. The line between living and dying can seem fragile. How can it be that one day I am sitting on my deck listening to nonagenarian Gleason Green recite Robert Service poems after he laments that there used to be a bumblebee on every single blossom of clover, and the next day I am hearing that when he got home, he felt a little funny and stroked out. And yet islanders work the sea, commercial fishing the highest-risk occupation, surviving frigid plunges and ferocious swells, grounding out on ledges and taking on rogue waves. The line between living and dying seems both a permeable membrane and a fiercely defended border. Some islanders believe in the afterlife. I don't know how many really think that our lost ones are up there in Heaven. There's a lot of Heaven talk. But my guess is that anyone who has lived very long in this place feels that the lost ones are still among us or "looking down on us," as people say, as if the dead were a mere thousand feet overhead. Memories become monuments in the landscape of a shared imaginary.

We flew low out from the island's shore, scanning the tapestry of greens and browns that stitch the intertidal waters. Islands lose their edge with the tide. Seen at the ebb, the rocky shore gives way to a long reach of musky yellow dressed in wrack. Is the moon pulling water away from us to the other side of the world? I find it so hard to imagine the planetary forces at play, though I watch the tides come and go, come and go, and I gauge my day by their tempo. The water is always in motion, always responding to invisible power, becoming powerful itself, becoming lax. The shallows shine. The depths resist light, hoard their darkness. Shoals and ledges, brackish brown, break through here and there. Nature is messy: there are no straight lines, no perfect curves. Deep water morphs gray-blue. Shallow water glows pale lichen green.

When we popped up to a thousand-foot altitude, forms began to resolve among the rock protrusions. The Seahawk tilted to catch the view. Patterns merged—circles, arcs, and bars of stone set in place more orderly than the sea could accomplish on its own. A huge circle, broken with a broad mouth. Two long, straight wings of stone stretching out symmetrically from the mouth. An invitation to schools of herring stemming the tide up the channel. Another hint of structure, then another, some legible, some largely erased. The ghost weirs butted up against each other, overlapped, one laid on top of the other, as they were built over time. Stone ballast is all that remains of the structures once lined with brush that served as nets, the herring harvested with buckets and pails and dories, men and oxen working in teams, a crazy quilt assembled by the generations that have gone before. My head was spinning as the plane circled and circled. Someone would say, What's that over there? Is that another one? And we would fly to the ruin, astounded by the abundance and craft. They're everywhere, someone would say, and then someone else would repeat it. We couldn't believe our eyes.

Russell's eyes must have seen more than mine. His grandfather perhaps was among the builders. These structures may have been in play as recently as the 1930s. The knowledge of sea and tides, herring and mackerel, the ability to read sky and wind, patterns legible to those who work the sea ("blows sou'west every afternoon about three thirty," a neighbor will say), all carried from grandfather to father to son to grandson. This is a bounty that gives weight and meaning to life, makes it possible to endure our losses, because people have shared what they know across generations, have built ways of living that make sense in their place and time. Of course, there are new tools and new skills: radar and sonar, fish finders and diesel generators to drive weir stakes into deeper offshore waters. There are seiners that chase shoals of herring out in ever deeper waters. There is our immense appetite that cannot quit its hunt for and decimation of bounty. But the ghost weirs speak of small-scale industry perfectly suited to its time and place.

The beauty of the structures says that the builders were masterful makers with complex skill who knew something profound in their bones about the relationship between form and function. The structures hold mystery. How deep is the learning that flowed into the craft of the weirs? Perhaps they speak of cross-cultural learning. Passamaquoddy people used weirs in coves and streams for several thousand years before Europeans settled in the region. During the American Revolution, thirty thousand Loyalists flooded the Fundy region. While the violence of that time inflicted deep wounds and loss, in the quieter recesses of a new cultural mixing, knowledge was exchanged about how to make a life within the terms that nature set in that place. Makers told their stories of harvest and hardship. Stories became adaptations. Adaptations became who we are today with ever more profound lessons to learn about the terms nature sets upon our lives.

We flew on from Cow Passage to circumnavigate all the weirs built that season, circling and dipping a wing and repeating their names: Mumps, Pat's Cove, Bradford Cove, Sea Dream, Jeff Foster's weir just going up in the pond at Dark Harbour, Money Cove, Wayne Green's experimental floating weir built with recycled materials off Eel Brook Beach, Whale Cove, Intruder,

Iron Lady (named for Margaret Thatcher), Cora Bell. Blackened stakes tracing the remains of weirs abandoned but still known by name: Jubilee, Turnip Patch.

No one knows the future of the Maritime herring fishery. The summer of our Seahawk flight was surprisingly abundant and led to renewed enthusiasm for weir builders. Herring showed up in weirs in July and kept coming well into the autumn. The first hauls were a pleasant surprise after nearly a decade of poor harvests. As they continued, one could feel people relaxing again into the feeling of natural bounty that had shaped the island culture. But for the Gulf of Maine, just south of our Bay of Fundy, the herring season was a bust. The gulf's water had been five degrees Fahrenheit above average. Above normal, I wanted to say, as if the sea had a fever. Both prey and predator had come north for the colder waters they prefer.

Atlantic herring are one of most abundant fish in the world. A shoal of herring might hold a billion fish. The weight of the eggs they spawn along the coast of Norway is three times greater than the weight of the Norwegian human population. Leif Andersson, a professor at Uppsala University in Sweden who specializes in genome biology, has led a study of herring that included sequencing Atlantic and Baltic herring. These fish are, he reports, "a near ideal model to study genes underlying ecological adaptation." Atlantic herring are highly adaptable because their population is enormous and they can spawn in a range of seasons, some in autumn, some in spring. Baltic herring adapt to high levels of salinity.

"The Atlantic herring has a rich toolbox composed of gene variants that underlies its ability to adapt to its environment," the research team reports. "I am convinced," Andersson continues, "that further research on this rich collection of genes associated with ecological adaptation will lead to new basic knowledge about gene functions that will be relevant also for human medicine since the majority of genes in herring are also found in humans and are expected to have similar functions." Herring, it turns out, are storytellers that have a lot to teach us about adaptation to climate change.

Ruins too can become storytellers. Sometimes they become repurposed in unexpected ways. A friend who spends his summers in southeast Alaska, knowing of my interest in weir fishing, recounted the story of a stone weir made for catching salmon built along the western coast of Canada. In high tides, the salmon entered. In low tides, the fish were stranded. The weir had been built and fished by Haida people, though at least a hundred years had passed since they had lived in that place. But the weir is still fishing, said my friend. Brown bears use it, splashing out at low tide to feast, leaving salmon carcasses all around their kitchen.

We do not have bears on Grand Manan Island. We no longer have many wild salmon. But we have a culture schooled by relationship with the sea, and that is a way of belonging to the world worth cherishing.

19

✳

Silk

We live in all we seek.

ANNIE DILLARD, *For the Time Being*

VISITING LIBRARIES IN PARIS IS A HUMBLING EXPERIENCE. THE Bibliothèque Forney is housed in a medieval residence, one of three surviving in Paris, the structure built in the thirteenth century. To get to the special collections room, I walked up a narrow spiral staircase, stone treads bearing the erosion of centuries. It felt like climbing the bell tower of a mini Notre-Dame. And I felt like a mini me, cowed by the weight of history. I don't really know what I had hoped to find there.

I had run through several theories of Louisa, none of which could be backed up with evidence. Had she come to New York to escape from danger? Until 1975 it was legal in France for a husband to kill his unfaithful wife, if he "shall have caught them in the fact, in the house where the husband and wife dwell." Suppose she'd had an earlier marriage to a distrustful husband who made threats on ungrounded suspicions? My mother had said that there had been "another family" in France. Or suppose Louisa had taken a lover (a woman with drive is a woman with desire)—a man who worked in his father's shoe factory (as had Arsenne, who would become Louisa's husband), with whom she later escaped to America? Or had she come for work, Napoleon III subsidizing French citizens to populate his new holding in Mexico, skilled artisans most desirable to help create the performance of aristocracy in Maximilian's court? A distant cousin had said that Louisa was a "follower of Maximilian." Or was she a pious woman? Louisa was born in Argenteuil, home of the learned and romantically doomed Héloïse. Educated in the convent there, Héloïse was fluent in Greek, Latin, and philosophy even before she met her tutor and lover Abelard. She named their son Astrolabe. Louisa would have known the story of this learned woman whose passion led her to great suffering. Did the story shape Louisa, leading her to become self-contained and imperious, as she looks in the two old photographs I have seen, one oddly torn in half at the neck? Or could the story of soulful, romantic martyrs have made her fearless in pursuit of passion? In her first poetic letter to Abelard, Héloïse wrote:

> You kept your silence, though, about most of the reasons
> why I preferred love over marriage,
> freedom over a chain.
> So I call my God to witness now:
> If great Augustus, ruler of the world,
> ever thought to honor me by making me his wife
> and granted me dominion over the earth,
> it would be dearer to me
> and more honorable to be called
> not his royal consort but your whore.

Had Louisa come as a single woman and met Arsenne in Manhattan, as my mother claimed? Or had they been married in Paris and crossed the

Atlantic together on their honeymoon, as my mother's cousin had claimed? Impossible now to know. Louisa was a pragmatic woman who took care of her needs. In her old age, my grandmother reported, when Arsenne, suffering from severe asthma, had to sleep upright in a chair, Louisa invited the family cook, Charlie Melino, into her bed "to keep her warm."

The only marriage certificate I have found makes a hash of my speculations. Arsenne and Louisa were married in Manhattan on October 6, 1886, more than a decade after their three daughters were born. The certificate lists this as the first marriage for both partners. Anyone who has searched census, birth, and death records knows not to trust the so-called data recorded on documents riddled with inconsistencies, written in haste with illegible handwriting and smudged ink. Worse for the seeker of facts, the marriage certificate said that Arsenne had married Louisa "Dalmont," whose mother was Sophie de Saint-Isle and father Prosper Dalmont. Why then would our family have always spoken of our great-grandmother as Louisa de St. Isle? And how, in fact, was this name spelled, as documents offer conflicting variations? The address on the marriage certificate was the same as the census noted for the family on West Eleventh Street, so at least that was right. I had an out-loud frisson at the Hôtel de Ville Library, finding an 1838 birth certificate for one Louise Anäis Saintisle, but I doubt that was my ancestor. No parents listed. The "Anäis" seems unlikely and the date is probably wrong and the spelling ... well, who knows? Other family documents contract the name to "de St. Isle"—an obvious space saver, but I'm not confident that search engines go along for the ride.

The Forney specializes in the decorative arts. In its collection I could swim through the waters of Louisa's milieu, get a feeling for the fashion and commerce of her time. Telling details often refracted fashion against politics. After Napoleon III made a trip to Algeria, dresses appeared featuring African motifs—sequins, golden crescents, bands of black taffeta. Advertisements about designs that would *éblouira les yeux* (literally, "blow out your eyes"). "The cut of the dress is strange—you will think it impossible!" Beasts and insects were in vogue. "So audacious you don't know how far it will go." The woman's body was an armature for sculptural expressions of bizarre extravagance. The length of a dress was a statement of privilege. When streets are full of horseshit and sewage, the woman who wears a floor-length dress is a woman who stands above it all. Huge department stores had begun to take over former palaces in Paris. Au Bon Marché, Les Grands Magasins du la Louvre. Some began to sell half-sewn dress kits that a woman could complete at home. The era of aristocracy was giving way to the era of consumerism.

As I leafed through the trove in the archival box labelled "1862," I couldn't contain my enthusiasms. The young man sitting across the wooden library table leafing through his own trove lifted his head.

"You're interested in dressmakers?"

"Yes, my great-grandmother—"

"I come from a small village. When I was growing up, every village had a dressmaker. And a hat maker. You did not go to church without a hat. It would be very immodest. You'd be an infidel."

His mother, he said, had all of the family's clothes made. Everyone had their dressmaker. Even people of modest means.

I found in the archive a fabric catalog from Labbey and Company based in Lyon—thin merinos and cashmeres. Strips of cloth three inches long and three-quarters of an inch wide had been pasted into rectangular windows on each page, so you could see and touch the range of textures and colors. Dust-resistant cashmere in a diamond pattern weave. Alpaca—rough. Indian cashmere—like skin. A box of six thousand fabric samples, an album of engravings with models, "reference knots" of four hundred colors of silk. Separate vendors sold fringes, bows, ribbons, corsages, *ceintures*, *baleine*, and black silk seam binding.

❋

THE WOMAN WHO VALIDATES MY TICKET MAY BE MY AGE—FACE beginning to deepen with lines and half circles underscoring her lower eyelids. She is lean, black hair loose and wavy at the shoulder. She wears a black jersey, red silk scarf ringing her neck. Red with tiny white dots. The scarf livens her face. Mirrors the red lipstick she wears. She is chic. Her energy is bright. I love seeing older women who are chic. Women who have the ability "to renew themselves at the fountain of their own lives." That's what James Baldwin said white people were no longer able to do. But the affect of the woman who validates my ticket for the Musée des Tissus in Lyon belies the age that marks her face. She does not fear her sensuality. She announces it with style. She walks me from the reception desk out the back door into a cobblestone courtyard surrounded with stately homes, two of them converted to museums. She crosses with me across to the entrance, as if I have come to her house for lunch. She has a quick but unhurried stride. She leaves me at the stone steps with a gesture of introduction toward the security guards. I love her just for that moment (*mon semblance!*) and then she is gone.

I've wanted to visit this museum, founded in 1864, since I had encountered catalogs of nineteenth-century satins and silks made by the *canuts* of Lyon during my visit to Paris with Lucinda. Ribbons of cloth affixed to the pages so that texture, density, and weight could be tested in the hand. An experienced dressmaker could translate the tactile encounter into gauging how the fabric would fold or drape or flow over a woman's body, how it would move as she moved, how it would catch and release the light. Such fabrics would have passed through Louisa's fingers hundreds of times.

Nothing matched silk, of course, *la grande fabrique,* for elegance and sensuality. Nothing matched the work of Lyonnais *canuts* after two Italian silk merchants settled in the city in the early 1500s and set in motion centuries of invention, innovation, and art in fabric making and design. The city's population grew within a few decades from thirty thousand to one hundred thousand inhabitants; the number of silk looms bloomed:

40 in 1541

1,000 in 1548

10,000 in 1802

30,000 in 1839

120,000 in 1877

Silk starts with silkworms, and silkworms start on mulberry leaves.

20,000 mulberry bushes planted in the Tuileries in 1603.

60,000 mulberry bushes planted in the countryside, most in the Rhône
Valley, then expanding to French-occupied Lebanon.

2.2 million kilos of raw silk produced in 1853.

1 kilo of silk requires 300 silkworms eating 104 kilos of mulberry leaves.

Silk. I had imagined bolts of diaphanous cloth, delicate and semi-transparent, Randall Jarrell's "Cloth from the moon. Cloth from another planet." But what I found at the Musée des Tissus told the story of a more complex art. Luxurious, heavy tapestries depicting a shepherd scene or wreath of roses; an ivory field of fallen rose petals or a black field patterned with a grid of golden beetles; flowers the size of trees or trees as ornate as flowers; a mandolin balanced upon a musical score; plumes of beige ostrich feathers tied with a beige bow. These fabrics had the detail of oil paintings, yet were woven of fine silk threads. All woven from the harvested saliva of silkworms. Already by the year 1606, one thousand master weavers worked in the city.

Lyon's looms were massive mechanical frames built of oak or walnut, some four meters tall, decked with harnesses, weights and counterweights, warp beams, hooks, and needles, with heddles controlling each individual thread, so that three or four thousand warp and weft threads could interlace as shuttles wound with various colors passed back and forth to create the weave pattern. A few looms from the 1800s are extant as demonstration looms at the Musée des Tissus and Maison des Canuts. The artistic intelligence and mechanical complexity in their design is staggering, as is the labor required of the weavers. Is it art or is it science that makes such invention possible? (As with the herring weirs of Grand Manan Island, it is both.) But the fate of the weavers suffered when a royal edict in the eighteenth century banned people from being both a master weaver and a master merchant, setting the conditions for a resistance movement that exploded in the nineteenth century.

The silk market relied upon the appetite of royal and papal courts for luxury fabric. Each boom in monarchy meant a boom in silk. Each wave of democratic revolution, a bust for silk. Even silk's commercial origin is linked to royalty, beginning in 2640 B.C.E. China, when Empress Xi Lingshi observed silkworms spinning cocoons on a mulberry bush. Silk became the property of the imperial family. Export of eggs and cocoons was banned. Nonetheless, by the second century, according to historian Jean Étèvenaux, silk appeared in Babylonia, Phoenicia, and the Roman Empire. By the sixth century, he writes, silk, "thanks to Emperor Justinian I (527–565), who sent two monks to collect silkworm eggs, sericulture, or the farming of silkworms, spread throughout the Byzantine Empire, then to the Arab world, then to Andalusia."

Silk nonetheless remained rare and valuable. Satin, a silk made with the warp threads floating over the weft to create its sheen, originated in the city of Quanzhou. Its Arabic name was Zayton, a major port in the maritime silk route. Hence, *satin*. "In the sixteenth century," Étèvenaux writes, "on the island of Rhodes, silk was reimbursed at the same price as gold and gemstones if a boat were to sink." Napoleon Bonaparte commissioned tapestries and furnishings and uniforms and gowns for the Tuileries and Fontainebleu and Compiègne, that panoply of royal residences and party houses for the aristocracy hobnobbing across the French landscape.

The rarest of silks were the patterned Jacquard weaves incorporating elaborate textured detailing of flowers and plants. Brocades and damasks. The Jacquard loom, invented in 1804 by Joseph Marie Jacquard, was an invention building on eighteenth-century precursors that made it possible for the weave's design to be stored in punch cards. The chain of cards was mounted on the loom to control which threads would go into which row.

One card for each row. Threading the warp on the looms required time and patience. It might take a week just for that preparation. But the Jacquard loom meant crisp details and a mechanical memory of the design, easing the creation of complex patterns of flowers and leaves and feathers and beetles. A portrait made in 1839 honoring Jacquard has the detail of a fine engraving—right down to buttons and buttonholes in his vest, calipers and chisels and compass, vice clamp on the workbench, cathedral spire out the window, woven entirely with silk threads. The pattern required twenty-four thousand punched cards. The Jacquard loom inspired Charles Babbage, British polymath and inventor, to conceive the first computer in his "analytic engine," which used punch cards to store memory. Babbage saw the device as useful for remembering numbers as measures of quantity: a calculator. When mathematician Ada Lovelace, daughter of poet Lord Byron, met Babbage, she realized his device could store numbers that stood for other things, like letters or musical notes: a computer. From silkworm to tapestry to calculator to computer, the making mind romped on toward the computer age. Babbage owned one of these woven silk portraits honoring Jacquard. A rack of punch cards laced together stands nearby, ready to flow into the loom.

A LA MÉMOIRE DE J. M. JACQUARD.

Joseph Marie Jacquard, inventor of the Jacquard loom. 1839.
Science Museum, London. Public domain.

Under Napoleon, the number of looms in Lyon tripled; foreigners were banned from entering textile schools so that jobs would remain in the hands of the Lyonnais. During the Second Empire, when Napoleon III ruled, silk production peaked in France. Empress Eugénie and her fashion-fierce entourage drove the industry. Dresses, dresses, and more dresses (350 alone ordered for the opening of the Suez Canal), tapestries, wall coverings, upholstery, beribboned uniforms. The demand put pressure on the weavers, already working long hours for paltry pay in miserable working conditions, with merchants clipping off the profits. Many of the looms were in weavers' homes with children assisting. Weavers had a shot at lifting themselves out of poverty with their talents, an opportunity for women who had little choice for work other than servant or whore. It was a step up, though working conditions for the weavers became intolerable as, increasingly, the profits went to marketers, not to makers.

In Lyon the history of silk weaving is bound up with social history. Silk signifies luxury, papal and royal. Silk signifies the rise of women out of misery and poverty into a middle class. Silk signifies freedom and a new social order that puts a value on labor. Silk signifies horticulture and sericulture—new relationships with the land. Silk signifies insurrection—the cry for justice and dignity for workers. Silk signifies the evolution of ideas.

Victor Hugo wrote of Lyon, "It's the city of the loom, the city of art where the machine follows the soul, it's the city where in the worker, we find a thinker." The first workers' newspaper in France was published by the *canuts*. *L'Echo de la Fabrique* was published weekly in the period between two revolts that erupted in 1831 and 1834. Étèvenaux writes that the *canuts* "had little in common with the poor, illiterate proletariat who were vilified in 19th century literature and propaganda." The paper was a forum for ideas as well as unrest. "The multitude of correspondents" debated such themes as "industrial association" and "mutual learning" in their newspaper. "They detailed events of the labour court and developed ideas of the social economy along with their poems, songs and charades, in addition to practical advice." The paper "was a reflection of social and intellectual agitation" and frightened the merchant authorities. Tempers rose. Bullets flew. Placards announced DU PAIN OU DU PLOMB and VIVRE EN TRAVAILLANT OU MOURIR EN COMBATTANT. And some did in fact die fighting as bullets flew. In the second *canut* revolt, hundreds of protestors suffered death, deportation, and imprisonment.

ALL ALONG THE RHÔNE BARGES WERE TIED UP FOR THE OFF-season during my visit. Work boats transformed into clubs for rock shows, jazz, tapas. Some Brutalist with battered sheet metal siding, some boho with batiks hung to cover the windows. Runners, walkers, scooter riders buzzed along the wide walkway that edges the river. Four years after the Bataclan attack, armed soldiers walked the more densely populated streets, places lined with upscale shops or medieval heritage sites, places where people were out for the pleasure of buying flowers and pastries, fresh blackberries and eggplant, endive and chicory, or dinner in one of the small *bouchons*. Weapons caches had been found in Lyon at the time of the attacks, so vigilance has not been relaxed either here or in Paris. The scene was surreal—paired soldiers bearing assault guns juxtaposed with street vendors manning a long table heaped with a dozen varieties of freshly harvested olives, green and brown and purple.

Downriver where the Rhône meets the Saône stands the Musée des Confluences, a weirdly biomorphic spaceship on legs that floats above the tip of the peninsula that separates the rivers. Confluence of rivers. Confluence of art and science. This used to be an area of shipyards and a sugar factory, a place where container ships stacked their cargo. Now it's been replanted with postmodern steel-plated cube-shaped office buildings—one bright orange and pocked with varied-size holes. Its nickname is "The Cheese." Another grass green with two big funnels diving into its side. Its nickname is

"The Speakers." Confluence of the ancient and the modern. Confluence of destruction and reinvention. Confluence of this urgency to believe we have a home in nature and the grief that we are leaving it behind in ruins. Still something organismic in us knows we *are* nature, because we dwell in the need to make and remake beauty out of ruin.

I TRAVELED OUT OF LYON TO VISIT A SMALL VINEYARD ALONG the northern Côtes du Rhône, home of one of the steepest wineries in the world, a site of viniculture for at least twenty-three centuries. The vines likely came originally from Italy, an outgrowth of Gallo-Roman culture as the Roman Empire engulfed Gaul and the two cultures then made a syncretic peace. The guide to the wine tour says viticulture signifies peace, which leads to more sophistication, which leads to more wine on the table.

The village of Condrieu is the home of Viognier grapes, the only grape permitted for Condrieu wine. In 1965 the grape became almost extinct, with only thirty acres in cultivation. It had been decimated by the phylloxera insect in the 1870s, along with nearly all the vineyards in France. The vines were reconstituted with stock from the United States. Then the vineyards were abandoned during the two world wars, men off fighting and dying, and the hills were overtaken by forest. The guide points to a dense seam of scrub and saplings that fills a crevice running down the slope, overgrowth interrupting the terraced rows of grape vines that traverse the steep hillside like a living topographical map.

In the 1960s, this entire hillside was covered with forest. Vintners are still working to clear the slopes. But the terraces—they have been here since Roman times. Yes, of course, they must be rebuilt year after year. There are now over 740 acres of Viognier in cultivation here, and the grape has been introduced in the Americas, Australia, New Zealand. But only here will you find Condrieu wine made from Viognier grapes. These sun-facing granite hillsides, a model of resilience in both nature and culture, are also the home of Côte-Rôtie—wine of the "roasted coast." I'd like to think that means they will manage to adapt to a roasting climate.

"But if you bring cabernet vines here," the guide says, "they will not grow. It's all about the place, the place, the place." Later the vintner, fourth generation of his family to work these hills, fleshes out the meaning of *terroir* so that it finally makes sense to me, rather than sounding like marketing hyperbole. Syrah grows in granite soil where the roots cannot go deep. Instead they extend laterally. "The wine is very soft," says the vintner. "You don't feel the alcohol. Drink it within three or four years to have the fruit. Keep the flavor in your mouth." He makes twenty-five thousand bottles a year. He has three workers full-time—himself, his brother, and one more. Otherwise he uses seasonal workers. He likes to pick the grapes early. He likes pruning. He likes to make the wine. He likes it all. The grapes that grow in schist soil where the roots can go deep—you can keep that wine for twenty years. "It's a masculine wine." The Asiaticus—a feminine wine—more earthy, more acid, stronger.

20

✳

One Thread

IN 1996 W. S. MERWIN PUBLISHED *LAMENT FOR THE MAKERS*, A MEmorial anthology of poets who had been important to him during his life as a poet. He was riffing on the idea presented by William Dunbar in his sixteenth-century poem "Lament for the Makaris." Both works find the death of influential predecessors to be a spur to speaking of what they value in their art. This memorializing impulse spurred my writing of *A Woven World*. In fact, throughout most of my research and writing I kept Merwin's title as my own. But the deeper I dug into the environmental and cultural histories this project explores, the more I felt that "lament" was inadequate to describe the complex emotions aroused. I could not bear losing (thank you, Gerald Stern, for that phrasing) my connection to either my matrilineal history in the fashion industry or the weir-based fishery of Grand Manan Island. Both seem brilliant adaptations to the demands of their times, both celebrated human inventiveness, both spoke of the resilience of certain microhabitats of human enterprise, and both stirred a fierce desire in me to hold these traditions close as sources of continuity and belonging in a time of radical discontinuities and threat. Yes, I wanted to participate emotionally with the past before it slipped away. But I wanted to move from lament to repair and the hope to be found in the human skill of making despite the painful fact that in nature and in culture the unmaking is always close at hand.

"LOOK AT THIS DRESS!" MY FRIEND GARY NABHAN ENTHUSED. I had come to meet him at the Agave Festival in Tucson. We met at Hotel Congress, where agave growers and mescal distillers had lined up their display tables in the courtyard and lobby, all these guys in broad-brimmed straw hats talking the trade of growing and making. Gary and I have been friends for years. As an ethnobotanist, he has taught me a great deal about arid lands and the people who have made their living in apparently inhospitable terrain for centuries. We have a writerly friendship in which we discuss our works in progress and egg each other on to pursue ideas that capture us, no matter how implausible they may at first sound. "Dressmakers and fishermen? That's incredible," he says. "I was just thinking . . ." and off we will go into the forest of ideas that only reveal themselves as you turn the next corner and the next on art's densely wooded trail.

I had told him about my great-grandmother and her dressmaking business in New York City. "That's incredible." And he told me about his "little Lebanese granny"—the grandmother of his Lebanese aunt—who had immigrated to Brooklyn in the 1890s. She had worked her way through college as a silk maker in Lebanon before leaving. The story had been slow to emerge in his family. The other aunts did not speak of it. "It was uncomfortable to have hookers in-house," Gary said, "when friends came by to play Scrabble." The former silk maker had made a business in Brooklyn as a lingerie dealer. She'd buy a couple hundred dollars of lingerie at Macy's and sell it to African American sex workers who could not get into the stores. These women had come in the great migration of Blacks who'd grown up in the South and come North to find their way in a free society. The "granny" could get into the stores. She was an Arab but she spoke French from her life in French-occupied Lebanon, and French was a signifier of class in the immigrant culture of New York City. All these resourceful women created new alliances and marginal businesses despite the obstacles thrown in their way. The "granny" lived to be 104, dying of respiratory disease, perhaps after smoking a bit too much hashish in her hookah.

Gary and I found a quiet corner in the Congress lobby. He pulled out the book. *A Red Like No Other: How Cochineal Colored the World, an epic story of art, culture, science, and trade*, published in 2015 in conjunction with an exhibition at the Museum of International Folk Art in Santa Fe, New Mexico. The book's editors, Carmella Padilla and Barbara Anderson, curated a dazzling collection of essays about the domesticated insect that gave the world its most precious reds.

Gary gives me a sheepish look.

"I was wrong about the details. I thought the dress was from the 1880s. A wedding dress. I thought a Navajo guy had gone to Lyon to study weaving and never left. I don't know if this will work for you. But take a look."

"No. No. I'm sure I can use this. I need a dress. One more dress."

The book is handsome and hefty, tracking the quest of painters, weavers, and designers over hundreds of years for the source of a perfect red. Red as the color of power, royalty, papacy, wealth, desire, life-giving and death-dealing blood. Natural dyes come from the earth—reds from cinnabar and hematite. But in the 1520s, the Spanish conquerors of the Aztec Empire found cochineal insects pressed into cake shapes in the Aztec marketplace. These insects grow on prickly pear cactus and had been cultivated in Mesoamerica for centuries. They produce the most prized and lasting deep crimson color. The Zapotecs had paid taxes to the Aztec court—twenty bags of cochineal every three months, thousands of peasant communities paying up. As with cultivation of silkworms in China and Europe, Mexican cochineal rearing required enormous amounts of labor; seventy thousand insects are required for one pound of cochineal red dye. Imported to Europe, the dye had a value second only to silver imported from Mexico. It became the coveted dye for church robes, textiles, and luxury fashion. The Spanish crown kept a monopoly on cochineal production—mostly located in Oaxaca—for two hundred years. The domesticated insects conquered the world of red, its tint spreading to France and China, Japan and Great Britain. British "Red Coats" who fought the colonists in Massachusetts wore uniforms dyed with cochineal red.

"But look at the dress," Gary enthuses. We flip to the book's last chapter, celebrating the cochineal-inspired dress of Navajo fashion designer Orlando Dugi. True, it was not a wedding dress. True, the Navajo had never moved to France to study weaving. True, the dress was made in 2014 and not in the 1880s. But were facts, after all, what we hungered for, both of us seeking stories of continuity and belonging, both of us egged on by beauty and friendship and work as counterweight to our age of elegy and diminishment?

Navajo weavers have long experimented with cochineal. In the nineteenth century, as the exhibition volume details, it was common practice for Navajo weavers to unravel threads from imported cochineal-dyed *bayeta* (baize) and reuse the precious red strands. A dye from the Americas moves to Europe, then moves back to the Americas. This globalization of culture stretched from the ancient Incas and Zapotecs, to the Spanish conquistadors, to the Lyonnais *canuts*, and back to the Americas in the red dirt terrain of the Navajo.

Orlando Dugi, a self-taught designer born in Gray Mountain on the Navajo Nation, brought the cochineal tradition into twenty-first-century fashion with his ten-piece Red Collection celebrating the power of women. "He imagined a pre-Columbian matriarchal society whose wealth and dominance was expressed in luxurious red gowns." His grandmothers wove textiles. His father and grandmother were bead artists who taught him to bead at five years old. He had learned to use a sewing machine in a home economics class in seventh grade. He loved the Navajo ceremonial tradition of "dressing for the holy ones," wearing satin and velvet with silver adornments. He learned about cochineal while working in a Santa Fe art gallery that exhibited historic native weavings made from the unraveled yarns of imported European *bayeta*. He had never worked with natural dyes, so he experimented with how the dye reacted to different fabrics, how different mordants (cream of tartar, tannic acid, sodium chloride) set the tints, how different waters (tap or distilled) changed the hue. He began dyeing swatches. "Purples first then reds, oranges, pinks. I played with it a lot, learning that the dye is really potent and really sensitive to anything that touches it."

Dugi's cochineal dress stands bodiless on a black page. The dress is a glory, a dress for the absent woman. Strapless bodice with a skirt that flows from waist to floor. It's a little too long for the floor, so that the fabric rests there, sprawls out a bit in graceful draping, as if to relax from the performance of itself. The bodice is heavily embroidered with beads and crystals, delicate silver, gold, and black designs threaded into place, the shapes reminiscent of feathers and leaves, derived from Dugi's favorite Pueblo Indian pottery collections—though to my eye the look is more Art Deco than Southwest. The bodice is so heavy with adornment it stands rigid. In the center, where the bodice might take a teasing dive down the chest, instead it rises on a gentle slope to form a central peak as if the bodice were a kind of body armor. The underskirt is heavy silk duchesse satin. To make the dress took "one month to dye and construct the gown, two months to bead the bodice, and time to hand-dye six spools of cochineal thread—thirty yards each—with which to stitch it all together."

Centuries and continents of conflict and difference are brought into brief and quiet accord in the hands of the maker. A quiet glow reflects off the satin, tempered by the overskirt of vaporous silk organza, fabric as delicate as a Scheherazade veil. Here is the diaphanous cloth of the moon. Copper moon. Salmon moon. Red of Chaco Canyon. Red of deep-sea coral. It's an evening gown. A red-carpet dress. A museum piece. A ceremonial garment. A holy vestment. See how the slightest breeze stirs it to life?

Pull one thread too many and the beauty will unravel before your eyes.

※

ACKNOWLEDGMENTS

I AM PROFOUNDLY GRATEFUL FOR A FELLOWSHIP FROM THE JOHN Simon Guggenheim Foundation that supported the research and writing of this book. Thanks also to the Agnese Nelms Haury Program in Environment and Social Justice and the Department of English at the University of Arizona for their generous support. The Costume Institute of the Metropolitan Museum of Art in New York City offered inspiration in their 2016 exhibition *Manus x Machina: Fashion in an Age of Technology*. Amanda Garfinkel, assistant curator, shared insights into Yves Saint Laurent's "sardine dress," the star feature of the exhibition. For research assistance in Paris, I am grateful to Jennifer Pinard for guiding me through archival collections. In Lyon the Musée des Tissus and Maison des Canuts proved illuminating, and I am grateful to them for preserving the silk-weaving heritage of that lovely city. The research of Judith G. Coffin and Nancy L. Green provided invaluable information regarding the labor issues for women in the garment industry. Thanks to historian Ed Berenson for a conversation on the history of French immigrants to New York City in the nineteenth century. Thanks to the Museum of the City of New York and New-York Historical Society for research materials and the space to reflect upon them. John R. Balow, curator for business, history, and social science at the New York Public Library, gave me much needed hope on my quest when I met with him, and he quietly reported, "I think I've found your great-grandmother." He sent me on a microfiche journey of discovery.

On the science side, I made ample use of materials from the Gulf of Maine Research Institute and Tides Institute & Museum of Art. Thanks also to the Grand Manan Museum and its director, M. J. Edwards, and archivist, Ava Sturgeon. Thanks to the Grand Manan Whale and Seabird Research Station and its director Laurie Murison. The knowledge and skill of fishermen on Grand Manan has been a gift to my understanding of the island's history and its great spirit of resilience. Special thanks to Russell Ingalls and Jeff Foster for taking me aboard on seining adventures at Pat's Cove and Money Cove. Unforgettable experiences, and I hope there will be more. Many other island friends and neighbors have nourished this work in conversation and friendship: Larry Small (builder of houses and teller of tales), Elton Greene, Allison and Janice Naves, Jimmy and Jonelle Hepditch, Peter Cunningham, Ara Fitzgerald, Carly Fleet, Bev and Amy Fleet, Wayne Green, Burt Green, David Ingalls, and Tom and Ann Wetzel. Peter Hoffman proved to be, unbidden, an able research assistant, sleuthing out fashion and family details. Thanks to Page Buono for research early in the game. Well, that is a start. Forgive me if I've not mentioned you. So many conversations fell into the book that at times it feels like a work of collective making.

A handful of writer friends have for decades been sounding boards for my projects in their early stages. Special thanks to Alan Weisman, Mitchell Thomashow, Gary Paul Nabhan, Scott Russell Sanders, Kathleen Dean Moore, and Robin Wall Kimmerer. My dear friend the writer Barbara Hurd came to visit on Grand Manan one summer as I was beginning my research on the matrilineal line of my family. We discussed our upcoming projects while walking among the abandoned fish houses in Seal Cove. Our conversation drifted to the history of the herring fishery on the island. "You should write about this! You know so much about it," she said. "Well, I'd like to, but I'm interested in these dressmakers . . ." "It's the same project," she said. And in that challenge, I began to see that a book that braided the worlds of dressmakers and fishermen might indeed speak to the larger issues of cultural and environmental loss. And that to give a presence to the spirit of invention and creation that shaped these cultures might inspire us to our better natures facing the uncertain future.

As I neared completion of the book, I asked Katharine Coles, a writer whose aesthetic judgment I trust without question, to read the manuscript and let me know what I had wrought. Her encouragements and insightful notes on the text clarified for me the final edits that needed to be done. I send boundless gratitude for her generosity and brilliance. And most of all for her friendship.

This book is dedicated to my brave and gifted daughter Lucinda Bliss. The joys of friendship with an adult child are an unexpected pleasure of parenthood, and I thank her for companionship on our travels to Paris, her keen editorial eye, her sharing of artistic life, and her love. Gratitude beyond measure.

I thank Laura Blake Peterson for believing in this book and finding its home with Counterpoint Press. I give heartfelt thanks to Jack Shoemaker, who I have admired for decades as a champion of writers and literary culture, for bringing the book to print.

Publications

THE FOLLOWING CHAPTERS HAVE BEEN PREVIOUSLY PUBLISHED, often in earlier versions. Grateful acknowledgment goes to:
"Driving the Cadillac to Valhalla," *The Arkansas International*
"The House Built of Herring" and "Herring Our King," *Prairie Schooner*

"A Portrait in Five Portraits," Meridel Le Sueur Essay in *Water~Stone Review: A Literary Annual*

"The Stone Weirs," *Carbon Copy*

"The Paris Notebook," *Solstice: A Magazine of Diverse Voices*

"Some of the Ghosts," terrain.org

"Invasive Beauty" and "Silk," *The Georgia Review*

Segments of an essay titled "Coming Home to Earth," published in *The Georgia Review*, have been repurposed here in several chapters.

© Bear Guerra

ALISON HAWTHORNE DEMING's most recent books include *Zoologies: On Animals and the Human Spirit* and the poetry collection *Stairway to Heaven*. The recipient of a Guggenheim Fellowship, Stegner Fellowship at Stanford University, National Endowment for the Arts fellowships, and Walt Whitman Award, she is Regents Professor at the University of Arizona. She lives in Tucson and on Grand Manan Island, New Brunswick, Canada. Find out more at alisonhawthornedeming.com.